Resonant
Leadership

Resonant Leadership

Renewing Yourself and Connecting with Others Through Mindfulness, Hope, and Compassion

Richard Boyatzis • Annie McKee

HARVARD BUSINESS SCHOOL PRESS

Boston, Massachusetts

Library of Congress Cataloging-in-Publication Data

Boyatzis, Richard E.
    Resonant leadership / Richard Boyatzis and Annie McKee.
      p. cm.
    ISBN 1-59139-563-1
  1. Leadership. I. McKee, Annie, 1955- II. Title.
    HM1261.B69 2005
    303.3'4—dc22
                                        2005007402

The paper used in this publication meets the minimum requirements of the
American National Standard for Information Sciences—Permanence of Paper
for Printed Library Materials, ANSI Z39.48-1992.

We dedicate this book to our parents:

Sophia and Kyriakos Boyatzis,

Catherine MacDonald Wigsten,

and

Murray Wigsten

Thank you for setting us on our paths, with love,

for guiding us to live mindfully,

with compassion,

and always with enduring hope.

CONTENTS

Foreword   ix

Acknowledgments   xi

 O N E

Great Leaders Move Us

1

T W O

The Leader's Challenge

13

T H R E E

Dissonance Is the Default

35

F O U R

Waking Up to Resonance and Renewal

57

FIVE

Intentional Change

87

SIX

Mindfulness

111

SEVEN

Hope

147

EIGHT

Compassion

175

NINE

"Be the Change You Wish to See in the World"

201

APPENDIX A

Power Stress, the Sacrifice Syndrome, and the Renewal Cycle

205

APPENDIX B

Additional Exercises

215

Notes   235

Index   275

About the Authors   285

SINCE I WROTE *Primal Leadership* together with my good friends and colleagues Richard Boyatzis and Annie McKee, we have been on podiums around the world talking about how resonant leadership can make leaders more effective. The one question we almost invariably face is: Yes, but how? Now Richard and Annie have answered that crucial question, with both vision and precision.

I've always learned a great deal personally from Richard and Annie. Each of them brings to life's raw data an exquisite sensibility, mixing the acumen of the scientist, the savvy of the practitioner, and the compassionate soul of their spiritual grounding.

They reveal that same sensibility in *Resonant Leadership*, and I feel as richly rewarded by this book as I have been through my work with them. Annie and Richard bring to this book the lessons learned on the front lines of businesses and organizations large and small, around the world—from schoolyards in South Africa to boardrooms in global centers of commerce. Drawing on their wide experience, they offer a compelling business case for qualities like benevolence and compassion, and for the utility of dreams, hope, optimism, and a strong ethical compass.

Leadership that gets results demands a social alchemy of sorts. As Richard and Annie show, the best leaders are not only highly motivated themselves, but able to somehow radiate that positivity, igniting and mobilizing positive attitudes in those around them. But leadership that works well goes beyond the image of the lone star somehow sprinkling magical pixie dust on others. True leaders know that they, too, are being led—that leadership operates on a two-way street. Any leader must listen and attune to others in order to pick up the signals that will help all those involved stay in step along the way. The best leaders know we're all in it together.

Here arises a leadership paradox: For leaders, the first task in management has nothing to do with leading others; step one poses the challenge of knowing and managing oneself. That includes connecting with the deep values that guide us, imbuing our actions with meaning. This self-engagement also demands we align our emotions with our goals—both to motivate and to keep our composure and focus. When we act in accord with these inner barometers, we feel good about what we do. And when our energy and excitement come spontaneously, they verify we are moving on the right track.

But for what? Here compassion enters the picture—not in the sense of charitable giving, but in terms of a benevolent attitude, a predisposition to help others. Compassion lifts us out of the small-minded worries that center on ourselves and expands our world by putting our focus on others. That simple shift allows leaders a sorely needed renewal of spirit, and that renewal, as it turns out, is crucial for leaders in sustaining not only themselves but also the efficacy of their leadership.

In an era when the business community has been badly damaged by the fallout when leaders fail to embody transparency and when the drastic consequences of leaders' arrogant self-absorption are greater than ever, the insights shared here are all the more valuable. If we need anything from leaders today, it is more leadership of the resonant kind.

—Daniel Goleman

ACKNOWLEDGMENTS

THERE ARE MANY VOICES whispering throughout the pages of this book—voices of wisdom, insight, experience, and support. These voices come from people who have touched us, taught us, moved us and inspired us—people whom we trust and treasure, and without whom we could not, or would not, have had the courage to write this book. We are deeply grateful for the support, encouragement, and commitment we have been so blessed to receive.

Our partnership with Daniel Goleman has been and continues to be a gift and a treasure. He has supported us every step of the way; we respect him, and care for him deeply. His positive energy is palpable—and contagious. Dan's resonant leadership continues to inspire us, and we are grateful and happy to share good times and good conversations with him.

The team at the Press has been fabulous. Each and every one is fun to work with, perceptive, astute, and creative. Special and abiding thanks to our editor, Jeff Kehoe for his thoughtful, incisive, and steady guidance; his good grace; and good humor. And to Hollis Heimbouch for deep commitment to both the content and the spirit of our work—she's a leader in her own right, and it shows. And, of course, thanks to Mark Bloomfield, David Goehring, Todd Berman, and Erin Brown for their belief that this book will make a difference to lots of leaders, in the business world and beyond.

Lucy McCauley, our hands-on editor and writing muse, is a special person indeed. Her help in crafting our message was invaluable, as was her belief that our work can really make a difference to thoughtful seekers, like Lucy herself.

Very special thanks to Teleos team members Gretchen Schmelzer, Neen Brannan, and Patrice Waldenberger. Each of them dedicated days—no, weeks—to the pursuit of knowledge in support of our work. Their serenity, intelligence, and good humor carried us through some difficult work and kept us on schedule, too.

We are fortunate to work with people who have dedicated their lives to the search for knowledge about great leadership. These people have shared selflessly of their experiences, their research, and their beliefs. They have inspired us and they have helped us. For this, we thank friends and colleagues in our institutions and study groups:

The Weatherhead School of Management, Case Western Reserve University, Department of Organizational Behavior: Melvin Smith, Diana Bilimoria, Poppy McLeod, David Kolb, David Cooperrider, Ron Fry, Eric Neilsen, Hilary Bradbury, Sandy Piderit, Susan Case, Danny Solow, Mihaly Maserovic, Neil Greenspan, David Aron, Deb O'Neil, and Betty Vandenbosch;

Teleos Leadership Institute: Co-Chair Fran Johnston and the team: Laura Peck, Eddy Mwelwa, Neen Brannan, Delores Mason, Richard Massimilian, Michael McElhenie, Bobbie Nash, Gretchen Schmelzer, David Smith, Felice Tilin, Patrice Waldenberger, and Amy Yoggev.

University of Pennsylvania: Peter Kuriloff, Greg Shea, and Kenwyn Smith.

ESADE: Ricard Serlavos, Tony Lingham, Bonnie Richley, Ceferi Soler, Carlos Losada, Xavier Mendoza, Joan Manuel Batista, and Jaume Hugas.

Inspirational colleagues: Tom Malnight, IMD; Anders Ferguson, Uplift Equity Partners; Sander Tideman, Insight Partners; Beulah Trey, Center for Applied Research; and Professors Babis Mainemelis, London Business School; Kathy Kram, Boston University; Jane Dutton, University of Michigan; James Bailey, George Washington University; Olga Epitropaki, ALBA Athens; Arnauldo Comuffo, University of Parma; Cary Cherniss, Rutgers University; Ken Rhee, University of Northern Kentucky; Jane Wheeler, Bowling Green State University; John Kotter, Harvard University; and Janet Patti, Hunter College.

We would also like to thank former and current doctoral students and members of the Coaching Study Group: Terrence Brizz, Brigette Rapisarda, Helen Williams, Elizabeth Stubbs, Edward De-Jaeger, Lindsey Godwin, Beatriz Rivera, Luis Ottley, Melissa Herb, Allece Carron, Ellen Van Oosten, Duncan Coombe, Darren Goode, Linda Robson, Anita Howard, Kleio Akrivou-Napersky, Loren Dyck, Margaret Hopkins, and Scott Taylor.

Many people have supported us behind the scenes, including Patricia Petty, Erato Paraschaki, Franco Ratti, Bernhard Urs, Lyle Spencer, Fabio Sala, Doug Lennick, Connie Wayne, Cindy Frick, Mary Burton, Hope Greenfield, Sharon Brownfield, Mary Ann Batos, Richard Alston, Sarah Drazectic, Charles Hennigan, Doris Downing, and Ruth Jacobs. We would like to express our appreciation to the Africa Foundation and their colleagues at the Conservation Corporation of Africa, and in particular Jason King, Jacqui McNaughton, Isaac Tembe, and Wendy Wood for the insight and commitment that has resulted in creating hope in so many children and their families in KwaZulu-Natal. Special thanks to Carlton Sedgeley and the team at Royce Carlton for helping us to find venues to share our messages around the world. And our attorney, Bob Freedman, for helping us anticipate possibilities and maintain clarity of purpose.

Although we can not thank them by name, we would like to express gratitude to the anonymous reviewers. Their care and attention enabled us to craft and sharpen our message.

We wish to thank our children, and our families. They've been with us every step of the way: Mark Scott, Rebecca, Sean, and Sarah Renio, Andrew Murphy, Rick, Matt, Mark, Robert, Jeff and Sam Wigsten, and Bobbie and Toby Nash.

And finally, heartfelt gratitude to our thought partners: There are no words big enough to thank the people closest to us, with whom we spoke endlessly and who shared their ideas, questions, wisdom, and love: Sandy Boyatzis, Eddy Mwelwa, Fran Johnston, and Melvin Smith. Our friends Fran and Melvin are precious. They inspire us to think beyond the boundaries of today's knowledge, and keep us grounded in reality as well. And Sandy and Eddy are our partners in everything so we thank them especially for inspiring hope when we were frustrated, compassion when we were anxious, and mindfulness during the all too frequent periods of mindlessness in our lives as we wrote and rewrote the book.

A final salute—to our partnership! We have been learning and writing together since 1987. We are friends. We treasure the creativity we inspire in each other, and enjoy every moment of our work and our relationship.

We welcome correspondence from our readers, and look forward to hearing from many of you through email: richard.boyatzis @case.edu, anniemckee@teleosleaders.com.

Resonant Leadership

ONE

Great Leaders Move Us

FOR THOSE BOLD ENOUGH to lead in this age of uncertainty, the challenges are immense. Our world is a new world, and it requires a new kind of leadership. Think about it: virtually everything we have taken for granted for hundreds, if not thousands, of years is in the midst of profound transformation. Our planet's climate is changing, and we are experiencing extreme, unpredictable weather and temperature changes that affect indigenous plants, farming, animals, and sea life. There is a rise in the number and severity of natural disasters—hurricanes, floods, and droughts. New diseases are on the rise, and HIV and AIDS continue to decimate populations of entire countries and all of sub-Saharan Africa.

And in our societies, across the globe, just look at what leaders are up against: a world that is more unstable, more dangerous than it was even a few years ago. Social systems in place for ages no longer meet the needs of families, communities, or nations. Conflicts that used to be local and for the most part containable are now global. They baffle our sense of reason and ignite panic and anger, as well as impulsive, ineffective responses. These conflicts do not lend themselves to traditional solutions. Around the world, a new kind of war has led to generalized anxiety that touches all of us, personally.

Along with the unprecedented changes affecting our physical and social environments, seismic shifts have shaken the business landscape as well. Our institutions struggle to keep up. Political, economic, technological, and social change are driving profound transformation of our organizational models, making predictability and stability elusive, if not impossible. The sheer complexity of our organizations has increased geometrically, resulting in confusing, albeit creative, organizational structures. Finally, whether we condemn new levels of globalization or laud ourselves for finally moving our organizations to touch the most remote corners of the earth, the fact is that even the simplest organizations are required to reach out and touch others in faraway places, requiring executives to routinely travel upward of two hundred thousand miles a year.

Of course, we have all heard the conventional wisdom: transformations of this magnitude bring with them tremendous opportunity. When the ground moves beneath us, the resulting fissures open up more territory in which to maneuver—more space to imagine possibilities and find ways to make our dreams happen.

The men and women we call *resonant leaders* are stepping up, charting paths through unfamiliar territory, and inspiring people in their organizations, institutions, and communities. They are finding new opportunities within today's challenges, creating hope in the face of fear and despair. These leaders are *moving* people— powerfully, passionately, and purposefully. And they do so while managing the inevitable sacrifices inherent in their roles. They give of themselves in the service of the cause, but they also care for themselves, engaging in renewal to ensure they can sustain resonance over time.

Great leaders are resonant leaders. They are exciting *and* get results. In our last book, *Primal Leadership: Realizing the Power of Emotional Intelligence*, coauthored with Daniel Goleman, we showed that great leaders build resonant relationships with those around them. We explained how emotional intelligence was a key ingredient in producing those relationships and described how to develop emotional intelligence in oneself and others.

We now apply our latest research and that from many fields to show *how* leaders can create resonance in their relationships, their teams, and their organizations. Research and study in fields as diverse as management, medicine, psychology, and philosophy show us the way. In this book, we synthesize key findings from these different fields, as well as from our experiences with leading executives, and show how good leaders can become exceptional by developing resonance in themselves and with others.

These resonant leaders are inspiring their organizations and communities to reach for dreams that even a few years ago were impossible. And these dreams are being realized. Today, we see new products and services available to more people than ever before. Organizational structures are changing dramatically, providing more opportunities for efficiency, effectiveness, challenging and rewarding work, and achievement of goals. New processes and procedures are being developed to cope with rising complexity and the need for speed.

Great leaders are awake, aware, and attuned to themselves, to others, and to the world around them. They commit to their beliefs, stand strong in their values, and live full, passionate lives. Great leaders are emotionally intelligent and they are *mindful*: they seek to live in full consciousness of self, others, nature, and society. Great leaders face the uncertainty of today's world with *hope*: they inspire through clarity of vision, optimism, and a profound belief in their—and their people's—ability to turn dreams into reality. Great leaders face sacrifice, difficulties, and challenges, as well as opportunities, with empathy and *compassion* for the people they lead and those they serve.

Along with all of this positive transformation, however, we have seen a coinciding, disturbing change among leaders with whom we work: they are finding it very difficult to *sustain* their effectiveness—and resonance—over time. We can understand why that happens to leaders who never practiced emotional intelligence in the first place; it is easy to see why those leaders might have trouble sustaining resonance and effectiveness in today's new uncharted waters. But, we wondered, how is it that even our best leaders lose their resonance? Why does this happen among leaders with vision, talent, and emotional intelligence—leaders who truly know better, who understand what it takes to craft great organizations and who have healthy and transparent relationships all around them? Before we look at those questions and some of the conclusions we have reached, let us examine more fully just what we mean by "resonance."

Resonance or Dissonance: The Leader's Choice

Resonant leaders are in tune with those around them. This results in people working in sync with each other, in tune with each others' thoughts (what to do) and emotions (why to do it).[1] Leaders who can create resonance are people who either intuitively understand or have worked hard to develop emotional intelligence—namely, the competencies of self-awareness, self-management, social awareness, and relationship management. They act with mental clarity, not simply following a whim or an impulse.

In addition to knowing and managing themselves well, emotionally intelligent leaders manage others' emotions and build strong, trusting relationships. They know that emotions are contagious, and that their own emotions are powerful drivers of their people's moods and, ultimately, performance. They understand that while fear and anger may mobilize people in the short term, these emotions backfire quickly, leaving people distracted, anxious, and ineffective. Such leaders have empathy. They read people, groups, and organizational cultures accurately and they build lasting relationships. They inspire through demonstrating passion, commitment, and deep concern for people and the organizational vision. They cause those around them to want to move, in concert, toward an exciting future. They give us courage and hope, and help us to become the best that we can be.

Resonant leaders help blend financial, human, intellectual, environmental, and social capital into a potent recipe for effective performance in organizations.[2] In other words, in addition to being great to work with, they get *results*. Of course, to be great, a leader needs to understand the market, the technology, the people, and a multitude of other factors affecting the organization. While this knowledge is necessary, it is not sufficient to produce sustainable, effective leadership. This is where resonance comes into play. Resonance enables the leader to use this expertise in pursuit of the company's performance. It allows the leader to engage the power of all of the people who work in and around the organization.

The problem, as we have said, is that being resonant is not so easy, and sustaining it is even harder—particularly in this new world in which leaders must cope with unprecedented demands and pressures.

Why is resonance so difficult? We think it has something to do with the nature of the job and how we manage it. Even the best leaders—those who *can* create resonance—must give of themselves constantly. For many people, especially the busy executives we work with, little value is placed on *renewal*, or developing practices—habits of mind, body, and behavior—that enable us to create and sustain resonance in the face of unending challenges, year in and year out. In fact, it is often just the opposite. Many organizations overvalue certain kinds of destructive behavior and tolerate discord and mediocre leadership for a very long time, especially if a person appears to produce results. Not much time— or encouragement—is given for cultivating skills and practices that will counter the effects of our stressful roles.

Add to that the increasing pressure on leaders to create predictable results: omnipresent and vigilant constituencies wait, ready to pounce on negative events, or even the hint of a problem. In the wake of the excessive and even criminal behavior of some business leaders in the late 1990s, scrutiny of financial and performance details is at an all-time high. Leaner organizations mean there is more work to do, and it is harder for people to hide. Somehow, we are expected to be strong enough to handle it all without paying much attention to managing the physiological and psychological ups and downs.

But when leaders sacrifice too much for too long—and reap too little—they can become trapped in what we call the *Sacrifice Syndrome*. Leadership is exciting, but it is also stressful. And it is lonely. Leadership is the exercise of power and influence—and power creates distance between people. Leaders are often cut off from support and relationships with people. Our bodies are just not equipped to deal with this kind of pressure day after day. Over time, we become exhausted—we burn out or burn up. The constant small crises, heavy responsibilities, and perpetual need to influence people can be a heavy burden, so much so that we find ourselves trapped in the Sacrifice Syndrome and slip into internal disquiet, unrest, and distress.

In other words, *dissonance becomes the default,* even for leaders who *can* create resonance. And, because our emotions are contagious, dissonance spreads quickly to those around us and eventually permeates our organizations.

Then, of course, there are the others—the many people in leadership positions who have never been resonant. Some should never have been in such positions in the first place. Others seek responsibility and power, but seem to lack a basic understanding of what leadership really is. For them, the dissonance seems to be just the way it is. So they live with it, not appreciating that life could be different and they could be more effective.

But whether they were once resonant or never so, dissonant leaders wreak havoc. They are at the mercy of volatile emotions and reactivity. They drive people too hard, for the wrong reasons, and in the wrong directions. They leave frustration, fear, and antagonism in their wake. And they are often completely unaware of the damage they have done.

The Cycle of Sacrifice and Renewal

We found one clue for why dissonance happens—a phenomenon that we call *power stress*: the unique brand of stress that is a basic part of being a leader, especially today. For people who head organizations, choices are rarely crystal clear and communication and decision making are incredibly complex; and such people often must lead with ambiguous authority. Add to that the loneliness that comes with being the person at the top, and you have the formula for power stress. In the last several years, we have observed leaders experiencing power stress day after day, fighting fire after fire—and then scraping themselves off the floor each evening. They go from occasional episodes of power-related stress to almost daily experiences of it. Ultimately this leads to a form of chronic stress.

We have watched as these leaders became increasingly dispirited. Some began to act out in unhealthy ways, forgetting what had once been their own most deeply held values. Others just burned out altogether.

The problem is not simply power stress, however. Stress has always been part of the leader's reality and always will be. The problem is too little recovery time. Many leaders fail to manage the *Cycle of Sacrifice and Renewal* that must be regulated in order to maintain resonance. Instead, leaders sacrifice themselves continuously to their jobs.

What can we do? To sustain effectiveness once it has been achieved, we need to manage the syndrome of sacrifice, stress, and dissonance—not be its victims. Returning to resonance again and again is the key.

Fortunately, we have some good models out there. We have seen leaders deliberately and consciously step out of destructive patterns to renew themselves physically, mentally, and emotionally. These leaders are able to manage constant crises and chronic stress without giving in to exhaustion, fear, or anger. They do not respond blindly to threats with fearful, defensive acts. They turn situations around, finding opportunities in challenges and creative ways to overcome obstacles. They are able to motivate themselves and others by focusing on possibilities. They are optimistic, yet realistic. They are awake and aware, and they are passionate about their values and their goals. They create powerful, positive relationships that lead to an exciting organizational climate.

Most important, we have found that leaders who sustain their resonance understand that renewing oneself is a *holistic* process that involves the mind, body, heart, and spirit. They see clearly that the self-sacrifice they inevitably must make in their jobs only works if the "self" is somehow still attended to. Without regular renewal the sacrifice becomes too great and dissonance results—with often devastatingly destructive results.

Great leaders understand this, even if they do not say it. They focus attention on developing their intellect, understanding and managing emotions, taking care of their bodies, and attending to the deep beliefs and dreams that feed their spirits. As we will demonstrate in this book, renewal can be a conscious process that actually invokes physiological and psychological changes that enable us to counter the effects of chronic stress and sacrifice. And it all begins with mindfulness, hope, and compassion.

Mindfulness, Hope, and Compassion: The Keys to Renewal

In our work with executives we have found that true renewal relies on three key elements that might at first sound too soft to support the hard work of being a resonant leader. But they are absolutely essential; without them, leaders cannot sustain resonance in themselves or with others. The first element is *mindfulness*, or living in a state of full, conscious awareness of one's whole self, other people, and the context in which we live and work. In effect, mindfulness means being awake, aware, and attending—to ourselves and to the world around us. The second element, *hope*, enables us to believe that the future we envision is attainable, and to move toward our visions and goals while inspiring others toward those goals as well. When we experience the third critical element for renewal, *compassion*, we understand people's wants and needs and feel motivated to act on our feelings.

As we will show in this book, the dynamic relationship among mindfulness, hope, and compassion sparks the kinds of positive emotions that enable us to remain resilient in the face of challenges, even in the unprecedented climate that leaders face today. Together these elements counter the destructive effects of power stress and keep us continually in a state of renewal, and thus they help to produce resonant relationships and great leadership while helping leaders and people around them to renew themselves.

But cultivating the capacity for mindfulness, hope and compassion—and creating or sustaining resonance—does not happen by accident. For most of us, developing ourselves this way requires a process of *Intentional Change*: deliberate, focused identification of our personal vision and our current reality, and conscious creation of and engaging in a learning agenda. This process, as we will show, is well researched and documented, and can support leaders in developing the capabilities necessary to cultivate and maintain mindfulness, hope, and compassion—and resonant leadership.

To summarize, then, leaders today face unprecedented challenges that can result in a vicious cycle of stress, pressure, sacrifice, and dissonance. To counter the inevitable challenges of leadership roles, we need to engage in a conscious process of renewal both on a daily basis and over time. To do so, most of us need to intentionally transform our approach to managing ourselves, and we need to learn new behaviors—practices that enable us to maintain internal resonance and attunement with those we lead. We need to cultivate mindfulness and learn to engage the experiences of hope and compassion. We need to focus deliberately on creating resonance within ourselves—mind, body, heart, and spirit—and then channel our resonance to the people and groups around us.

In the following chapter, we will describe the leader's primary challenge—that of igniting people's passion and mobilizing the resources of the organization toward the emerging and protean future. Then in chapter 3, we will explain how dissonance is the default and how easy it is, even for effective leaders who *can* be resonant, to slip into dissonance with themselves and others around them. This will include a discussion of the Sacrifice Syndrome and a review of its toxic effects on the leader, as well as on others.

In chapter 4, we turn to the possibility of leaders moving into resonance, or even rediscovering it after slipping inadvertently into dissonance. We will look at the critical process of renewal, examining the neuro-endocrine aspects of *physiological* renewal and explain its subsequent effects on the leader's mood, feelings, perceptions, and behavior. As part of this chapter, we will explore how hearing wake-up calls is a vital aspect of the self-awareness that enables a leader to move into renewal and manage the sacrifice and renewal cycle—rather than be a victim of it.

In chapter 5, we review the process of Intentional Change and how it leads to sustainable changes in one's habits, perceptions, and moods. Chapters 6, 7, and 8 explore exactly how you can engage in and move into resonance through the three essential paths to resonance: mindfulness, hope, and compassion. We will explore each of these three primary ways leaders can work through sacrifice to renewal and how they can work on these paths, both within themselves as well as with others around them. The last chapter will ask you to consider how this starts with you.

Thoughts on How to Use This Book

We take the business of counseling leaders very seriously, and this book is intended to provide you with solid advice. Throughout these pages, you will find stories of real people facing real challenges, people who struggle with the most difficult leadership issues. Our recent work and research are supported by an amazing convergence of the latest findings. Recent studies in management science, psychology, and neuroscience all point to the importance of the development of mindfulness and the experiences of hope and compassion. We will show how our ideas can help leaders be more effective and more successful in their roles and even in their lives. We will also provide clear guidance about how you, as a leader, can put some of our ideas into practice.

There is lots of information out there on leadership—some of it is excellent, and some of it is pure hogwash. We believe that there is a big difference between good advice on leadership and the trendy, empty words we so often read. How do you make the distinction?

Good advice should be verifiable. In other words, there should be solid research to support key ideas, concepts, and practices. Our ideas are born of years of research—our own and others'— in the fields of management, psychology, organizational behavior, education, and neurophysiology. In each of the chapters and in extensive endnotes and the appendixes, we have cited and carefully explained this research. We want you, the reader, to be able to see the logic and the empirical support for our ideas and advice. We want you to understand and be able to explain to others what enables a leader to be effective and what gets in the way.

Good advice should also be relevant and applicable. Our ideas, concepts, and practices make sense and can be easily adopted in the context of a leader's work and world. Almost all the examples we share are stories about people we know well and respect tremendously. We have learned a great deal from them, and are deeply grateful for their willingness to share details of their professional challenges and their lives as a way to bring our concepts to life. We hope you will be inspired by these stories, and will learn from them as we have.

In addition to examples you can relate to and that bring the concepts to life, we have included exercises and activities at the end of various chapters and in the book's appendixes. You can use the reflections these exercises inspire to better understand your approach to leadership, to evaluate your current situation, and to move deliberately toward the future of your dreams. These exercises and activities are tried and true. We have used them ourselves, as well as extensively with our clients and executive students.

Depending on how you prefer to learn, you might like to glance at these exercises and even do some of them before you start reading. Now that you have an idea about where we are taking you, you might like to see how some of the concepts apply to you even before you dive into the stories and the research. Some of you may prefer to do the exercises as you read each chapter, others after reading the entire book. Suggestions about each of the exercises will appear at the conclusions of various chapters. In any case, we strongly urge you to take the time to do at least some of them. Give yourself the gift of a few hours of self-reflection. You will be glad you did.

Let us begin now with an in-depth look at two real leaders—one who slipped into dissonance and one who understood the cycle of sacrifice and renewal and how to maintain resonance—even in what is probably *the* most stressful job in the post–September 11 world: running an airline.

TWO

The Leader's Challenge

"EDUARDO" had just been promoted to lead a very visible division of a well-known international NGO (nongovernmental organization).[1] An economist, Eduardo was assigned to a country with a fragile, newly democratic government—formed from opposite sides of a decade-long war that had finally reached resolution. His division's challenge? To help the new government ministries to coordinate their strategies as they built their democracy in this war-torn, poverty-stricken part of the world. His staff of fifty local, well-respected professionals—many skilled in diplomacy—was well suited for dealing with the NGO's "clients," members of a government who until very recently were literally trying to kill each other.

Eduardo, a leader on the fast track who'd had three jobs on two continents over the past six years—all apparent successes—intended to get results and get them fast. At first, he seemed to do all the right things. He met his new team members and began to establish good, friendly relationships with them. He organized his staff for specific tasks, clarified assignments, and established standards of excellence. He drafted a work plan. He made the rounds, meeting key ministers and community leaders. But Eduardo quickly became impatient and a bit skeptical; people seemed to want to move so *slowly*. Privately, with his staff, Eduardo scoffed at the notion that local leaders could really help. He saw their typically long-drawn-out meetings as a huge waste of time, and the emotional discussions a bit embarrassing.

He knew that he needed to move quickly to help the government's ministries formulate a clear agenda for the future. He crafted a research project to investigate and then integrate different community objectives and concerns, as well as to address the inherited conflicts among the country's different cultures. He set a demanding timetable. He worked long hours, stayed focused on outcomes, and demanded the same of others. Within a matter of weeks, people were working at breakneck speed, day and night. This was a familiar pattern for Eduardo, and it had worked for him many times before. But the effects of the heavy demands on Eduardo, his staff, and their clients soon began to show. Tempers were short, communication was curt and devoid of details or social niceties—resulting in misunderstanding and hurt feelings.

Throughout the few months it took to do the study, his staff came to him numerous times trying to share what they had learned about the *real* needs of the new government and the various ministers' opinions about the approach the NGO was taking. They believed it was critical to establish better relationships with key ministers and community leaders. Eduardo, who by this time was extremely frustrated, chastised them for wasting time, derisively calling the meetings they attended "chicken parties" because of the nonsensical "cackling" he believed they encouraged. In the interest of efficiency, he also forbade them from attending state functions or having other contact with government representatives beyond the requirements of the research project. When, after a while, Eduardo began to notice that there was considerable resistance to his approach among his staff, he responded by working harder and demanding ever more of his people. He became increasingly impatient and saw only incompetence and lack of motivation all around him.

Meantime, Eduardo was unaware that the government ministers and other leaders were questioning not only his tactics, but his motives; many believed him to be overly concerned with his own career ambitions, rather than focused on collective goals. This was not completely true, of course. Eduardo was committed. The problem was that he was off-kilter—out of sync with his clients' needs and his employees' work style, and people simply could not understand why he was so caustic and difficult to deal with. Before long, quiet whispers of confusion and uneasiness were turning into a roar of complaints. He did not see that, with few exceptions, he was alienating his counterparts in government and even his staff. Soon, many of the latter were actively siding with their colleagues in government.

Less than a year later Eduardo was sidelined in the country, and the few staff who had followed his lead publicly were discredited. The strategic plan they had written was not used. The NGO was out of favor, and the government ministers did not get the support they needed. Worst of all, there was no logical way to determine how to allocate resources, infighting was on the rise, and communities continued to go without critical health, education, and other services.

They Do Not Call It Blind Ambition for Nothing

What went wrong? In his new assignment, Eduardo did exactly the same kinds of things he'd done in the past to succeed. He assessed the situation, pinpointed what appeared to be time-wasters, and made sure he avoided them. He focused intensely on his goals and drove his people hard to get the job done. Yet this time what he thought were all the *right* moves were actually *wrong*; he failed—and he wasn't even sure why.

One problem was simply that the world he entered was vastly different than that of his previous assignments, making Eduardo's usual formula for success questionable. Those "right moves" he had made in the past had appeared to work just fine in his old organizations. But this country was a much more complex place. People in this client "organization"—a newly democratic government—had only recently put down their weapons against each other after a protracted war. Old rules and traditional ways of solving problems simply weren't going to work here. And, despite the prominence of the NGO and Eduardo's role, his political clout held little appeal for the real decision makers—the ministers and community leaders. They operated informally, as often as not, and almost outside the boundaries of organizations. No clear organizational lines existed, yet Eduardo acted as if there were clear hierarchies. He came in with his eyes closed, focusing on his assigned mission rather than what was really happening.

In essence, Eduardo totally missed the *emotional reality* of the community and the country.[2] He was under a lot of pressure to get results and did not see that *relationships* were the currency and the vehicle for change in this setting. He did not see that when people met to discuss strategies, they were doing at least two things at once: finding common ground so they could make decisions, and healing the wounds of the past. What he dismissed as meaningless "chicken parties" were actually a key means for bridging gaps of understanding between the previously opposing sides. He totally missed the fact that relationships needed to be healed and rebuilt—*before* any formal plan could be conceived. And as the pressures mounted and the complexity of the situation increased, his intense focus on outcomes as opposed to relationships became more and more ineffective.

Without even realizing it, then, Eduardo had slipped quickly into *dissonance*. The mystery here is that even though he had demonstrated good leadership in some of his previous situations, in this job he acted without emotional intelligence. He neglected to listen to his people or even to his clients, and was blind to how his behavior ultimately set the failure in motion. Worst of all, Eduardo's ability to manage his own emotions, attitudes, and behavior *decreased* just when he needed to be most effective.

Eduardo was caught in the *Sacrifice Syndrome* to which so many leaders succumb. His two previous jobs had been "career builders"—tough, visible, calling for everything he could give. He had moved his family several times, disrupting his wife's career and his children's schooling. Each new job brought more responsibility, and that special kind of stress that comes along with power and leadership. With all the excitement of that lifestyle came a high price—prolonged, unremitting pressure at home and at work. In his new NGO job, he felt the responsibility of actually rebuilding a country's infrastructure. He cared deeply about his work and its outcomes, but he perceived himself to be in a race against time. His emotional and physical reserves were depleted, and yet he drove himself relentlessly for weeks on end, continually sacrificing himself to the project and taking no time for the equally necessary periods of rest or reflection. And he demanded the same of everyone around him. In the end, the pressures inherent in Eduardo's life and leadership went untended, causing him to literally close down. His focus narrowed, his emotional intelligence diminished, he lost sight of the reality of the situation and his part in it. He lost his way.

It's Only Human

Perhaps you read Eduardo's story and were immediately able to pinpoint the flaws in this leader's behavior and how they led inevitably to his downfall. And you might have also found yourselves nodding your head in recognition. The fact is that leaders like Eduardo are not at all unusual. Nor are they stupid or evil. Indeed, in today's tumultuous environment, many of us have found ourselves caught up short by what seems to be the continually moving target: challenge after challenge, heavy responsibilities, and new and ever more impossible goals every few months. And all in response to the changes occurring around us—from shifting organizational structures to shifts in the organization of entire nations. It never seems to stop, and sometimes it feels as if there is no room to breathe.

Many of us, like Eduardo, find ourselves in a succession of jobs (often on a fast track), moving our families and changing our priorities every year or so. The demands of these jobs are high, and each success brings loftier expectations and more responsibility. Sometimes we attempt to deal with sacrifices and stress by oversimplifying our tasks, doing the minimum required to get the job done. Maybe we get tunnel vision and focus on a technical approach to getting results, to the exclusion of heart, body, spirit, and relationships. Maybe we just tune out any messages that do not jibe with our sense of what needs to happen. We are exhausted, and we shut down.

Like Eduardo, we miss the *real* goals and create dissonance along the way. Our negativity causes us to close down and to stop functioning effectively. At the same time, our stress and negative emotions are actually contagious, so our people also begin to feel frustrated, empty, and unfulfilled—not to mention ineffective. It becomes a vicious cycle: power stress, sacrifice, dissonance, more stress, and more sacrifice.

The result? Dissonance is more common than resonance, poor leadership is evident more often than good. In this environment of unprecedented change, dissonance has become the default mode, and even good leaders find themselves slipping. And that's the challenge of being a leader today: how to manage the Sacrifice Syndrome, to build and sustain resonance in the face of great trials.

Had Eduardo balanced all of the stress and pressure with regular rest, reflection, and contemplation—had he managed what we call the *Cycle of Sacrifice and Renewal* with which every leader must contend—he might not have missed the signs that he was about to go down. Had he taken regular time to renew himself mentally, physically, emotionally, and spiritually and allowed those working for him to do the same, he'd have realized what was happening. Perhaps he might have even stopped and listened to the critical insights his people were trying to share with him. Instead, Eduardo lost the capacity for attending to himself and others.

Clearly the Eduardos of the world do not want to fail. They do not want to create dissonance, or environments in which people feel disconnected, threatened, overworked, and undervalued. They do not intend to foster a sense of doom or threat. Every leader wants to be effective, and underneath all the bad behavior most dissonant leaders are actually good people.

Successfully managing the inherent stress of leadership *over time* enables us to leverage our strengths and compensate for our shortcomings, even when things are tough, as they were for Eduardo. Had he maintained balance and resonance within himself, he would have been more likely to remain open, strong, and grounded in the face of the new challenges of his position. He would likely have taken more, and more appropriate, steps to build the right kind of relationships with the right people. As it was, he just did not have the emotional energy to think clearly or take the right actions.

So what happens? What enables some people to successfully manage the leader's challenge and consistently develop and sustain resonance in themselves and in their teams and organizations, while so many others slip into dissonance? To begin exploring that question, let us look now at a very different kind of leader—one who illustrates that, although dissonance is all too typical in the rough-and-tumble environment of recent years, *resonance is possible*—and leads to infinitely better results. What's more, it's possible even in an industry that arguably has faced the toughest challenge of all when it comes to doing business in the current climate: the airline industry.

Flying High

Back in the 1970s, Colleen Barrett would hardly have guessed that she would one day be president of an airline. At the time she was a legal secretary and her boss, Herb Kelleher, asked her to help him and a small band of committed friends and colleagues fulfill a dream: to launch a company that they would call Southwest Airlines. It looked like a David and Goliath story. The big airlines naturally did not want competitors homing in on their business, and they did everything they could to stop Herb and his team. "They fought us every step of the way," Colleen recalls, "and some of it got really ugly. But the more arrogant the 'bad guys' became, the more they tried to break us, the more committed and united we became as a team."[3]

Herb and Colleen and their team could see a new and very different kind of airline—great services *and* a great place to work. The commitment they had to one another was tangible. They resonated with each other and as a team they resonated with their dreams. They consciously defined how they would work together—team spirit was high on the list, as was "do unto others . . ." They focused on doing the right thing for themselves, the business, and the customers—and not necessarily in that order.

They had noble values. But even the most inspiring values are not easy to sustain over time, when everyone is under a lot of pressure and the business is growing by leaps and bounds. Early on, Colleen—who had become Herb's right-hand person, idea generator, and implementer—recognized this. And she saw something else too: she realized that the resonance they had created in the team and the small company might well be part of the reason it was fast becoming unique—and thus so successful.

Colleen recognized something that many leaders miss. She saw that effective teams and powerful, positive organizational cultures do not happen by accident. It takes time, effort, planning, and even a strategy to create and sustain the healthy working relationships and norms that foster effectiveness. She determined that creating a great company meant more than developing great services—it also meant paying attention to the emotional reality of the organization and deliberately creating a great culture. To make sure the company never lost its magic, she began organizing systems, processes, and rituals that would essentially create and preserve what we would now call resonance. She took charge of many of the processes that guided people's behavior within the company and with customers. Rather than institutionalize the vision and the mission, however, Colleen deliberately created systems based on the *spirit* of the company; she put a premium on esprit de corps and on treating one another with compassion; she minimized the company hierarchy and emphasized individuality; and she made sure that amid all the hard work of getting a startup airline flying, she and the team had regular opportunities for fun and reflection.

With such a culture in place, one with resonant leadership and in which all members from the CEO on down regularly treat each other, their customers, and their suppliers with respect and compassion, it's no surprise that this airline got off the ground. But the question is: How has Southwest *sustained* its success over thirty-plus years? How has it continued to do this even in today's troubled times and in an industry in which every year another competitor grounds its airplanes—permanently? In contrast, Southwest has consistently shown profit and met goals, quarter after quarter. The company's customer service is legendary. There has never been an involuntary layoff—even after September 11, 2001, when many U.S. airlines cut back drastically. Employees are committed and passionate about their work. They see it as a cause, not a job, and it shows.

They are doing something right at Southwest, and we think it has a lot to do with resonant leadership and the climate Colleen has so deliberately created over the years. Research corroborates our thinking: studies show that the culture of an organization, and in particular the way people feel about the climate, can account for nearly 30 percent of business performance.[4] As a resonant leader, then, Colleen has helped to craft a climate that translates into results. Today, Colleen's efforts show up in day-to-day practices as well as the principles and values of the company. Indeed, despite being named one of the "Fifty Most Powerful Women" by *Fortune* magazine in 2003, she has not lost the down-to-earth common sense, authenticity, and profound commitment to people that she started with during the airline's early days.[5] Colleen defines the culture at Southwest. She guides people's passion, energy, and activities in a positive direction.

We know when we are around resonant leaders like Colleen—they bring out the best in us. They help us to see when good fortune is smiling on us and they make us feel good about our efforts and ourselves. People follow resonant leaders because the leader's *heart* is so clearly in the work.

As we have already pointed out (and it bears repeating), resonant leaders manage their emotions well and read individuals and groups accurately. They consciously attune to people, focus them on a common cause, build a sense of community, and create a climate that enables people to tap into passion, energy, and a *desire* to move together in a positive direction. They are optimistic and realistic at the same time.

If you wonder whether you or someone else is a resonant leader, ask yourself these questions:

- Is the leader inspirational?
- Does the leader create an overall positive emotional tone that is characterized by hope?
- Is the leader in touch with others? Does the leader know what is on others' hearts and minds? Does the leader experience and demonstrate compassion?
- Is the leader mindful—authentic and in tune with self, others, and the environment?

Colleen's success is in part due to the fact that anyone observing her could answer "yes" to those four questions. In other words, her success is due to her ability to create and sustain resonance, just as Eduardo's failure was in part due to his slipping into dissonance. And both resonance and dissonance develop because emotions are *contagious*.[6] Yes: research indicates that there are actual physiological reasons behind the spreading effects of either resonant *or* dissonant leadership in an organization.

Resonance Is Contagious— and So Is Dissonance

The notion that emotions are contagious and that the human brain has an "open loop" system when it comes to sharing emotional clues and ultimately feelings and moods has been researched extensively in recent years.[7] We are literally "wired" to pick up subtle clues from one another—and therefore, in a sense, we are dependent on one another for our emotions. We gauge our emotional response on the feelings we notice in the people around us.

Our emotions can also convey our intentions to others, thereby enabling smoother communication and interaction. For example, fear may signal the need to mollify, defend, or flee; joy may indicate a chance to share good fortune or a desire for contact and connection. Our bodies respond to our emotions in subtle as well as obvious ways; things like facial expressions and tone of voice are fleeting but important signs of the emotions that drive a person's behavior.[8] The more subtle clues—flushing or paling, minute facial expressions, and some aspects of posture—are very difficult to control and are strong signals to other people of our true emotions. Our bodies tell the truth, and even when we do not intend it, we send messages about our true feelings.[9]

We are not always conscious of the messages we are sending or receiving about emotions. Nevertheless, we are very good at reading each other. This is likely related to survival mechanisms that have been in place for thousands, if not millions, of years.[10] We attend to each other constantly, attempting to predict one another's behavior so we can tailor our responses accordingly. Even if we do not understand the source of another's feelings, we generally can tell when he is in the grip of strong emotions, even when he is trying to hide them. Furthermore, we actually catch the emotions of people around us, even when communication is completely nonverbal.[11]

This is especially true when it comes to our leaders—we watch them very carefully, and we can smell their emotions a mile away.[12] They have a lot of power over us, and we want to be able to predict, as best we can, what they want and what we should do. When a leader (like Eduardo) is impatient, frustrated, or fearful of failure, we begin to feel exactly the same way. We become defensive and self-protective, or we do whatever we can to get away from the source of our distress. This is the beginning of a dissonant climate.

On the other hand, when we sense that our leader is excited and hopeful, we feel invigorated and motivated. When our leaders exude enthusiasm, realistic optimism, and genuine concern for us, we have more energy for our work and can face challenges more creatively. This is what it feels like to be around Colleen Barrett. We want to be around people like this, and we want to join in whatever they are doing—especially if the cause jibes with our values.

Demonstrating what most of us know from experience, professor Nadia Wager and her colleagues have been studying the effect of negative versus positive managerial styles on the blood pressure of the people around the leader.[13] They found in one study that subordinates' blood pressure went up dramatically when dealing with a supervisor whose style was not respectful, fair, or sensitive to others. Their blood pressure would drop to normal when they worked with a different supervisor whose style was more thoughtful and sensitive.

Having seen Colleen Barrett in action with people at Southwest, we are convinced that the messages she personally sends to the people around her go a long way toward creating resonance. She is passionate about what she is doing, and it shows in her excitement, hard work, and dedication. She likes working as part of a team, and she cares about her employees and customers. Her powerful, positive belief in the company and its people are tangible and contagious—and evident in how people treat each other.

At Southwest, people start with a fundamental, shared commitment to their cause and to each other. Even in brief encounters about normal daily business, employees treat each other with friendly respect. There is a clear sense of team spirit and that people want to help one another. The golden rule is alive and well: people treat one another as they'd like to be treated themselves. That's why both inside and outside the company, with customers, vendors, and contractors, the customer service relationship is real and has a human face. When one person told us "We are in the customer service industry. We just happen to fly planes," we believed her.[14] It was clearly more than a company line, because the statement was evident in people's attitudes and behavior. We could see it and feel it in every interaction. We could also sense it in the very atmosphere at Southwest's headquarters at Love Field in Dallas, Texas. Reports from within Southwest Airlines suggest that this atmosphere as well as Colleen's style helps people to feel excitement and commitment and to *want* to rise to the inevitable challenges they face every day.

The contagious nature of resonance often translates into what we might think of as intangibles. Just look at Southwest: the first thing you notice is the light—bright and sunny; something about the place feels vibrant and alive. Thousands of pictures and framed letters on the walls show celebrations of achievement, special events, and ordinary, everyday workers being honored. Everywhere you go in the building, people are talking and laughing together and clearly having a good time. The way people dress is striking too: no corporate stodginess at Southwest. You'll see everything from casual suits to jeans and t-shirts. Mainly, you'll see everyone looking busy, happy, and comfortable.

Most important, people's behavior at the company reflects the values and mission that Colleen's contagious resonant leadership has helped create. Resonance is a way of life, not just an abstract goal. People demonstrate obvious, tangible care and concern for one another, and yet they are direct and hold each other accountable for getting the job done and living the company values. It seems that people are really paying attention—to their work, their attitudes and values, and their relationships. There is a sense of pride and hopefulness about the future. Common sense and good judgment are expected, cultivated, and celebrated. Passion for the work and the company as a whole is evident, and it is deliberately kept alive in hundreds of small and large ways. Information flows freely; there is very little second-guessing about where the company is going or how it is going to get there. This frees up a lot of energy for actually doing the work and successfully moving forward. Colleen and her team are clearly managing the emotional reality at Southwest—and it is resulting in consistent victory in the marketplace.

The flip side of the contagious nature of emotions, however, is that dissonance is infectious as well. When we sense a leader's distress, we generally will not ask what is going on, we simply adjust our behavior. We respond emotionally and almost automatically, either catching our leader's moods or trying to protect ourselves from whatever may be disturbing him or her.

This is certainly what happened in the case of Eduardo, whose story we recounted at the beginning of this chapter. He had been capable of generating resonance, but except for a few attempts at the beginning of his tenure at the NGO, he became trapped in the Sacrifice Syndrome and could not sustain effectiveness. And the effects worsened as the pressure of his new role became evident. Somehow, he could not tap into his leadership skills. When he stepped into his new post people knew little or nothing about him—his personal challenges or his professional dilemmas. What they did know was that the man was anxious and under a lot of pressure. They caught the brunt of his stress every day, and avoided him as much as they could, even on those days when he was relatively cheerful and calm.

This is because our response to one another is not dictated only by what we pick up in any one encounter. According to numerous studies, emotions can be linked to longer-term attitudes as well as in-the-moment responses. Because of this, emotions indirectly affect people's judgments about social situations and impact their behavior as well.[15] In one study, during a negotiation exercise, when people were made what they considered an insulting offer, their brains showed the same electrical activation as when people experience strong negative emotions like pain, disgust, and distress.[16]

When we apply these findings to relationships at work, we see that if we are sometimes confused by someone's anxious or inauthentic behavior (causing distrust and feelings of unease or fear), we may come to habitually approach that person cautiously, no matter what their mood in the moment. We avoid them, or we play their game, colluding with their pretense, and begin to engage in a less-than-authentic way ourselves. So, when the leader is inauthentic or overtly expressing destructive emotions, dissonance in the team and even in the organization is almost inevitable.[17] The outcome when a lot of people act this way is pretty ugly—unpleasantly political at best, toxic at worst.

Think of how, in contrast to Colleen's encouragement of a team spirit at Southwest, Eduardo communicated both nonverbally and verbally that he had no interest in working as part of a team. This was not because he categorically dismissed the importance of teamwork—in fact, in the past, he had managed teams very well. But, as the pressure mounted, he began to see the stakes as too high, and his judgment about how to accomplish his goals became skewed. He was not seeing clearly. Given his limited line of sight, he actually began to believe that he alone knew what the project demanded, and his interest in what his employees and his clients had to say diminished and then disappeared. As a result, his people grew more and more frustrated and despondent; and they felt helpless about their ability to do anything to turn the situation around. In the end, of course, neither they nor Eduardo could complete the mission with which they'd been charged.

Eduardo drove people's emotions in a negative direction. As the very real challenges of the situation and the press of responsibility increased, and as the repercussions of years of coping with the Sacrifice Syndrome set in, he began to slip into a state of chronic nervousness. His emotions were contagious to the point that people became paralyzed, or began to actively resist his leadership. At this point, neither Eduardo nor his staff could tap into their creativity, energy, or problem-solving skills—they were too focused on dealing with negativity and dissonance. In fact, one person told us that nearly half of everyone's time was taken up by complaining, political infighting, or simply hiding out. Needless to say, this kind of situation, which is common in dissonant environments, does not lead to collective success.

The difference between Eduardo and Colleen is that resonant leaders like Colleen drive their own and others' emotions in a *positive* direction. They create healthy, vibrant cultures and climates, and they get results. And it all begins, at least, with emotional intelligence.

Emotional Intelligence: A Good Place to Start

As we have pointed out in previous writings, emotional intelligence (EI) accounts for 85 to 90 percent of the difference between outstanding leaders and their more average peers.[18] EI includes four domains: self-awareness, self-management, social awareness, and relationship management. The first two domains determine how well we understand and manage ourselves and our emotions; the latter two dictate how well we recognize and manage the emotions of others, build relationships, and work in complex social systems. As shown in Table 2-1, these four "quadrants" house eighteen leadership competencies, all of which support the development of resonance.[19]

The fact that EI is a determining factor in excellent leadership does not mean that intellect is unimportant. Clearly, we need to be smart to deal with the complexities and challenges our organizations face. We need to be able to see patterns in seemingly unrelated bits of information. We need to understand strategy, markets, finance, and technology and to be able to use what we know quickly and efficiently, and communicate our knowledge with others. In fact, two cognitive competencies, *systems thinking* and *pattern*

TABLE 2-1

Emotional intelligence domains and competencies

Personal competence: These capabilities determine how we manage ourselves.

Self-awareness

- *Emotional self-awareness*: Reading one's own emotions and recognizing their impact; using "gut-sense" to guide decisions
- *Accurate self-assessment*: Knowing one's strengths and limits
- *Self-confidence*: Having a sound sense of one's self-worth and capabilities

Self-management

- *Emotional self-control*: Keeping disruptive emotions and impulses under control
- *Transparency*: Displaying honesty, integrity, and trustworthiness
- *Adaptability*: Demonstrating flexibility in adapting to changing situations or overcoming obstacles
- *Achievement*: Having the drive to improve performance to meet inner standards of excellence
- *Initiative*: Being ready to act and to seize opportunities
- *Optimism*: Seeing the "up side" in events

Social competence: These capabilities determine how we manage relationships.

Social awareness

- *Empathy*: Sensing others' emotions, understanding their perspectives, and taking active interest in their concerns
- *Organizational awareness*: Reading the currents, decision networks, and politics at the organizational level
- *Service*: Recognizing and meeting follower, client, or customer needs

Relationship management

- *Inspirational leadership*: Guiding and motivating with a compelling vision
- *Influence*: Using a range of tactics for persuasion
- *Developing others*: Bolstering others' abilities through feedback and guidance
- *Change catalyst*: Initiating, managing, and leading in a new direction
- *Conflict management*: Resolving disagreements
- *Building bonds*: Cultivating and maintaining a web of relationships
- *Teamwork and collaboration*: Fostering cooperation and team building

recognition, consistently show a strong relationship to leadership effectiveness. [20]

That said, most cognitive abilities are baseline—you'd better have them, or you cannot (or should not) be in a leadership role. What makes the most difference once you're in that role is *how* you use your knowledge, not what you know. This is where EI comes in. In most cases, we feel before we think or at least feel and think at the same time (the sequence often occurs in miliseconds). The parts of our brains that deal with emotions and those that deal with cognition and rational thought are intimately linked. In many cases, emotions will indeed drive our behavior, especially when we are in crisis or feeling threatened.[21]

In this time of uncertainty, in today's complex and challenging environment, and with the stress inherent in leadership, leaders are constantly feeling threatened in one way or another. Now, more than ever, EI is key. It enables us to monitor our own hot buttons, so we don't fly off the handle and react without thinking. Developing self-awareness and self-management enables us to capitalize on our strengths and manage our emotions so we can feel—and create—passionate commitment to our goals. Understanding others enables us to more effectively motivate individuals and guide groups, teams, and organizational cultures.

Looking again at our examples of Eduardo and Colleen Barrett, you can see right away the differences in their EI levels—and the effects on their organizations. When under pressure, Eduardo defaulted to a simplistic way of understanding influence: he valued organizational hierarchy (with himself as boss), for example, over the idea or practice of any kind of team spirit. Colleen, on the other hand, is consistently balanced and resonant within herself, enabling her to effectively employ her considerable skills in building and maintaining relationships while engaging in complex influencing strategies.

And, Colleen's emotional intelligence and internal resonance translates to organizational resonance. Hand-in-hand with the team spirit she helped instill at Southwest goes an egalitarian work ethic featuring minimum hierarchy. Instead, the culture places a

premium on individuality, which you can see in the casual atmosphere of the company headquarters and how people dress. People's
individuality is respected and even celebrated at the same time
that collaboration and teamwork are a given. Several people con-
fided to us that if asked, most people would not even be able to
identify each other by title, but they *do* know what people do well
and they know their names. They know each other as people and
for what they can do. Personal relationships are encouraged—employees often get together for after-work barbeques and parties
at the office, celebrating small wins, holidays, birthdays, and the
like. The egalitarian spirit seems to free people to build relationships, and get work done, in unusually creative and flexible ways.

People truly appreciate one another at Southwest, just as they
appreciate their customers. In another demonstration of how to
sustain resonance, Colleen recently found a great way to institutionalize appreciation. Southwest is unique in the airline industry, and
its flexible and friendly service surprises customers. Many of them
write to senior management to thank them for the special attention they receive. Colleen has made it a habit to *use* these letters
as a way to renew herself. In the quiet early mornings, or when
things get hectic and stressful, Colleen takes time to read every one
of these letters. Reading the stories connects her with her dreams,
her vision for the company and the people it touches. In the letters
commending employees and the company there are messages of
hope. The small and large contributions people have made in the
spirit of respect, empathy, and care for customers are the epitome
of the vision Colleen and others hold for Southwest.

These letters help Colleen to feel excitement and hope, even
on those days when things are tough. Hearing about employees'
challenges and their responses keeps Colleen in touch with her
people's lives in the trenches. She empathizes with them, and feels
compassion for the difficulties they and the customers have faced.
She will often pen handwritten notes to her employees, commending them for their creativity and hard work. This, we know, means
a lot to people. So, as Colleen renews herself, she also *shares* the
renewal. And once a month Colleen sends employees the most

inspiring letters from customers. This "Packet of Good Letters" enables her to build resonance by inspiring in Southwest's employees hope, care and concern, and awareness of how good they can be as a company. Colleen knows that when they read the letters, they will feel as she does: renewed, hopeful, passionate, and in touch with the best of who they are as a company.

In contrast, think of Eduardo, who not only had a hard time showing (and certainly did not institutionalize) appreciation, but often showed a complete lack of respect for others' viewpoints when it came to how to get the work done. He didn't even allow for open communication, much less a forum for dialogue and sharing of hope and pride about the work his people were doing and the goals they hoped to meet. He may not have meant to do this; he had just lost the capacity to create a positive emotional climate as a result of succumbing to the Sacrifice Syndrome. He had neglected renewal for too long.

What we are saying, then, is that given the inherent pressures of a leader's role and the demands of today's environment, *EI alone is not enough to sustain resonance.* How, then, do leaders like Colleen Barrett do it?

Sustaining Resonance Through Renewal

To create resonance in a culture, and success in the business the way Colleen and her team at Southwest Airlines have, you have to attend to yourself. Otherwise, you will find yourself at the mercy of the stress of your job.

Think again of Eduardo. He drove himself relentlessly to achieve his goals, and he drove his people right along with him. The end result? Stress, dissonance, burnout—and failure. What Eduardo didn't understand is that for leaders to sustain their effectiveness, they must learn how to sustain themselves.

Colleen, in contrast, has figured out that *being* emotionally intelligent simply is not enough to sustain resonant leadership—not today, and especially not in an industry like hers. She has learned, therefore, how to manage the inevitable sacrifices of leadership, to renew herself, and to create and sustain resonance in her organization. In short, she has learned to manage the Cycle of Sacrifice and Renewal that we will continue to explore in these pages.

Knowing that emotions are contagious, Colleen pays attention to her feelings and her mood. She is mindful of personal ups and downs, and works not only to understand herself but to take care of her own emotional needs. She knows that certain aspects of her work, such as close connection with people and customers, make her feel hopeful, inspired, and ready to face challenges. Care and concern for the needs of others actually renews her. So she makes sure she has lots of direct contact with people. As a counterbalance to stress and to ensure time to regroup, she deliberately builds in time to be alone and reflect: early mornings, a protected hour here and there, are dedicated to thoughtful reflection, writing warm personal notes to employees, and other sustaining activities. Colleen has learned how to create and sustain resonance in herself and with others through a conscious process of renewal—she takes time to care for herself, get in touch with what is important to her, and to connect with people she cares about.

We will soon look more closely at this idea—how great leaders create or sustain resonance through renewal. But first let us examine how easy it is to slip into dissonance, especially in today's climate, even when our intentions are good and our talents are many. In the next chapter we will look at one good person who, in the end, failed as a leader. We will see how this happened to him—and can happen to the best of us, when we do not counteract the pressures and sacrifices that are inherent in our roles.

THREE

Dissonance Is the Default

FOR MANY YEARS, "Karl," a managing partner in a well-known professional services firm, exemplified the qualities of an exceptional leader. His reputation for not only bringing in clients but also keeping them happy was legendary. He was a stellar role model, therefore, for young new associates, whom he often would take under his wing, creating opportunities and guiding them up the company ladder. Karl worked hard to manage both himself and his relationships in an insightful way. Managing client projects in the region he led had become second nature—he could almost predict the pattern of team dynamics and ongoing negotiation with clients about deliverables and next steps. He was generally upbeat and creative, even during the times of year when the workload peaked and nerves were frayed. He held people accountable, while ensuring that they got what they needed and developed their skills along the way. People below him responded to his guidance, peers trusted him, and the board respected him.

But all of that began to change—slowly at first and then more radically—when his industry came under siege amid several high-profile scandals involving unethical behavior and illegal actions that toppled companies and careers. Karl felt a new level of pressure to generate business and manage increasingly low morale among partners and associates alike. Then he was moved to a corporate role to support the senior team in managing the crisis. He welcomed the change; though he loved his work, the job had become excruciatingly stressful over the last year or two—and this move seemed like an important stepping stone.

Soon, however, reality set in as he found himself cut off from the work he loved. It was hard for Karl to fathom how this office, a mere five hundred miles from his region, could be so completely different. Here he was, in the same company, with some of the same people he had known for years, and yet the rules of engagement were completely alien. And he was working harder than ever.

Around the same time, Karl's wife took on a leading role at a startup company and seldom made it home for dinner herself. The distance between them grew, and, buckling under the pressures of a disintegrating home life coupled with his new work demands, Karl soon stopped doing some of the little—and big—things that he used to rely on as a resonant leader. For example, he stopped paying as much attention to the dynamics between people with whom he worked. Whereas, out in the regions, he had made it his business to know who worked well with whom and where the rivalries were, in this new role he ignored these subtleties. He just did not have the patience anymore, and he felt that the games that were played were beneath him. When he had occasion to step into the middle of a long-standing conflict between corporate lifers, he did not attempt to smooth things over; instead, he barely concealed his scorn for what he saw as immature behavior and posturing, losing the trust and respect of both parties.

Karl was also ignoring the cultural messages, which were very different in headquarters than in the regions. His focus was on surviving his disappointment with the new job and the unpleasant business environment, not on managing politics. One fateful day he got tired of it all. He decided to share a piece of his mind with the board and wrote a scathing letter criticizing the political environment at headquarters. He knew, of course, that he was violating a cardinal rule of business wisdom by putting such opinions in writing, but he no longer cared.

It became more and more uncomfortable to be around Karl. His conversation circled largely around himself: what he was doing and how well (very well); and how underappreciated he was by his colleagues (they had no idea how good he was, they were all jealous of him, etc). His disdain for colleagues and clients came across. Karl didn't have a good word to say about anyone. His body language, tone of voice, and even his choice of words indicated a host of disturbing emotions: anger, hostility, jealousy, pride, and a deep sense of resentment at being treated unfairly.

The change in his behavior surprised everyone: this was not the cool, collected, and emotionally open Karl whom everyone had known for so long. Clearly, the last several years of turbulence in the industry had become too much even for this star performer. Some people stopped trusting him, and clients no longer seemed very interested in his offers of social evenings. Yet no one seemed able to approach him about his behavior; the firm's other partners were too embarrassed to confront their colleague, and his subordinates felt too intimidated.

Those close to Karl noticed another change: his lifestyle was becoming excessive. Despite his wife's objections and dire signs in the economy, he insisted on buying the most expensive house in the best neighborhood near headquarters, even though it meant a hefty loan. He started joining young associates on nights out, drinking too much and getting involved in conversations he probably should have stayed well away from. He shared too much information, was too free with his opinions about the firm and clients, and was too often just this side of propriety in his behavior, especially after a few drinks. One evening two female associates got sick of his tired jokes and hints: they spent the better part of the next week talking through their options with human resources.

The financial services environment worsened: a few leaders had been tried, convicted, and jailed. Karl's firm had avoided major problems so far, and senior management wanted it to stay that way. As they diligently reviewed partners' behavior, values, and style, they found themselves in the awkward position of finally having to deal with Karl—a member of their own team. His behavior had become too egregious to ignore. His questionable management style and the way he pushed the envelope with employees and clients were no longer tolerable.

No one could understand what had happened. He was as smart as ever, but somehow he was stumbling—making bad decisions, alienating people, and generally creating dissonance. It seemed that all of a sudden, Karl's brilliance just was not good enough anymore.

Clueless Coping

When we met Karl, his management team had recently made it clear that his behavior was no longer acceptable and he must either change or leave. He was trying desperately to avoid being fired—and he was completely baffled. It was clear to us that he had slipped from resonant leadership into a vicious cycle of power stress, sacrifice, dissonance, and more stress—and he was at that point in the Sacrifice Syndrome where he was not able to see for himself what was happening. The stress was blinding him, and so was history. After all, he had been one of the best managers in the firm, had been moved to corporate because of his success, and had consistently been rewarded for his performance—until now. The problem was that his industry was being forced to change, the pressure was extreme, and Karl was not able to martial the personal resources he needed to change himself.

Instead, he fell back on old habits—ones that had worked early in his career when he felt pressured and had to prove himself. Hard work had served him well before, he reasoned, and he believed more of the same would bring success. He thought that simply upping the intensity and his pace should do the trick, not reflecting that his current role was now in leadership, not client management. He tried to deal with the constant pressure at work by turning up the heat—on himself. Karl's intense focus caused a kind of mindlessness, a concept we will explore in depth in chapter 6. Under stress, he was closing off to exactly the information he needed to pay attention to—a fatal error, and one many of us make when we become trapped in the cycle of stress and sacrifice that is so common among leaders.

When we spoke with Karl, and then with his CEO and colleagues, it became clear that Karl had become blind. He had a wildly inaccurate view of how others perceived him, and was unable to recognize that he was causing people to be uncomfortable and anxious. Over time, Karl had lost touch with what he was feeling. He was clueless about his own (now usually negative) emotions and how they showed in his facial expressions and body language. When asked, he could speak elegantly, even passionately, about his beliefs and values, but as he told stories about his recent escapades, it was very hard to see evidence of those values. Karl was a walking, talking contradiction and he did not seem to know it.

Over the past few years, he had slowly lost touch with reality. He had created a self-image that served to protect him. He had stopped seeing other people clearly, and whatever capacity he had for empathy was buried under warped judgments and self-serving interpretations of events. He had chipped away at people's trust to get the results he wanted, damaging relationship after relationship.

In the end, Karl was not fired (last we knew). But he was relegated to a low-visibility, low-impact management position in a far-off regional office. He was on a kind of probation: one wrong move and he would be out. Karl's career was just about over at this firm, even if he did have a job.

When Stress Becomes Dissonance

We have all known people like Karl—bright, successful leaders who lose their resonance when faced with a prolonged period of pressure, becoming irritating, abrasive, and oblivious. We shake our heads, amazed that they simply do not see how people are reacting to their negativity and self-centered behavior. It is more disappointing than watching those leaders who have never or seldom been resonant with others. We almost expect bad behavior from these people and we are not surprised at their mindlessness. But in the case of leaders like Karl, we are confused: How did it happen, and why doesn't anyone stop them? We predict that eventually they will fail, and we are often surprised at how long they are able to avoid failure. How is it possible, we wonder, that they are so clueless, and how is it possible that our organizations tolerate such behavior for so long?

We see three major reasons that so many people sink into dissonance and are allowed to remain in that state. First, there is what we have termed the Sacrifice Syndrome, an outgrowth of power stress when it goes unchecked.[1] Power stress is endemic to those in positions of responsibility whose jobs depend on them exercising influence (or power) with and over others. Leaders are called upon to wield influence every day, and with power this particular form of stress is inevitable. For a leader such stress can become chronic over time, because our bodies are just not designed to deal with the unremitting pressures that go along with the leadership role. Second, many people cope with their stress by developing what are called defensive routines—bad habits that keep us in denial about what is really going on inside us and around us.[2] And finally, our organizations create their own monsters—some of the worst, dissonant behaviors are actually encouraged in the workplace, especially in the tense environment of the last several years.

Power Stress and the Sacrifice Syndrome

As leaders, we face crises, small and large, as part of a day's work. We find ourselves putting out fires, running from one crisis to the next. And we are good at this: the most talented among us are smart, focused, independent, and high energy. We have a great deal of self-control and are effective in managing our impulses and leading others. We give a lot, strive for excellence, achieve our goals, and get results. We are influential, and we use our power for the greater good. And like Karl, we are effective leaders—for a time.

Paradoxically, it is our effectiveness that contributes to the Sacrifice Syndrome. It goes like this: in the process of giving of ourselves, we give too much, leading us to ultimately become *in*effective. Over time and unchecked, the physical and emotional toll of even resonant leadership limits our ability to sustain high performance, as shown in figure 3-1.

Leaders like Karl have tremendous responsibility, and the more senior they are, the heavier the burden. They need to exert influence over others, engaging with them and guiding their behavior towards challenging goals. Good leaders need a great deal of self-control, which takes emotional energy and effort. When you add it all up and throw in a real crisis or two, leaders will experience what we call chronic power stress.[3] In fact, scientists studying stress would call leadership a role involving "chronic stress with periodic occasions of acute stress."[4]

When effective, the normal demands of a leader's job arouse power needs and cause our minds and bodies to be constantly on high alert.[5] This is stressful. In this state, a part of our limbic brain,

FIGURE 3-1

The Sacrifice Syndrome

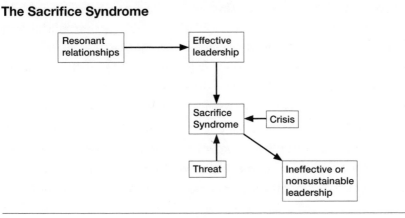

called the amygdala, is aroused. It activates neural circuits that increase electrical activity in the right prefrontal cortex (behind the forehead).[6] At the same time, a set of hormones are released into the bloodstream that invoke the "fight or flight" response. These neural and hormonal processes protected early man from dire and immediate physical threats. In those days, stressful events were usually separated by long periods of gathering food or doing uneventful routine work, like stripping hides to make clothing, and play, such as socializing with friends and family.

In today's stressful world, however, we are in very complex and often threatening emotional situations, both at work and in our lives. We are frequently at the mercy of rapid change, needing to take big risks and make decisions that feel like life and death for ourselves and our organizations. In recent years, the immediate pressures at work and in our busy lives are set against a backdrop of global unrest: wars, terrorism, environmental changes, and unpredictable events that spark fear and confusion. And, as humans, we have the distinctive ability to create our own stress, with its full bodily response, merely by thinking about or anticipating future episodes or encounters that might be stressful. This means that we are likely to be in a state of high alert much of the time. This condition is magnified for leaders who, in addition to all the normal stress, also have tremendous responsibility and who face real crises almost daily.

This was the state in which Karl found himself once his industry came under increasing pressure and he was moved to a job he did not like and was unsuited for. The trouble is that neither our minds nor our bodies were designed to deal with such relentless stress. To cope and keep ourselves on an even keel we have to constantly employ emotional self-control, which in turn causes more stress.[7] The net effect: many of us are fighting stress most of the time, and it can wear us down physically and psychologically. This, again, is even more true for leaders. Let's look at how this happens.

Stress arouses the sympathetic nervous system (SNS), which activates sets of hormones, or endocrines. One set, epinephrine and norepinephrine, elevates blood pressure while blood is channeled primarily to the large muscle groups (preparing the body for fighting or running away). It seems that the brain simultaneously shuts down nonessential neural circuits, meaning we are less likely to be open, flexible, and creative.[8]

Other hormones are released that help fight off damages from inflammation (like swelling muscles).[9] These hormones, called corticosteroids, have several damaging effects. First, they lead to a reduction in the healthy functioning of the body's immune system. Second, they inhibit creation of new neurons and appear to overstimulate older neurons, causing shrinkage or possibly death of the tissue.[10] In our earlier book, we reviewed the research showing that the adult human brain generates new neural tissue on a regular basis.[11] Under stress, not only does the brain shut down and lessen our ability to function, it also loses capability to learn.[12] As a result of this activity, we begin to feel more anxious, nervous, stressed, or even depressed. In this agitated state, we have an increased tendency to feel we are losing control and to perceive things that people say or do as threatening or negative. This can be magnified for leaders. On any given day, they are faced with unrealistic demands, manipulation, and judgment. Even the best leaders can begin to feel uncertain at times, to feel somewhat out of control of events, or to interpret people's actions negatively.

Studies have shown that uncertainty and situations we view as uncontrollable arouse stress, as do situations in which we believe others are evaluating us.[13] When we feel our understanding, control, or impact on events slipping away, we slide into a stress response. Our bodies, minds, and emotions lose resilience and creativity. We begin to see the world as more threatening. This adds to the Sacrifice Syndrome, causing us to experience stress in situations or interactions that may not be as bad as they seem to us.

The research says that sooner or later, when trapped in the Sacrifice Syndrome, most of us will burn out or burn up and begin to create dissonance, even when we do not intend to and even if we are capable of resonant leadership. This is exactly what happened to Karl. Like Karl, we may not recognize that this is happening because the toll of constant sacrifices does not show up right away. Burnout is insidious and its manifestations are different from person to person. Over time, though, one thing is clear: sacrifice, unchecked, leads to less effective leadership and dissonance.

Still, it seems amazing that Karl did not see what was happening to him or around him. But unfortunately Karl is not unusual. As we have seen, the physiological effects of power stress are very difficult to deal with, and many people do not realize that they are actually suffering from those effects until they have already become ineffective, dissonant leaders. This is because once we are in the grips of the Sacrifice Syndrome, we can find ourselves caught in an insidious and even seductive negative spiral. We often realize that things are not as they should be and may secretly feel quite unhappy. And, when we are in the grips of our own anxiety and unhappiness, our lives can become somewhat mechanical, seeming meaningless and detached from our dreams. We literally talk ourselves into settling for what we see as inevitable: stress, unease, and discontent. We justify our behavior and we even blame others for the problems we encounter. And sometimes we begin to rely on psychological defense routines to cope, which spiral us even further downward.

Defensive Routines and the Negative Spiral

When we get stuck in the Sacrifice Syndrome, many of us cope by reverting to or creating ineffective habits of mind and behavior. These habits, which psychologists call defensive routines, are coping mechanisms—they serve to protect or distract us from the discomfort of our current emotional state. For example, some people attempt to cope by overreacting to situations, or they begin to take foolhardy risks just to feel powerful again. Others become habitually cynical; still others find excuses and blame others for the problems they see as too difficult to tackle. Some of us start doing things that do not seem to fit who we are (or who we thought we were). When feeling like this, it becomes increasingly difficult for most people to maintain focus, think clearly, or make good decisions.

Far from offering solutions, however, defensive routines usually catapult us into further distress. That's what happened when Karl began to spend too many evenings out with young associates—a dangerous move in regard to both his work and home life. Yet Karl justified it to himself as a distraction he deserved from his stressful job and because of his wife's busy schedule. He also began to ruminate on how unfair life was. After all he had done, he often thought, why were things turning out to be so complicated? He dwelt on his current difficulties, blaming the business environment, his senior managers, and even his wife. This train of thought inevitably resulted in his feeling despondent, angry, and just plain fed up, which in turn led to more negative thoughts and rationalizations.

When we are in a downward emotional spiral, feeling confused, unhappy, or ill at ease, we often end up playing and replaying mental "tapes" that actually accentuate our negative emotions and feelings of hopelessness.[14] Some psychologists call this "self-talk." When we are feeling down over a long period of time, this self-talk centers on messages that undermine us and, in turn, our power to change bad situations ("It's not my fault" "My life will never be really happy") or messages that weaken our sense of efficacy ("This situation is beyond my control, I'm just stuck with it").[15]

When we get caught in this prison of our own making, we lose the ability to see ourselves, others, or our environments as they really are. We see the world through filters that may not have a basis in reality, and we begin to make decisions based on what we *think* rather than *what is*. We forget to engage in that other kind of self-talk: hopeful, affirming thoughts about ourselves and compassion for others.

This situation becomes quite painful, even intolerable, and many people respond by sinking into denial. The mistake so many of us make, and that Karl made, is to bury our feelings, avoid the issues, and attempt to continue as before, often setting up an elaborate façade or adopting a jovial, devil-may-care stance.

Many successful leaders literally bury themselves in their jobs (often compounding problems elsewhere in their lives). Why do we do this? Most of us want to feel good about who we are, to maintain a positive image of ourselves. And many talented professionals do not let things slip at work for a long time, no matter what else is happening in their lives. They maintain a reasonable level of effectiveness and an aura of success. By over focusing on work, especially during tough times, people can avoid facing the real problems in life outside work while maintaining a reasonably positive self-image.[16] In Karl's case, we suspected (and it was later confirmed) that he had not been doing all that well even before moving to headquarters. He had done a yeoman's job of keeping up appearances, but in retrospect, quite a few people close to him admitted that they saw the façade crumbling long before he actually hit real trouble in the new job.

Adopting a façade is a common tactic for people grappling with the Sacrifice Syndrome. And in fact it may be easiest for successful people to deny that anything is wrong with their lives, or even their performance at work, over a prolonged period, sometimes years. This is because accomplished leaders usually get almost exclusively positive feedback at work, and at home things look right. Most of the time, things seem to go very well.

Successful people also fall into the trap of believing that their accomplishments are solely their own doing, and failures are the result of others' mistakes or the environment. Psychologists call this the "fundamental attribution error" and most of us are guilty of it at one time or another, especially when caught in the grip of the Sacrifice Syndrome.[17] Leaders are especially apt to fall prey to this error because, for various reasons, people around them constantly and insidiously feed their egos and keep the myth of single-handed success alive. For Karl, it was easy to believe that his stellar career was the result of his own hard work, creativity, and talent. He attributed his success to intellect, a bit of luck, and having found a perfect niche for himself.

One of the problems with attributing success to our own efforts and failure to others' shortcomings is that, under stress, we end up seeing the world in very black-and-white terms, and we slowly lose the ability to see ourselves, or those around us, realistically. We miss a lot. Then, when things do go wrong, it is very easy to continue to blame others, and feel sorry for ourselves as things deteriorate—especially when the downturn feels like a surprise and follows a period of denial. So it was with Karl. His early success had actually caused him to be unaware of his impact on people, thoughtless about how he affected them, uncaring about their particular situations. Then, when the pressure mounted, he tried to ignore it and adopted defensive routines that kept him in the dark about his own behavior.

Sometimes, when we look back on a period of mindlessness, we find it difficult to believe that we really did not know what was happening to us. But as Karl was eventually forced to realize, when we live in a state of denial, pretending to be something we are not, we lose contact with ourselves—our emotions are a roller coaster, with wild ups and downs that seem to be disconnected from our lived experience. Or we stop feeling entirely. We justify behavior that is counter to our values, finding lame excuses or blaming others for our actions. Some people get depressed. Some people turn to painkillers of one sort or another—excessive drink, drugs, sex, food. When we live like this, we often find ourselves becoming a shadow of who we thought we were.

Whether we dive into our work, play a role at work and at home, blame others, or simply tune out the irritating messages that tell us something is wrong, we are in essence using an age-old line of defense: denial and pretense. We start by denying truth to ourselves, then extend the lie to colleagues, friends, and loved ones while we try (desperately) to keep a semblance of normality in place. The problem with this strategy is that it takes a tremendous psychological and physical toll. And, ultimately it does not work. All the typical ways to rest—long weekends, vacations, and the like—do little to make up for the effects of chronic power stress. Whatever clever defenses we try to employ, our emotions are evident and our bodies betray us. People sense there is something wrong and that we are no longer at the top of our game. We are off balance, out of whack, off-kilter, and it shows. As we saw, no one—not his colleagues or clients (or, presumably, his wife)—could miss it in Karl's behavior.

In the end, of course, we can not hide from ourselves, either. Whatever is wrong continues to plague us and for even the most resilient among us, small cracks begin to appear in whatever façade we have created.

But there is yet another piece to this puzzle, another element that often contributes to even a resonant leader's defaulting to dissonance: the very organizations for which they work.

How Organizations Create Their Own Monsters

Our organizations often encourage us to remain clueless and stuck in a cycle of sacrifice and dissonance. This happens for a couple of reasons. First, many organizations overvalue achievement, and are willing to tolerate dissonance if the short-term results seem to be there—until there is a big problem. Second, it is often difficult, if not impossible, for leaders to get the message that they are creating toxic environments and must change. Why? Because no one will tell them. Let's go back to Karl to see how this played out.

Karl had been a star for years. He had been rewarded in his early life and career for being smart. He did well in school, and on paper he looked like a great job applicant. After graduating from a good university, he held a series of jobs; first as an analyst in a large accounting firm, then in a similar job in an insurance company, and briefly as an assistant bank manager.

Lots of people make moves like this right after college, so Karl's pattern was not suspect. In fact, he usually left with good references. His managers appreciated his achievement drive, his keen intellect, his willingness to work hard, his friendliness, and the fact that he got things done. Interpersonally he was sometimes rough around the edges, especially when the pressure was on, but his managers wanted the results and wrote off his occasional episodes of bad behavior as youthful exuberance. Some bosses even encouraged it: they saw his brashness as chutzpah and a display of strength of purpose. In those early jobs, Karl took on the tough assignments, succeeded, and usually moved on quickly.

His first few years at the firm at which we met him were without notable incident—he basically fulfilled the financial goals set for him and went about his business. In the 1990s, there was a lot of money floating around in the industry Karl specializes in, and getting the splashy accounts was valued tremendously by his firm. He was handsomely rewarded with bonuses and promotions. Most of his team members loved him and felt he created an exciting, resonant environment and inspired them to ever better performance. And although some subordinates had difficulty with his behavior and the somewhat questionable decisions he made with regard to client work, his bosses more or less ignored this noise; Karl stirred up a lot of dust with these team members, but they were in the minority—and he got money in the door.

Let us not forget that while most managers are rewarded for getting results, in too many of our organizations, they are rewarded for *short-term* results, and the means to the ends are not always evaluated as seriously as the ends themselves. Being smart, quick, and efficient in meeting objectives is prized, and people are literally trained to achieve short-term goals at almost any cost. In fact, in many companies there is an implicit "whatever it takes" rule.

Over time, this pattern tends to chip away at people's capacity for awareness—it is very difficult to stay open, curious, and mindful when the press of work and expectations, and the need for speed require absolute efficiency of thought and action. So there are a lot of people out there, especially people who have a strong achievement drive, who develop and refine a narrow set of skills related to specific results or efficiencies. A consequence is that this specialization and focus often dampens their innate ability to remain open to new information. These people operate on autopilot

and are, most of the time, largely unaware of what is going on inside themselves or around them other than the excitement they get
from being in the game. They are somewhat mindlessly focused on
getting things done.

We suspected Karl's drive for achievement was a notable
strength and clearly part of the reason he had accomplished so
much. However, like any strength taken to the extreme, his desire
to meet objectives had become a liability. His concentration on
goals and results was so strong that other motives and even values
were pushed aside. This became a serious issue when he moved
from a line position to a functional role. The environment had
changed dramatically, and goals were no longer clear and predictable. Still, Karl was not a *totally* clueless leader—remember,
he started out as resonant. Normally he watched people pretty
carefully, read situations fairly accurately, and, at his best, created
an environment where people felt safe talking straight with him.
Even when in the grips of the Sacrifice Syndrome he sensed that
his relationships were not as good as they had been, although no
one seemed to be treating him differently.

This is where another organizational reality kicks in: what we
have called in previous writings "CEO Disease." [18] Even if leaders
sense that they are not at the top of their game, and even when
others can actually see that they are slipping into dissonance, it is
unlikely that anyone will tell them the truth about what they see.
People simply do not treat those with power the same way that
they treat others. They tend to be cautious and somewhat self-
protective, even to the point of not sharing complete (or even accurate) information. And people tend to think leaders are omnipo-
tent. As a leader, you will likely notice that people seem to hold
back, or become very careful, or they act as if they do not care
about your feelings. Somehow, the power that goes along with
leadership causes people to believe that the leader is somehow
"above it all," and does not feel things as keenly as normal people.
Merely because you hold the leader's role, some people come to actively dislike you. Or idolize you. In either case, real connection
and real relationships are very hard to find and keep. All too often

this translates into cautiousness or callousness—and very little straight talk.

Most leaders, like Karl, are susceptible to CEO Disease, so not getting enough, accurate, or timely information is a common problem. And when the leader is anxious or has a style that is deliberately or unconsciously distant and remote, the problems are compounded.[19] When a leader habitually orders people around, demands perfection, or is emotionally neutral or unavailable, people tend to feel frightened and very reluctant to engage. Sometimes people become openly defiant and deliberately withhold information. So for a very long time people did not confront Karl, and it was easy for him to assume that his friends were loyal and true, and that his changing style was not only acceptable but valued.

The Slippery Slope

Breakdowns in communication, such as those resulting from CEO Disease, occur because the Sacrifice Syndrome is a slippery slope. It often starts when we are doing the right things, such as reaching for our goals and trying to create the life of our dreams. When we realize what we are doing—or not doing—and that we have given up too many of our dreams, many of us react by trying to deny that anything is wrong. But even if we ignore, deny, or pretend we can live with constant sacrifices, stress almost always leaks out somewhere, in us and with others. We can become stuck in a negative spiral, inadvertently and sometimes unknowingly creating dissonance in our relationships and our organizations.

As Karl's story shows us, the ultimate result of enduring a prolonged period of sacrifice, emotional turmoil, and unrest is that it becomes increasingly unlikely that leaders will sustain resonance in their teams and organizations, or among family and friends. When we are in emotional turmoil and under stress for protracted periods and are sowing the seeds of dissonance in those around us, it becomes difficult to maintain top form personally or with the people around us. For the most talented and resilient among us, this deterioration can take time—even years—but ultimately negativity, unhappiness, and anxiety take their toll and permeate all areas of our lives. Even so, it is surprising how long it takes for us to realize that we are in trouble.

For Karl, the slide into dissonance damaged not only his perceptions and his relations with others, but also his physical self. When under stress, our bodies become susceptible to disease. Like many leaders, Karl began to suffer physical problems. Some leaders, like Karl, have gastrointestinal difficulties. They are so typical that prescriptions for Tagamet and Zantac to prevent the development of stomach ulcers were once a sure sign of being a leader. Now Acephex or Nexium, which counteract other common stomach problems, have become associated with chronic power stress. Some leaders suffer from high blood pressure and are at risk for strokes, heart attacks, and other cardiovascular diseases. The Sacrifice Syndrome manifests as a breakdown of the body's immune system and results in an increased susceptibility to genetic predispositions. In fact, many diseases have been directly linked to chronic stress, including diabetes and bacterial and viral infections. Moreover, growing and recent research shows that depression and other complex disorders of the mind and body are exaggerated and made worse under conditions of chronic stress.[20]

Stopping the Sacrifice Syndrome before it starts is simply common sense, and a part of a leader's job. Maintaining health, both physical and emotional—as well as intellectual top form—is in part dependent on how we manage the inevitable pressures of our roles. (If you are interested in exploring how the Sacrifice Syndrome may be affecting you, personally, you may want to try some of the exercises at the end of this chapter and in appendix B.)

Before we leave this discussion, we should mention how the Sacrifice Syndrome may unfold for *ineffective* leaders. So far, we have been gentle with leaders and assumed that many were effective at some point and slipped into dissonance. But actually, our observations are less gracious. There are many people in leadership positions who are not adding value and even hurting their organizations.[21] These leaders are dissonant, and some are demagogues—they are clearly not resonant. Many of them get caught in the same spiral as Karl (or Eduardo in the previous chapter) and suffer from the Sacrifice Syndrome.

And then there are those ineffective leaders who are so mindless that they do not even experience the responsibility of their roles. They habitually misuse power, singlemindedly pursuing personal goals or ineffectively managing their own, and others', focus. In fact, some are so well defended that they are able to avoid even feeling the effects of power stress—they are oblivious to it. These people are extremely well defended psychologically, and when problems become too big to ignore, they inevitably blame others.

Unfortunately, while these people may not be personal victims of the Sacrifice Syndrome, they are carriers. That is, they inflict stress on others around them. They are direct creators of dissonance, and the people around them suffer. People who report to these leaders and have to interact with them daily or weekly become victims of chronic stress. Under such leaders, the performance of the organization is almost always less than it might have been. And if the company does profit in the short term simply as a result of the talented people around such a leader, this is usually a short-lived phase. Most of the time, even good people have a very difficult time maintaining top performance, and adapt much less quickly to changing conditions in the absence of resonant leadership.

Fortunately, our organizations are becoming far less tolerant of extremely poor leadership. But, as we have seen, dissonance can be the default even for people who have demonstrated excellent leadership for most of their careers. In the next chapter we will look at one resonant leader who, for a time, lost his way and became trapped in the Sacrifice Syndrome. We will look at how he slipped into dissonance. Then we will see how, unlike Karl, he woke up to the realities of his life, and how he deliberately charted a path to renewal, great leadership, and a deeply fulfilling vision of the future.

An Exercise on the Sacrifice Syndrome: Where Am I?

A S WE HAVE SEEN, the Sacrifice Syndrome can be insidious, and it is sometimes hard to tell we are slipping into it until we are "caught." If we are vigilant, however, we can see signs that we are heading in the wrong direction, before it becomes a problem. Check the following list. Many of these "clues" can help you determine if you are heading in the wrong direction, so you can catch yourself before you slide into dissonance.

Am I:

- Working harder with less result?

- Getting home later or leaving home earlier each day?

- Feeling tired, even after sleeping?

- Having trouble falling asleep, or waking up in the middle of the night?

- Finding less time (or no time at all) for the things that used to be enjoyable?

- Rarely relaxed, or only really relaxed with alcohol?

- Drinking more coffee?

Have I noticed changes in myself or my relationships, such as:

- I can no longer really talk about my problems with my spouse.

- I don't care what I eat, or whether I eat too much or too little.

- I can't remember the last time I had a long conversation with a trusted friend or family member.

- My children have stopped asking me to attend their functions or games.

- I no longer attend my place of worship or find time for quiet contemplation.

- I don't exercise as much as I used to.

- I don't smile or laugh as much as I used to.

Do I:

- Have frequent headaches, backaches, or pain?

- Routinely take over-the-counter antacids or painkillers?

- Feel as if nothing I do seems to matter anymore, or have the impact I want?

- Feel as if no one can understand what I need to do, or how much work I have?

- Sometimes feel numb or react to situations with inappropriately strong emotions?

- Feel too overwhelmed to seek new experiences, ideas, or ways of doing things?

- Frequently think about how to "escape" my current situation?

FOUR

Waking Up to Resonance and Renewal

NIALL FITZGERALD, chairman of Reuters, is known as an engaging leader who gets results—and he exemplifies holistic, resonant leadership. But it has not always been that way. For a time, Niall was caught in the Sacrifice Syndrome and slipped into dissonance. This is the story of how that happened and how he learned to renew himself and to sustain resonant leadership.

Until the fall of 2004, Niall was co-chairman of Unilever. After he joined the company in the early 1970s, his rise was meteoric, marked by one triumph after another until the early 1990s, when he was clearly marked for succession to the chairman's role. Everything Niall had ever done in his business had worked out like a dream. He had had no major failures, nothing to tarnish his record. He had given his all—with great results—in the service of building the business. He put the organization's needs ahead of his own, and took his responsibilities very seriously. He faced challenges and threats creatively and, more often than not, successfully. He managed his influence well, regularly engaging tremendous self-control in order to stay the course, create resonance, and get results. It seemed he could do no wrong. His personal life seemed fine, too: great kids, personal finances on target, and a relationship with his wife that appeared to friends and colleagues to be sensible and solid. Niall's life was on track and the future looked bright.

Or so it seemed. Many of us have learned (the hard way) that you do not have the kind of business success Niall had, or pursue that success as single-mindedly as he did, without it taking a huge toll somewhere in your life. The constant sacrifices and stress inherent in effective leadership can cause us to lose ourselves and sink into dissonance. And, paradoxically, the most successful among us are often the ones who most easily lose ourselves along the way. Usually as a result of good intentions and doing what we are supposed to do—building a great career, committing to an organization, having a family,—we can easily create fairly narrow, one-sided lives.[1] Slowly, over many years, we can lose touch with who we are at our core and what we really care about, and one day find that we are not ourselves anymore.

The result? As we saw in the last chapter, an inability to manage the Sacrifice Syndrome can mean that dissonant leadership becomes the default. And in many cases, people's psychological or physical health suffers. They live with stomach problems, high blood pressure, or heart disease; or they eat and drink too much and exercise too little, if at all. Some people lose sight of everything other than their work—or the trappings of success—and live shallow, less meaningful lives. Other people sacrifice relationships.

So it was with Niall. With all the pressure he faced, he rarely took time to renew himself in any real way, much less to manage the inevitable Cycle of Sacrifice and Renewal that comes with being a leader. Niall, like all leaders, had to cope with power stress and the ups and downs of an executive role and the accompanying lifestyle. Some of Niall's stress was a result of positive events; his successes, for example. Some of it stemmed from difficulties at work and at home. Some stress was extreme and relatively time-limited. As we saw in chapter 3, when we slip into dissonance as a result of power stress, the problem is often compounded by our organization's expectations and our own dysfunctional coping mechanisms. Indeed, Niall's organization was, for the most part, delighted with his hard-working, results-oriented approach. For many years, there was little or no encouragement to adopt new management practices or to deliberately cultivate resonance in himself or with others.

Other situations, at home for example, caused slow-burning chronic stress. Despite appearances, the fact was that Niall's marriage was in trouble. The press of work, raising children, constant moves, and just day-to-day living had taken a toll. In retrospect, it is easy to see how the really important things—like keeping his marriage vibrant—had slipped. Communication was reduced to surface logistical concerns about the house and kids. Decisions were made based on the children's needs and Niall's career. Sadly, the couple's relationship often took a back seat to all the other priorities.

The result of both of these situations, at home and at work, was extreme pressure. Niall attempted to deal with it, of course, but to no avail. He had become trapped in the Sacrifice Syndrome and simply could not seem to find a way out.

The Slip into Dissonance

Not surprisingly, Niall was becoming a dissonant leader. Looking back, he says that while it may have looked like he was extremely successful, even then he knew that something was very wrong. In quiet moments, he began to wonder if maybe many things were wrong with this life that looked near-perfect. The optimism that had been a guiding force in his life and his leadership was dwindling. It was taking an awful lot of energy to stay focused. Decisions were harder to make, and he just was not as confident in either his reasons for making them or the intended outcomes. He had always taken his values for granted and his beliefs had been his rock, guiding his decisions and actions. But he was beginning to see that sometimes his behavior was not in line with his beliefs. In fact, over time his values had actually taken a back seat to his drive for achievement and success, to the point where he ended up becoming a shadow of his true self both at home and at work. His spiritual and emotional life felt a bit barren, and relationships were not as fulfilling as they had been. Physically, the toll of an executive lifestyle was beginning to show. Niall recalls that, at the time, these feelings and his insight into what they meant were somewhat vague. They were more a rumbling of growing uneasiness and dissatisfaction than clear understanding.

Niall found himself longing for more depth, connection, and intimacy in his personal relationships. For a long time, he could not bring himself to fully acknowledge the fact that he was not able to rekindle this kind of meaningful relationship in his marriage. As he lost hope, he began to shut down even more at home, and turned increasingly only to close friends outside his marriage for emotional support. All the while, he kept up pretenses at home and among his colleagues, further disconnecting from himself and those around him.

At work, he went into a similar sort of disengagement. While directing Unilever's laundry products business, Niall and his team launched a new and seemingly revolutionary laundry soap. It looked great on paper and the marketing campaign was nothing short of brilliant. Championing this product was an oasis for Niall and a wonderful escape from his growing unhappiness. He jumped in with all he had, literally burying himself in the details. He was on the front lines, leading, and it was exciting. This is one of the great traps for successful leaders: we often think that doing more of the same will continue to bring us the results we crave, even when it is becoming obvious that the constant sacrifices over many years have finally come home to roost.

At first, things seemed fine. The product was welcomed by the market, the numbers looked great, and everyone was very excited.

Then, a few warning signs popped up; there were more than the usual number of complaints about the soap; employees who tried it reported that it seemed to be harsh and that it was actually damaging their clothes. It even became kind of a joke around the office. For months, as the data about the product began to trickle in, Niall led his team in a fight against what he thought was bad press brought on by the competition's dirty tricks.

Denial, then, was his first response, on both the work and personal fronts. He also tried, many times, to revitalize himself through rest and relaxation. He planned and sometimes even took vacations and long weekends. But these coping mechanisms do not make up for years of power stress and sacrifice. He was beyond tired; he was exhausted, and it was beginning to show in the decisions he made. As we mentioned, the Sacrifice Syndrome shuts down our ability to see possibilities because the effects of anxiety, fear, nervousness, and the physical damage to our brains are very real. Mere rest does not lead to recovery from the ravages of the Sacrifice Syndrome.[2]

The Antidote: Renewal

Niall needed more than just rest and relaxation. He needed *renewal* to sustain himself. Reversing the slide into dissonance and keeping yourself energized as a leader are possible only through a renewal process. The effects of chronic power stress do not allow the mind, body, or heart to flourish, and as a consequence even the spirit may wane. When we engage in personal renewal, we are better equipped to deal with the challenges and sacrifices inherent in leadership. Let's look at why this works.

Recent research shows that renewal invokes a brain pattern and hormones that changes our mood, while returning our bodies to a healthy state.[3] This sets into motion a chain reaction that evokes changes in perception and eventually in our behavior, as shown in figure 4-1. It puts us back into a state of mind, body, and heart that allows for the restoration or building of resonant relationships so critical to leadership effectiveness.

FIGURE 4-1

The Cycle of Sacrifice and Renewal

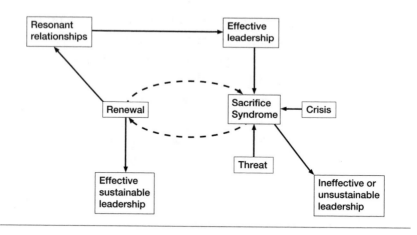

Renewal begins as certain experiences arouse a different part of our limbic brain than that involved in stress responses. This in turn stimulates neural circuits that increase electrical activity in our left prefrontal cortex, leading to arousal of the body's parasympathetic nervous system (PSNS).[4] A different set of hormones is released into the blood stream than when the sympathetic nervous system (SNS) is aroused (see discussion in chapter 3), including oxytocin in women and vasopressin in men. These activate another set of hormones that lower blood pressure and strengthen the immune system. The person then feels elated, happy, optimistic, positive, or amused—an experience which in the recent psychology research is termed a "sense of well-being."[5] Once in this emotional state, a person is more likely to perceive events as positive rather than negative or threatening, further enhancing the condition that we call *renewal*. These processes are explained in detail in appendix A.

As we will explain in later chapters, the experiences of mindfulness, hope, and compassion foster and provoke arousal of the PSNS and the condition of renewal. Then a positive cycles sets in: being in renewal feeds the experiencing of hope, compassion, and mindful attention to self and others while it counters the detrimental effects of stress.[6] So among other things, to renew ourselves, we need to remain hopeful even in the midst of real difficulties. We need to truly care about the people we are leading and we need to experience compassion—both directed toward other people *and* coming from people to us. We need to attend to ourselves and to others in mind, body, heart, and spirit. Mindfulness, hope, and compassion enable us to be resilient and function effectively even in the face of challenges.

Therefore, sustainable, effective leadership occurs only when the experiences of the sacrifice and stress of leadership are interchanged with those of renewal.[7] While resonance will lead to effective leadership, unless a leader moves in and out of renewal, he or she will not be able to sustain it.

How do you know when you need to act to invoke renewal? It will not occur by itself. Turning renewal into a habit or way of life usually means waking up to the realities of our current life and deliberately engaging in intentional change and personal transformation. You have to *do* something that will invoke the renewal that will counteract the Sacrifice Syndrome.

Becoming Aware That You Are Not Aware

We have seen many leaders who, arriving at the point of dissonance that Niall had reached, simply rationalize or ignore all signs of problems and numb themselves to the consequences of their actions (much as we saw in the case of Karl in chapter 3). But some people, like Niall, recognize and hear "wake-up calls"—clear signs and messages that their lives have become something they do not want. These calls can be a first critical step to intentional change.

Sometimes, of course, big or unexpected life events such as marriage, divorce, birth, death, or a colossal failure or opportunity at work can be a wake-up call. Most of us have experienced a time in our lives when we have been forced to look at ourselves differently—say, when our first child is born or when we take a new and challenging job in an unfamiliar part of the world. How we deal with these life events, these wake-up calls, depends in large part on how carefully we are attending to ourselves and the people close to us.

The interesting thing about personal transformation, however, is that it is not always linked with life events. In fact, wake-up calls and change can often be traced to a cycle. Whether it happens in the seven-year cycle alluded to in the Old Testament, or the cycles discussed in more recent works by Erik Erikson, Dan Levinson, or Gail Sheehy, we each seem to have a rhythm to our lives.[8] For many of us, cycles of personal transformation occur over periods of about seven years. The sound of the wake-up call from these cycles is harder to hear.

At the end of this chapter, we offer several reflective exercises that may help you distinguish where you are in your life and career cycle at present. These exercises can help you become mindful of the need for a change. So instead of acting out a particular point in your life cycle unconsciously—with inappropriate, dysfunctional, or wildly expensive adventures—you can become mindful of the cycle and what to do about it.

Sometimes we find ourselves at a low point in a cycle, or possibly adrift as a result of unexamined choices along the way. When we find ourselves in this situation, we can feel stuck, or even trapped. Our energy may have dwindled, and we may experience a kind of soul-destroying boredom at work or even, sadly, at home.[9] When caught in this spiritual blackout we feel as though the fun and fire have gone out of our life or work. Restlessness and even sadness pervade our lives, and we may feel as if something is missing or feel something akin to homesickness, even in our own homes. As we become aware of this feeling, we often feel shocked, as if we have slept our life away.

At times, however, we cannot trace a wake-up call directly to a normal life cycle, and it is not triggered by an event as dramatic as a breakdown or significant failure. Rather, the cause is simply that the Sacrifice Syndrome has driven us to exhaustion—the breaking point. In fact, this is common. Many leaders experience a slow, steady decline in effectiveness, health, and happiness. It happens over many years, simply as a result of the constant pressures and the need to give so much of oneself. The trouble is, the subtle messages that tell us something is not right are often just whispers. It is easy to miss them until we are literally trapped in the Sacrifice Syndrome. Then, one day, we find ourselves waking up to the fact that we are worn out, tired, or just unable to give anymore—simply burned out.[10]

As we have noted in our earlier writings, long before we figure it out cognitively, there are often clues that tell us that we have lost ourselves and need to engage in renewal and make some changes in our lives.[11] Most of the time, the clues are emotional or physical. They are vague or easy to miss because they can be attributed to living a busy, stressful life. But if we are paying attention, we might notice disturbing feelings of being stuck—a prisoner of decisions we have made or events that seem out of our control.

Let's go back to Niall to see how he woke up and found his way to renewal and to sustainable resonance and effectiveness. As we have seen, for a long time he was closed off from himself—his feelings, his awareness of what kind of life he wanted to have, even his behavior as a leader. He could not see himself, other people, or the world around him very clearly.

His situation points out the paradox: in order to wake up and do something to counter the numbing effects of the Sacrifice Syndrome, you have to *become aware that you are not aware*. Fortunately, Niall began to recognize the wake-up calls that had long been trying to get his attention. There were at least four separate calls, and they came over a period of a year or two. Some calls he heard right away, and some he ignored at first, but eventually he was able to act on them and change his life.

Trouble in the Business—the First Wake-up Call

The first wake-up call came in the form of Niall's first ferocious failure at work. The problems with the laundry soap that his division was championing finally came home to roost. Despite

Niall's efforts to contradict damaging data regarding the product, and despite the fact that if used as directed the product was fine, one memorable day the competition managed to get the papers to print pictures of tattered clothing: the clothes *had* been washed with the product, and they were ruined.[12] But instead of withdrawing or improving this obviously flawed product, Niall and his team fought back with everything they had. They knew there were some issues but, they reasoned, it was also true that if used correctly the product was fine. So, under Niall's leadership, they stood by the product until the bitter end, when customers, suppliers, vendors, and even friends began to denounce it.

Niall had not always been a clueless leader, but at this point he was closed down and shut off, from himself and with others. He had become difficult to deal with, and people found it hard to confront him. His distress was becoming more obvious, even as he tried to maintain a façade of normalcy. To many people, it seemed as if he was just acting a part, which made it difficult for them to know where he stood or how he might react to issues. This was confusing and unsettling.

Lots of people could tell that something was wrong with Niall, but nobody knew what it was. What they did know, as one colleague said, "He was impossible to deal with. It was always 'his way or the highway,' and watch out if you tried to change his plans. He had a terrible temper." So, it is no surprise that CEO Disease had set in—few people could, or would, tell Niall the truth.[13]

Eventually, even CEO Disease could not protect Niall from what was happening. If nothing else, the competition was delighting in airing their version of the facts. Niall and his team could no longer deny the evidence. When used incorrectly, the product was destructive and possibly dangerous. They had failed miserably in the product launch and even more miserably in their inability to admit mistakes early on and curb the damage. It was a very public and humiliating failure. For the press, it was a feeding frenzy of bad and embarrassing news.

This began what Niall describes as an avalanche of problems, and more wake-up calls.

Friends Abandon Ship—the Second Wake-up Call

When the product failed, Niall looked around for support and found that many of his friends had disappeared. As one colleague put it, "We needed him, so we put up with him, but at the first hint of trouble everyone took the opportunity to abandon ship." People who had supported Niall for years simply stopped calling. This was a big shock; it had never occurred to him that people would abandon him when the going got tough.

The turmoil in his personal life had hit the boiling point as well. He was seriously unhappy at home and wracked with guilt about what a mess he had made. For the first time, Niall found himself really questioning who he was as a leader and a person. Niall *had* to wake up. He started asking himself: "What is it about *me* that caused the business failure? That caused most of my friends to disappear and my marriage to slide into disrepair? Have I ever been as good a leader as I thought? Why have I ignored so many messages? Did arrogance start driving my decisions? Why did people stop giving me information and why did they abandon me when I needed them most?"

Niall was beginning to feel some desperation, and turned to a couple of close friends to talk through the problems. He stopped denying everything and started talking about *his* part in the situations. He also began to focus on health and took up distance running. His health began to improve, and gradually he noticed an added benefit: when he ran, he found he had the time to reflect and think through what was happening to him.

Slowly, he started to realize that he had lost his friends because they were no longer friends at all, and that this was *his* fault. He had not consistently cultivated the friendships, or nurtured them. He had taken for granted that people wanted to be near him, and he had treated people as conveniences, not as treasured human beings with whom he could enjoy mutually supportive relationships. Although the situation was more complicated, he suspected that the same slow process had disrupted his marriage: he had never seriously worked on this relationship, and years of inattention resulted in the couple's growing apart. At this point, they each had grown into people who did not know each other very well, and intimacy had dwindled.

As Niall tells it, he was awakening to the fact that he was not the person he wanted to be. He began thinking back to the passions and values of his youth, and saw that somehow he had let them slip—he was no longer acting on them, even at home. He was painfully aware of the way things had slipped at work, and that relationships there had suffered too. He realized that what was now guiding him was some combination of "shoulds" with respect to his role at work, and probably within his family. He vowed to change.

A Bad Compromise—and a Third Wake-up Call

At home, Niall tried one solution after another, each worse than the last. At one point, he crafted the ultimate compromise, making arrangements to live away from home during the week and return home to his family only on weekends. Of course that was not a solution at all; it was simply a way to lessen his guilt and to ensure that he maintained some semblance of normality. As he describes it now, he was so focused on doing the right thing he was doing absolutely nothing right. His emotions careened wildly up and down, as did the feelings of the important people in his life. Life was just so *dramatic*. He alternated between guilt about his family situation and bouts of self-pity because of his own unhappiness. He began to realize that he was driven by destructive emotions—he was hurting himself and others.[14]

It became increasingly difficult for Niall to deny that he was hurting everyone he loved. Paradoxically, the fact that people in his life actually accepted the lifestyle compromise was the wake-up call that he finally heard. He finally got it: by selfishly and frantically trying to keep up appearances, he was causing pain all around. His back-and-forth living situation meant he was inconsistent in his relations with his wife and children too, and everyone ended up feeling confused, rattled, sad, and angry most of the time.

As the ugly reality of the situation finally sank in, he asked himself "What am I doing?" He describes this awakening as a huge release, as if a heavy burden had been lifted from his shoulders. Niall was finally looking at his behavior, his values, his impact on others. He was opening up to reality—first, the reality within himself, including his emotions, his honest reflections about his life, and the toll his current situation was taking on his mind, body, heart, and spirit. He began to see how his decisions at work and with his family and friends were not only flawed, they were in some ways disastrous. As he became more aware, he began to direct his attention more consciously, and began seeking real solutions instead of Band-Aids and compromises. He began to see things that he had missed for many years, giving him deeper insight, more choices, and the beginning of wisdom.

A Friend's Dying Words—and a Final Wake-up Call

Then Niall had an extraordinary experience that finally, once and for all, woke him up. His best friend, Peter, had became very ill and had moved back to London. Despite his busy life and the stress of his current situation, Niall felt deep love and compassion for his friend, and he spent as much time as possible with Peter.

The two friends spent many hours together during the long months of Peter's illness. Niall found he could talk to Peter about what was happening in his life, the mess he had made, the pain he felt. Something about this particular situation, and this particular friend, enabled Niall to really open up. Until this time, he had been on a see-saw, alternately trying to figure out what had gone wrong and what to do, and then denying it all. In these conversations with Peter he found his voice, and it was as if a dam had burst—all the pain, all the self-loathing, and the deeply hidden hopes he had for life and for the future came out.

One night as the two friends talked, Niall found himself asking, "Peter, are you afraid of death? Are you afraid of what is to come?" Neither man had any way of knowing it, but it happened that this would be Peter's last night on earth.

Peter answered that indeed he was not at all afraid, because he had had time to make peace with himself. Then, with passion, Peter turned to Niall and said, "I have finally come to realize that what they say is *true*: life is not a rehearsal. This is all we have, this is it. There is no second chance. I have realized this too late, and I have had to find peace with this. But it is not too late for you. You are not living the life you want to—not in your personal life, not in your work. If this is not the life you want to live, then you *must* change it. You must promise me, you owe it to me to take this realization of mine and act on it."

Peter's words shook Niall to the core. Peter was right. In that moment, Niall decided that he would find himself again, no matter what. He began to realize that personal integrity, authentic relationships, and intimacy were far more important to him than success or doing what others expected. He would begin living the life he should live, the life he *wanted*. He would find his soul again. Niall felt as if he was a bird, and someone had let him fly free. He would live his life *as himself*, not as some shadow. He would stop living in fear.

Peter's friendship, his message, and his death opened a door for Niall to begin to find truth and to make the most difficult choices. Over the next year or so, Niall managed to act on the awareness he had finally found about his life and the changes he needed to make.

How did Niall do this? It is one thing to hear wake-up calls; it is quite another to act on them, to become a resonant leader who is able to sustain that resonance through difficult times. The leaders we have observed do it through a process of intentional change and engaging in a continual process of self-renewal. That is something that Niall had long ignored; failing to manage the Cycle of Sacrifice and Renewal that all leaders inevitably face is what had gotten Niall into trouble in the first place. But as he began to "wake up," so too did he begin the path to renewal, and ultimately, sustainable resonance.

Resonance and Renewal Through Mindfulness, Hope, and Compassion

As we have seen, the Sacrifice Syndrome can derail even good leaders like Niall. But that is not the end of the story. In our work with leaders, we have watched the best among them learn how to manage the downside of leadership through engaging in a process of intentional change and continual renewal. They are able to intentionally strive toward resonance and retrieve it—or create it anew in the present conditions. As Richard Boyatzis's research indicates, individual change is not always easy—and it does not happen by accident. In fact, to engage in *real* change—the kind that enables us to manage the inherent stress of leadership, for example—we must engage in a process over time to capture our dreams and chart a course toward them. We will discuss intentional change in depth in the next chapter, but for now, suffice it to say that once we have woken up as Niall did, we need to articulate for ourselves a dream of a future that is personally meaningful and compelling. We need to look at ourselves realistically and identify aspects of ourselves that we know we must change, or enhance, in order to reach for our dreams. We need to plan an agenda for learning, and we need the support of people around us as we begin the change process.

To return to resonance and counter the Sacrifice Syndrome, we need to make renewal a way of life. This requires conscious action and, for most people, intentional change. We have seen, and the research supports our observations, that there are actually concrete ways to achieve resonance. These are the same ways to interrupt the Sacrifice Syndrome, enter into renewal and sustain resonance personally and with the people around us. Specifically, resonance and renewal involve three experiences that we introduced in chapter 1—*mindfulness, hope, and compassion*—that we can, with practice, cultivate as a way of life, as shown in figure 4-2.

Mindfulness, hope, and compassion spark positive emotions and healthy relationships that enable us to be resilient and function

FIGURE 4-2

Sustaining resonance and effectiveness through the Cycle of Sacrifice and Renewal

Effects internal (within) the leader are marked by dashed lines and arrows. Social, interactive effects between the leader and others are marked by straight lines and arrows.

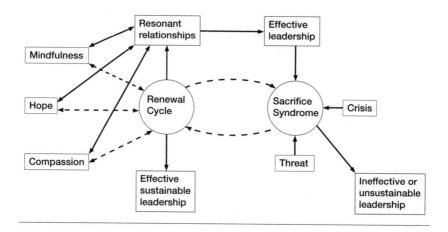

effectively even in the face of challenges.[15] Renewal is a dynamic process in which mindfulness, hope, and compassion restore us and counter the destructive effects of power stress, even as the renewal itself feeds the experiences of mindfulness, hope, and compassion (as shown in figure 4-2).[16] So among other things, to renew ourselves, we need to remain hopeful even in the midst of real difficulties, to truly care about the people we are leading and experience compassion, and to mindfully attend to ourselves and to other people holistically.

Some people seem to renew themselves naturally—it almost looks effortless. These people seem to be able to withstand tremendous pressure without harming themselves or others. In psychological terms, they are called hardy, or resilient. Recent research shows us that such people do not necessarily have special traits or characteristics, but they actively engage in various activities, including mindfulness and engaging hope and compassion, to renew themselves continually. They may even engage in these activities somewhat unconsciously—they have made renewal so much a part of their lives they do it without too much effort.[17] The examples in this book help to explain that being able to renew yourself is not a single characteristic. It is a variety of experiences and processes that any person can learn, engage, and practice, which can eventually become an unconscious, or natural, element of that person's style.

In chapters 6, 7, and 8, we will discuss mindfulness, hope, and compassion in detail. Now, however, let's look at each of these elements of renewal and how they helped Niall get back to resonance in life and as a leader.

Mindfulness as a Source of Renewal

When we talk about mindfulness, we mean living in a state of full and conscious awareness of one's whole self, other people, and the context in which we live and work. This means developing our intellect, taking care of our bodies, using the power of our emotions, and attending to our spirituality. We define mindfulness as *being awake, aware, and attending*—to ourselves and to the world around us. Mindfulness enables us to pay attention to what is happening to us, and to stop the Sacrifice Syndrome before it stops us. Being mindfully aware of ourselves and our surroundings, human, and environmental, invokes the capacity for renewal.

But, you say, this sounds like self-development—and we say, yes, that's it exactly! Mindfully attending to all aspects of our humanity enables us to reach our full potential as individuals while becoming more fully engaged with people, with our communities, and with our environment.[18]

Leaders are often advised to focus on the rational mind and on the mechanics of business—planning, organizing, and controlling resources (including people)—and to leave the soft stuff alone. They are told to ignore the body, heart, and spirit or, better yet, leave them at the front door when entering the office. But bringing only parts of ourselves to work leaves us feeling lost, dull, or as if we are running on a treadmill. The resulting disconnection with ourselves, our colleagues, our customers, and even friends and families results in increasing isolation and dissonance.

Instead, people need to cultivate mindfulness and seek resonance in themselves and with others. This is what it takes to be an effective leader and to sustain effectiveness in the face of constant pressure. Those of us who cultivate mindfulness have more cognitive flexibility, creativity, and problem-solving skills.[19] In other words, leaders who pay attention to the whole self—mind, body, heart, and spirit—can literally be quicker, smarter, happier, and more effective than those who focus too narrowly on short-term success.

Back to Niall for a moment: part of the reason for his success was that he *has* the capacity of mindfulness. The problem was, as the pressure increased and as a result of becoming more powerful, he had let his attention to himself and others slip. He had lost the habit of attending to the nuances of his internal state. Similarly, he had stopped working as hard as he used to on understanding others and their messages, as well as the messages from the broader environment.

So, for Niall, the question was, "How can I re-engage my capacity for mindfulness?" He started with a lot of reflection. He built in time to think—and to concentrate on getting clear about what he was feeling and what he was doing. And he did this while running, so the physiological effects of the exercise literally helped him to think more clearly. He also reached out to one or two people and used them as sounding boards to check on his reflections. He took the risk of being vulnerable with his closest friends—admitting that maybe he was making mistakes that needed fixing (at work or at home), and he asked for opinions and help.

Hope as a Source of Renewal

Although renewal begins with mindfulness, such awareness is not enough. Renewal is sparked by positive emotions. In particular, the experiences of *hope* and *compassion* actually cause changes in our brains and hormones that allow us to renew our minds, bodies, and hearts. We can be more resilient and have more capacity for creating resonance when we are optimistic and when we experience hope and compassion. And these feelings—or more accurately, the *experience* of hope and compassion—are the basis for leaders' creating resonant relationships with those around them.

When we experience *hope*, we feel excited about a possible future, and we generally believe that the future we envision is attainable. Hope engages and raises our spirit and mobilizes energy. It causes us to want to act and enables us to draw on personal resources in the service of moving toward our goal. Beyond this, hope, and the visions that come with it, are contagious. They are powerful drivers of *others'* behavior. Hope is an emotional magnet—it keeps people going even in the midst of challenges. A leader's hopeful outlook enables people to see beyond today's challenges to tomorrow's answers. Hope binds people together and helps us move in concert toward a desired end.

In Niall's case, hope was in short supply for a while. At Unilever, the laundry product situation looked pretty bad and it would have been easy for Niall, then the team, to sink into despair. But, two things stopped this slide. First, Unilever's leaders did not lose faith in Niall. Then, Niall found energy to direct the team's efforts toward the future. Let's look at how this played out.

Even during the worst days of the debacle, Unilever's leadership still believed that Niall could become the next chairman. This surprised him, and he was appreciative. It was a dream he had had for many years. But what good is a dream if you feel you do not deserve it? Niall had a huge mess on his hands. It just did not seem right to win when in fact he was in the midst of a colossal failure. He did not know it at the time, but the fact that he was beginning to be honest with himself and to hold himself accountable for living up to his values actually sparked a bit of hope. He saw a future that was more than simply getting the brass ring, that chairman's position.

All of this led Niall to begin to seriously question his decisions in the laundry soap business. He saw that his stance on the doomed product had hurt lots of people—customers, his team, and colleagues—and the business itself. He looked at this situation and the possible solutions from many different perspectives and let go of the single-mindedness that had characterized his treatment of the problem. He took responsibility for his part, deciding to stay with the business and see it through. He did not have to do this. He could have easily gotten out of it, moved on, and let someone else clean things up. But instead he asked Unilever's board for permission to stay in the business, to see it through until things began to turn around.

Niall's hopeful view of the future and his actions inspired commitment and ultimately sparked resonance on the team. And as the vision of what to do and the belief it would lead to a better situation began to develop, Niall began to feel once again that he had some control over his life. He was regaining a bit of self-respect. He felt emotionally ready to work on the other serious problems in his life. As he began to act on his values more deliberately at work, Niall talked himself into believing that despite the problems and the bad choices he had made, he could right the wrongs in his personal life as well.

The image of the future that Niall generated was realistic—difficult, but possible. This meant that his hope was based on an optimistic, but reasonable, vision, and thus he felt he had the ability to move toward—and achieve—this feasible set of goals.[20] In other words, he was dealing with reality, not fantasy. And the feasibility of his dreams supported his feelings of hope—sparking a positive cycle that continued to generate hope and energy during the process of making changes in his leadership and his life.

Here's where resonance comes in: as Niall began to imagine a different—and feasible—future, his hope became contagious. At work, others began to understand and see his vision and realistic possibilities about the future. And he carried this realism and hope into his personal life. Although for a time it was extremely difficult, he was finally able to act on mistakes and chart a different, more promising path for himself and those close to him.

Compassion as a Source of Renewal

When we experience *compassion*, we are in tune with the people around us. We understand their wants and needs, and we are motivated to act on our feelings. Like hope, compassion invokes renewal in our mind, body, and heart. And, like hope, compassion is contagious.

If asked during the years of struggle and confusion, Niall would likely have said that he still felt tremendous compassion for the people in his life who were so hurt by his actions, at work, and at home. But compassion is different than sympathy, or even empathy, in that it goes beyond understanding. Compassion is a combination of deep understanding, concern, *and a willingness to act* on that concern for the benefit of oneself and others. What made the difference for Niall and helped him step into renewal was that at a certain point he stopped simply feeling sorry for himself and merely feeling sympathy for others. He acted on his feelings and began to make changes that would ultimately lessen people's suffering and bring them closer together.

Conversely, as much as we need to show compassion in order for renewal to take place, we also must receive it. When we are in emotional turmoil and especially when we find that some of our life's foundations are crumbling, we need to know, if we are to repair this situation, that we are not alone. As we are cultivating mindfulness and beginning to feel a glimmer of hope, we also need to know that others care, that they are offering us their concern, compassion, and love. We need others' positive regard, even respect, in order to hold on while we figure things out and find ourselves again.

Maybe Niall was lucky. Even though many friends had eventually deserted him, there were a few who did not abandon him. They seemed to understand him not just as a person who had made a mess of things, but as a truly good man and a good businessman. They saw him as someone who had made some bad choices along the way—but also as a person who could, and would, right the wrongs of the past and return to more balance and resonance. The knowledge that a few people still trusted and liked him gave Niall some breathing room.

One of those people was Peter, Niall's dying friend. And conversely, Niall's compassion for and with his friend opened the door to ultimately feel compassion for himself. This profound experience, along with the love and support of others, fed his growing sense of hope and prepared him to design the future he wanted to unfold.

Personal Renewal and Professional Excellence

Niall FitzGerald is an outstanding leader, and in other, more personal roles in his life, he is living up to his own high standards. We have seen him in action—he really does create resonance, whereas in the past he could easily create dissonance. People in the business world look up to him, and he is having impact on social causes that are close to his heart. And maybe most importantly, his personal life is now vibrant and happy.

In the end, Niall has found a path that is right for him, and he treasures it. He has learned that the dangers of being seduced by the pressure of the leadership role and one's own power are constantly present at work. And that ignoring one's most important relationships leads to disaster at home. He has crafted a life in which he focuses constantly on being honest and true to himself. And Niall is at last living a personal life that reflects his values and his beliefs. Although sadly his first marriage was lost—a casualty of Niall's years of dissonance—he has learned lessons from that collapse. He now works very hard to maintain a close relationship with his children. He is married again, and this time he takes nothing for granted. He focuses a tremendous amount of time and energy on this relationship, working hard to keep it vibrant, meaningful, and close.

For Niall FitzGerald, getting back in touch with his values—what he truly, deeply believes to be important—was at the center of his renewal. In his moments of greatest self-doubt and uncertainty about the future, he began to reconstruct a life of meaning from his values. The lesson to be learned is this: whether it is to help you hear a wake-up call or to reaffirm your core values as a basis for entering renewal through mindfulness, hope, and compassion, it is useful to review what your values are from time to time.

At the end of this chapter and in appendix B, we offer several exercises that can help you to explore your values and philosophy. There are also exercises to help reveal the rhythms in your work and life; these may also add insight into when you may expect a wake-up call, or signal the faint echo of a wake-up call. At the minimum, they can help you keep in touch with possible changes taking place inside.

The End, and the Beginning, of Niall FitzGerald's Story: Sustaining Resonance

Transformations like Niall FitzGerald's do not happen overnight. In fact, it takes years for old habits and old patterns of behavior to disappear and for new ones to take their place. Once awake, it takes vigilance to remain so. Niall admits to slipping into old habits at times. During the years he was chairman at Unilever, and now at Reuters, he consciously and deliberately works to be the best leader he can possibly be. He strives to be courageous and willing to take chances, authentic but even vulnerable in his relationships, honest, compassionate, and consistently challenging people to find their passion and reach for their dreams. He has consciously developed his emotional intelligence, or more accurately reinvigorated the competencies he had demonstrated effectively and repeatedly in the past.

During his awakening, Niall cultivated new habits that enable him to renew himself continually. He continues to run marathons, and combines this with raising money for charities that attend to the needs of children around the world. He has rekindled an interest in studying spirituality—he reads widely across a variety of spiritual traditions and works to bring their wisdom and practices into daily life. He and his wife focus on friends and relationships as a central part of their life; on most weekends, you will find friends sitting around their kitchen table engaged in deep conversation on everything from the world's events to the welfare of children to life in general.

As we have seen in Niall's story, even those of us who *can* create resonance will at times lose our way. This is why we need to catch the Sacrifice Syndrome before it starts and do something about it. To learn how to counter the Sacrifice Syndrome and engage in renewal, most of us have personal *work* to do. We need to find our passion, take a good, hard look at who we are and the life we are leading, break old patterns, and get rid of old habits. We need to cultivate mindfulness and learn how to engage hope and compassion, even (maybe especially) when we are under extreme pressure.

We will devote the next part of this book to showing just how the process of intentional change works and how the experiences of mindfulness, hope, and compassion foster and provoke the condition of renewal. We will look at exactly how some leaders, like Niall, have "cracked the code" and learned to manage the Cycle of Sacrifice and Renewal.

Exercise 1: Is That a Wake-up Call?

SOMETIMES, wake-up calls come in the form of a dramatic life event such as the birth of a child, a death in the family, or an unexpected change in job. Other times, wake-up calls are more subtle and come as a result of gradual changes in life or work, or as a result of a combination of a few, seemingly minor, alterations to a familiar lifestyle. Monitoring the big—as well as the smaller—changes in work or personal life is a way to stay tuned in to our own wake-up calls, and to have more control over our present as well as our future. Consider the following examples of common wake-up calls. Have you experienced any of these in the recent past, or are you experiencing them now? Are there other, more subtle, life events not on the list that could be a wake up call for you?

- Divorce or separation

- Move to a new home

- Death in the family or support network

- Promotion

- Significant medical diagnosis

- Physical injury

- Significant loss of physical capacity

- Anniversary of a significant event

- Car accident

- Marriage

- Significant job change

- Job loss

- Birth of a child

- Significant financial loss or gain

- Life cycle changes (children leaving home, etc.)

- Significant success or failure in a project

- Change in the amount/type of medication

- Significantly more time away from home (e.g., travel for work)

- Significantly less quality time with family or friends

- Important new relationship (love, friendship, boss)

- Noticeable gain or loss of weight

- A sense of boredom or frustration with life or work

- World events that have impacted me personally (psychologically or otherwise)

- Disruption or dissatisfaction with an important relationship (spouse, child, friend, boss)

- Completion of a major project

- Change in lifelong habits (e.g., exercise, spiritual practice, hobbies)

Exercise 2: Your Moral Core

THE OBJECTIVE of this exercise is to help you clarify your values or beliefs. Since our values and beliefs change from time to time, often after reflection or certain events, it is useful to review and consider our values and beliefs regularly.[21] Being mindful of your values requires periodic reflection about your beliefs and their importance to you at this point in your life.

Below we present a list of values, beliefs, or personal characteristics for your consideration, along with steps to help you identify which are most important to you as guiding principles in your life. You might find it useful to determine degrees of importance by considering whether you would be upset or elated if your present state or condition in life would change if you could no longer act on a particular value. You might at times find it helpful to consider two values at a time, asking yourself about the relative importance of one over the other.

1. Identify the fifteen or so values that are most important to you, and mark them with an asterisk or circle them.

2. From this list, identify the five that are the most important to you.

3. Third, rank each of the five with "1" being the most important value to you to "5" being the least important of these five important values.

List of Values, Beliefs, or Desirable Personal Characteristics

Accomplishment	Control	Independence	Recognition
Achievement	Cooperation	Improving society	Reliable
Adventure	Courage	Innovativeness	Religion
Affection	Courteousness	Integrity	Respect
Affectionate	Creativity	Intellect	Responsibility
Affiliation	Dependability	Involvement	Restrained
Ambition	Discipline	Imagination	Salvation
Assisting others	Economic security	Joy	Self-control
Authority		Leisure	Self-reliance
Autonomy	Effectiveness	Logic	Self-respect
Beauty	Equality	Love	Sincerity
Belonging	Exciting life	Loving	Spirituality
Broad-mindedness	Fame	Mature love	Stability
Caring	Family happiness	National security	Status
Challenge	Family security	Nature	Success
Cheerfulness	Forgiving	Obedience	Symbolism
Cleanliness	Free choice	Order	Taking risks
Comfortable life	Freedom	Peace	Teamwork
Companionship	Friendship	Personal development	Tidiness
Competent	Fun		Tenderness
Competitiveness	Genuineness	Pleasure	Tranquility
Contribution to others	Happiness	Politeness	Wealth
	Health	Power	Winning
Conformity	Helpfulness	Pride	Wisdom
Contentedness	Honesty	Rationality	

This is not an easy exercise. Most people find the first step easy, but the last step is difficult, if not uncomfortable. That is because the reflection forces us to reconcile a number of potentially divergent aspects of our current lives. First, when you develop the final list of five values and rank them, you inevitably keep asking yourself, "Does this placement of the value reflect how I act or how I would like to act?" In other words, does the ranking of the value represent the person you are today in your actions and decisions? Second, if it does not, does it represent the person you would like to become? You might also wonder, does the assignment of value in the ranking reflect my current preferences, attitudes, actions, and decisions? Or it is a better reflection of the way I was a few years ago—a past, earlier me?

Understanding what is important to us becomes a moral rudder, helping us steer our path through confusing and sometimes conflicting moments and decisions.

Exercise 3: Rhythms in My Career(s)

THIS EXERCISE presents a worksheet for recording your career history.* Each horizontal line in the figure represents a job/role of your career or careers. The vertical lines represent transitions, such as a promotion, job change, organizational change, career change, or professional preparation period. Starting with the present, please complete this form by writing the year of each career transition and a brief description of the transition on the vertical line. Write the jobs, roles, or activities along the horizontal lines. Complete the chart backward in time from the present to the point at which you first entered the full-time workforce, or to the age of twenty-one, whichever came first. Please include all work and roles that you consider meaningful, even, for example, a part-time job.

After filling the lines and transitions, examine the number of years between major changes. A major change is not necessarily every job change or even organization change, but one that means

If you need more lines or space, insert a blank page and draw your career history.

you are approaching work differently. Does this reflect a rhythm in your cycle of interest and boredom in work? If so, where are you in the current cycle? When might you approach a transition period and listen for a wake-up call?

*© Richard E. Boyatzis, 1996.

Exercise 4: Rhythms in My Life

ON A SHEET of paper, write the current year at the top of the left-hand side of the page. Underneath it, write the years in descending order from this year all the way back to when you were born. Next to any of the years, write any event or experience that you considered at the time or now consider to have been important in your life. The years are listed as a memory aid; it is not necessary to write something into each year. Possible categories reflecting aspects of life to consider in completing this list are: physical or personal health events (e.g., turning 50, surgery); relationship events (e.g., marriage, birth of a child, divorce); spiritual (e.g., finding and joining a church, temple, mosque); emotional (e.g., death of a parent, a vacation or trip that opened a new horizon in life); intellectual (e.g., a book that inspired a new way of looking at life); financial (e.g., being laid off, achieving a major financial goal); avocational, such as hobbies, interests, or sports (e.g., shooting under 80 at golf, writing a song that was recorded, skydiving); and so forth. But they should be important events in your life.

A hint about this form: most people find that in completing this form, they do not follow a logical time sequence as they did for the career history. In other words, you may remember or think of a major event that occurred ten years ago that reminds you of something that happened earlier and another event that happened more recently. Feel free to add items to this list in whatever order works for you. It may require several sessions in which you reflect on your life and think about the events mentioned on this list. Do not feel constrained by the space provided for any given year. Use additional paper to add items for particular years. Most people find it useful to note items going back to their twenties, but some find it important to go back further. Add more years if necessary.

Look at the number of years between major life events. Is there a rhythm to when you feel the need for a change or when changes seem to occur? If so, where are you in the current rhythm and when should you listen for a wake-up call?

FIVE

Intentional Change

M EANINGFUL AND IMPORTANT CHANGES do happen by
chance. Without a high degree of awareness, we may not
notice the changes for a long time—or until others comment on
them. In this sense, desired changes often appear discontinuous.
In complexity theory, these surprises are called "emergence." For
most of us, though, the important changes in our lives feel like
epiphanies; they are truly discoveries. With increased mindfulness,
the process of change seems smooth or even seamless. Part of the
challenge of creating and sustaining excellent leadership is to recognize, manage, and even direct one's own process of learning and
change. People who manage their own development intentionally—
as Niall FitzGerald ultimately did and as he does today—are poised
to make good choices about what they need to do to be more effective, and more satisfied with their lives. Drawing on decades of
research, much of it conducted by Richard Boyatzis, we can now
say with some certainty that the Intentional Change Model can
help people to engage in personal transformation successfully, and
with excitement and enthusiasm.[1]

Longitudinal research studies in the last few years have shown that sustainable change occurs as we focus on five major discoveries:[2]

1. The *ideal self*, or what you want out of life and the person you want to be—leading to your personal vision.

2. The *real self*, or how you act and are seen by others; the comparison of the real self to the ideal self results in identification of your strengths and weaknesses—leading to your personal balance sheet.

3. Your *learning agenda* to capitalize on your strengths and move you closer to your personal vision while possibly working on a weakness or two (or working to maintain the ideal current state of your life and work).

4. *Experimenting with and practicing new habits* or reinforcing and affirming your strengths.

5. *Developing and maintaining close, personal relationships*—resonant relationships—that enable you to move through these discoveries toward renewal.

These discoveries are shown in figure 5-1 as a cyclical process. Your path to renewal and resonance involves cycling through these discoveries to become the person you want to be and live the life you want to live.

But as we have said, dissonance is the default. Without intentional effort to move into resonance or remain there, we can miss opportunities for personal transformation, and our relationships will slide into less effective and less fulfilling interactions. On the path to resonance with self and with others, hope is the driver, compassion enables it, and mindfulness makes the path smoother and more understandable. Only with these elements can we sustain personal health, effectiveness, and resonant relationships. But it is not easy. It takes commitment and courage.

Let us look at an example of a classic high-achieving, action-oriented, successful man who dramatically improved his already good leadership through engaging in intentional change to develop his capacity for renewal and resonance.

FIGURE 5-1

Boyatzis's Intentional Change Theory*

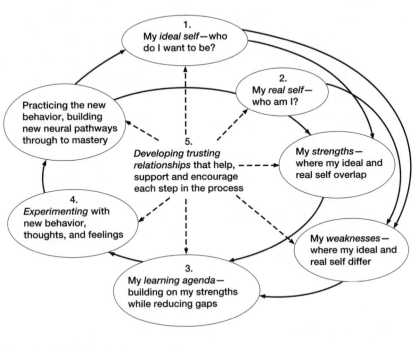

* Formerly self-directed learning theory.

A Leader's Journey to Renewal

As CEO of Italy's UniCredit Banca, Roberto Nicastro stands out. He is young to be in his position—barely in his forties. His ruffled hair, quick smile, and restless inclination to act make him appear to be in perpetual motion, driven as he is by a powerful desire for excellence. And while he is likeable, friendly, and confident, Roberto is also a leader whose mental sharpness has brought him and his company much success.

For example, recently Roberto was instrumental in enabling UniCredit Group to engage in an ambitious international expansion. In only three short years, the group took a solid but very bold acquisition strategy from vision to reality. Starting with just a minor interest outside the Italian borders, Roberto's business acumen, emotional intelligence, and sheer energy enabled the bank to develop partnerships with several significant financial services institutions in Central and Eastern Europe. Moving across cultural barriers is not always easy, and it is often difficult to establish trust, but Roberto quickly built solid relationships during the merger and acquisitions processes in sensitive situations that could have become contentious. He found novel solutions to management dilemmas. He built new systems, both human and organizational.

Given his obvious success as a leader, when we met Roberto we found it fascinating (and admirable) that he had decided to focus his energy on developing himself. After all, he was doing great, leading this new, exciting division with a very promising future in the industry. He and his family were also happy in their personal life. So why change?

Step 1: The Sparks That Ignite the Passion to Change—Finding Your Ideal Self

Roberto Nicastro described his awakening to the need for a different kind of happiness as a Maslovian process.[3] Early on, he was meeting modern basic needs: starting his career, doing well in his field, courting his loved one, getting married, having a family. All of these had been achieved some time ago. But, in quiet moments of honest reflection, Roberto knew deep down that he was not totally at peace with himself. He recognized that he was on an emotional roller coaster much of the time, pushing up hills and careening down—not feeling out of control, really, just not peaceful. It was starting to seem as if this roller coaster might be all there was to his life, and it was just not enough. Even though to everyone around him—up, down, and around in the organization—he seemed to be totally in control and very successful, Roberto knew that he was beginning to be caught in the Sacrifice Syndrome. This is, as we have seen, the trap into which many leaders fall when they give too much without renewing themselves on a regular basis.

To his credit, Roberto saw what was going on long before it negatively affected him or his leadership. And, interestingly, he was not driven to change by any sort of fear of impending failure. In fact, the impetus was just the opposite: instead of being driven by a need to compensate for weaknesses, he wanted to build on his strengths. The spark that ignited Roberto's commitment to develop himself was a desire to be the best *person* he could be.[4] As he began to realize that he was indeed achieving the goals he had set for himself with respect to career and family, he found himself free to think a bit more expansively about life. He began imagining a future that included physical health well into old age, deeply fulfilling relationships at home and at work, and even making his mark in the world—his legacy, if you will. Roberto began to imagine a bigger future that was ripe with hope.

The new image that emerged of the person he wanted to be was what we call the *ideal self*. It was a vision that ignited hope—a powerful driver of behavior. His vision and hope actually motivated his change process, and constituted the first epiphany he had on the journey.

This kind of discovery—this awareness of what could be—that Roberto experienced was the first step in his becoming mindful of his personal change process. This process begins with identifying your dream—for yourself, your life, and your work.

The last twenty years have seen considerable research done on the power of positive imaging and visioning. The research in sports psychology, meditation, and biofeedback indicates that we can access and engage deep emotional commitment and psychic energy if we engage our passions and catch our dreams in our ideal self-image.[5] Surprisingly, even though we know the importance of considering a positive view of ourselves and our future, we often skip this step. We take on others' hopes for us, maybe, or we simply let ourselves become numb to our own dreams. So, your first challenge: find *your* dream—your *own* vision for yourself and your life.[6] You may want to start this process now. If so, take some time to look through and work on the exercises at the end of this chapter and in appendix B.

Step 2: Confronting Your Real Self—
Finding Your Strengths and Weaknesses

As Roberto worked to clarify his vision, he felt excitement, hope, and a compelling desire to move toward the future. Along with excitement from his hopeful vision came energy and a commitment to look at what might get in his way, what was preventing him from creating the life he dreamed about. He started looking at himself holistically—mind, body, heart, and spirit—and came to the conclusion that in fact some of his greatest strengths were now becoming liabilities.

Becoming aware who we are *now*—what we call the *real self*—is the next step in intentional change. To move from where we are now to where we want to be, we need to have a sense of how others see us, and how that image matches (or does not match) with how we see ourselves.

This is an important aspect of mindfulness and requires deep self-awareness and the willingness to be vulnerable. Becoming clear about oneself and how others experience us is difficult and takes courage. Why? Because over time, we build a certain (usually positive) self-image, and our psyche actively protects that image from harm or change by preventing us from taking in all of the information about ourselves, especially negative or disconfirming information. This defense mechanism serves to protect us, but it also conspires to delude us into an image of who we are that feeds on itself, becomes self-perpetuating, and eventually may become dysfunctional.[7] So in order to really see ourselves as we are we have to let our defenses down.

Roberto was a prime candidate for playing out this dynamic. Everyone had always praised his creativity, energy, drive, and ambition. In his early career these characteristics were the source of his success, and he certainly did not want to put out his own flame. Yet during this time of visioning, he found himself to be more open and willing to let his defenses down, increasing his capacity to look at himself realistically. He began listening to his emotions, his body, and to what people did *not* say to him. He began to realize that his strengths—notably his creativity, action orientation, and speed—were also at the root of some of his problems. Roberto's adrenalin was constantly pumping—he was in a physiological state of high alert most of the time. His body was beginning to revolt: irritating stress-related illnesses were becoming more common with each passing year. He realized that his intensity, focus, and creativity were sources of personal satisfaction and success but also at the core of some of the internal unrest and stress he habitually experienced. He noticed the effects of power stress and the beginning of the Sacrifice Syndrome.

Moreover, his intense style was beginning to cause a few problems with his work relationships. At the height of his fast-paced, action-oriented, hurricane era, Roberto inspired admiration, awe, frustration, and sometimes fear. His tendency to constantly move toward novelty and to always have lists of new ideas and projects became overwhelming for the people around him. Some could not keep up and began to feel exhausted, inadequate, or decidedly uninspired.

At around the same time, there were a couple of difficult personnel situations that were not, in fact, helped by his intensity. He came to see that part of the problem was that he moved too fast, with such impatience, that he could lose sight of the people around him. In his search for excellence and the next best idea he was running right over people—not really understanding their experience and often quite callously ignoring his impact or the impact of what he set in motion.

As he moved up the hierarchy, he realized, his style might become a liability.[8] Even though so many strengths—such as initiative, drive, and the quest for excellence—actually do lead to success, they can also become very problematic for a leader and the people around him when left unexamined. In fact, people who have a strong achievement motive often find themselves pushing so hard for excellence that they actually sabotage their own and others' efforts—not very effective in leadership situations. It is particularly damaging when dealing with strong individuals at the top of a large organization, where relationships are key.

When we finally recognize that we are heading for trouble, we often wonder why we did not see it sooner. In fact, however, seeing yourself as others see you and honestly considering your internal states, beliefs, emotions, and so forth is probably one of the most difficult developmental challenges. Many of us know this phenomenon as the boiling frog syndrome. Simply put, if you drop a frog into a pot of boiling water, the frog will immediately jump out. But place a frog in a pot of cool water, and gradually raise the temperature to boiling, and the frog will remain in the water, unaware of the rising temperature, until it is cooked to death.

Several factors contribute to humans becoming boiling frogs. People around you may not let you see yourself or the world clearly; they simply do not give you feedback or information about how they see you. This is particularly true if you have power over them—as a parent or leader, for example. Or, they may be victims of the boiling frog syndrome themselves, not seeing you or the world all that clearly. And some people are enablers: they deliberately avoid sharing the truth. They may be frightened of repercussions, want to avoid conflict, or be unwilling to change themselves.

We also miss clues about our real selves because when we attempt to change and develop, all too often we focus only on our deficiencies rather than our strengths. Organizational training programs and managers conducting annual reviews often make the same mistake. There is an assumption that when it comes to talents and strengths, we can leave well enough alone and get to the areas that need work. So, at best, people are faced with negative and disconfirming information about themselves, with little or no attention paid to their strengths. They then become trapped by negativity, which has a powerful and destructive effect, as we will see in chapter 7. They lose the passion for change, become resentful, or even opt out from their jobs, psychologically if not physically. It is no wonder that many of the leadership programs intended to help a person develop result in the individual feeling battered, beleaguered, and bruised, rather than encouraged, motivated, or guided.

As Roberto's story illustrates, for you to truly consider changing yourself, you must have a sense of what you value and want to *keep*. Roberto started with a sense that quite a lot was working well with respect to his leadership and his life. He began examining himself holistically—looking at what he valued in himself as well as what he might need to change. He took a balanced approach, focusing on what we call *strengths* and *gaps*.

The areas in which your real self and ideal self are consistent and congruent can be considered strengths, and you are likely to want to preserve them. You will also need to consider weaknesses: areas where your real self and ideal self are not consistent, or deficiencies that you wish to change or adapt in some manner (these deficiencies are often referred to as *gaps* in organizations). Then you have to turn your insight into an actionable plan—a personal vision and a learning agenda.

It takes courage to change patterns that have always worked well, to let the old behaviors and attitudes go and try new ones. It is particularly difficult to modify one's strengths—after all, we do not want to obliterate the very characteristics that have enabled us to succeed. Difficult as this kind of change can be, it is important to start with a highly motivating vision—this is exactly what the ideal self is, and why the hope it generates can provide the fuel that drives the engine of personal transformation.

It takes inner strength to look at your real self. That is why you need to look at the ideal self *first*. This gives you a powerful, positive, and motivating sense of what could be that sustains you through the hard work of looking at your current reality. Discovering the real self, then, begins by looking closely at your ideal self. We have included exercises for insight into your ideal self at the end of this chapter and in appendix B. These activities are personal and the outcomes can be elusive, so the work of exploring your ideal self must take place in psychologically safe surroundings.

These exercises and tests can help by making explicit the dreams or aspirations you have for the future. Talking with close friends or mentors can help, if both you and they agree to candor, honesty, support, and confidentiality. Allowing yourself to think about your desired future, not merely a prediction of your most likely future, is difficult but quite possible if you diligently consider your real dreams and consciously stay open to possibilities.

After you have discovered your ideal self and begun to gain insight into your real self—and your strengths and weaknesses— you might want to begin systematically collecting information from others, perhaps through 360-degree feedback, which is popular in organizations. Other sources of insight into your real self may come from behavioral feedback through video- or audiotaped interactions and other exercises done in assessment centers, career centers, and coaching relationships. Again, good friends and loved ones can help if all parties take the exploration and conversations seriously and treat one another with compassion and sensitivity. Various psychological tests, such as those that look at values, philosophy, traits, and motives, can also help you determine or make explicit inner aspects of your real self. In fact, reflecting on your core values and operating philosophy is a good way to begin this process. You may want to explore this now, using appendix B.

Once we have these insights about our strengths and weaknesses, and the context of our personal vision, how do we get there? Developing a learning agenda makes it possible.

Before we see how Roberto's story has played out, let us now move to the case of how another executive remade herself into a resonant leader.

Step 3: Creating a Learning Agenda for a New Future

"Ellen" is a general manager of a small business within a *Fortune* 500 company that makes a variety of automotive and truck components. Little did she know, when she took yet another promotion in 2000, that she was about to have an epiphany that would bring her strengths and weaknesses into stark relief. Her appointment as head of sales and marketing at one of the parent company's large divisions followed the latest of what had been a series of star performance reviews. In this review, her boss, the general manager, gave her the first "1" performance rating he had awarded in his twenty years of managing for the company.

Success was not new to Ellen. After getting a BA in biomedical engineering and one MA in finance and another in operations, she was on the fast track—changing jobs about every year and a half. She wanted to be the best she could be at any job and enjoyed the steady movement up the ladder toward general management. Her duties were challenging, including orchestrating layoffs and restructuring. Following one particularly difficult turnaround period, a new HR manager came into the division. He approached Ellen on a Friday and said, "We have a problem." He had reviewed exit interviews with people who were laid off and handed her a list of things people had said about her.

The list devastated her. People had said things like, "I can't trust Ellen." "She doesn't care about her people. She only cares about results." "She's intimidating to work for." "She expects a lot out of people without taking the time to develop them." The shock permeated Ellen's every waking thought for the weekend. She could not believe it. She had always done what was needed or expected of her and gotten results. Her performance was exemplary and had won her accolades. Bosses had consistently praised her.

Ellen approached her boss on Monday and asked him what this meant. He was angry at the HR manager for what he had done (without his knowledge), and furious at the way he had done it. He reiterated all of her strengths, as he had a few months earlier at the time of the promotion and most recently at her annual review. But he then told her that although she always got results, "You have to get your people to be as results driven and passionate as you are—then, you'll be ten times more successful." He handed her a book on emotional intelligence and suggested that she read it and consider its implications for her style.[9] As we all know, reading a book—any book—is rarely enough to get us to change. But, as Ellen read, she was also crafting a vision of her ideal self, and a vision of her future. She saw that some of the attributes of great leadership, including empathy, would be essential if she were to achieve her dreams. This was her wake-up call—and she heard it.

Over the next few weeks, Ellen came to realize that her new mission was to get results through others. As she will say now, "For many years, I demonstrated very little empathy at work. In fact, in my efforts to demonstrate strength and courage in a male-dominated environment, I had convinced myself that empathy was a sign of weakness and did not belong in the workplace. As a result, I was very unskilled at being an empathetic manager." And this despite the fact that at home with her husband and children, and with her friends and extended family, she was tuned into others. "The book," she said, "convinced me that emotions had a place at work."

Her learning agenda started with getting help. When she asked, her boss encouraged Ellen to go ahead and find a coach. She did, and worked with him to refine her image of her ideal self. In particular, her coach helped her realize that she could not achieve her dreams unless she really focused on and fixed the problem she had showing empathy. She and her coach engaged in long conversations and even exercises that enabled her to explore empathy and to practice it at work and at home. The exercises sounded simple, but they were not easy for someone who had never thought this way—at least not within the work environment. They had a powerful effect on Ellen's awareness and growing talent for understanding others' feelings and tuning into their moods. For example, the coach once asked her to describe what others' feelings and thoughts were likely to be during an upcoming meeting, *before* she went into the meeting. She did this before each meeting for a few weeks. At first, it seemed awkward and an interference in her tight schedule, but she kept repeating to herself that she had to tune into the others to be able to motivate them.

Then Ellen visualized customers' thoughts and feelings through role play. Soon she felt confident enough to begin to use the new insights and techniques with her internal customers.

Next, she asked for her next two promotions to be in staff positions. In these roles, she had no direct subordinates, but had to use her interpersonal sensitivity and skills to get things done. She continually practiced her new-found talent. Eventually, she found that she did not have to spend so much conscious effort. She seemed to be aware of how others were feeling and their moods while looking at them or just being in the room with them.

About two years later, when she was offered the challenging job of turning around an old-line business, she felt ready, but nervous. She took the job as general manager of the business unit. Had her transformation worked?

Now, with over one hundred people reporting to her, Ellen says, "I am having more fun than I ever imagined . . . I love the people I'm working with . . . because, in part, we have good relationships while getting results." Her division and her company have turned around financially. But, you might ask, what is different? What's different is Ellen—how she is leading, and how people experience her leadership.

We had the pleasure of observing Ellen recently when she received anonymous 360-degree feedback from all of her direct reports, as well as peers and her boss. It confirmed that her intentional change had worked. As she opened her 360-degree report, her face broke into a smile. She had done it. In all of the six emotional intelligence competencies related to relationship management, including developing others, inspirational leadership, and teamwork, her direct reports and boss assessed her at or above the target point for outstanding leaders (see chapter 2 for the full list of EI competencies). With regard to empathy, her direct reports gave her an almost-perfect score.[10] In the open-ended comments, people praised her and used words like "inspirational" and "exciting" to describe her leadership. She had become a resonant leader!

What worked so well for Ellen can work for others—but not

always. Even when we have the intention, courage, and energy for change, it is easy to become distracted and focus on the wrong things. Lots of times, when we realize that our style is beginning to cause problems for us, we turn to coping strategies—exercise, a better diet, a holiday. In extreme cases, we have known people who quit their jobs, ended marriages, or took other drastic measures to try to alleviate their distress. While all of these things are sometimes necessary, and in particular the healthy coping mechanisms are probably things we should all do, the reality is that if we do not find the true source of our distress, anxiety, or our shortcomings, no coping mechanisms or extreme measures will really help. A great exercise program is just a Band-Aid if we have internal drivers that cause us to be forever dissatisfied and striving. Leaving a job might ease things for a while, but most people we know who do this without getting at the real issues eventually end up in another situation as stressful as the one they left.

While Ellen's challenge was to become mindful of others and work on her empathy, Roberto's was to become mindful of himself and work on his self-awareness. Let us return to him now to see how he used personal transformation to accelerate his success at work—and at home.

To Roberto's credit, he saw that if he wanted to be content, to have some measure of peace in his life and to achieve his dream, he needed to attend to himself holistically. His challenge was to become mindful of himself—his emotions, his drives, how he made sense of things, his habitual patterns of behavior. Taking up a new sport or building in more time for family and enjoyable activities would not be enough. He needed to address the issues from the inside out.

After his initial self-diagnosis, Roberto turned his drive for excellence inward, on himself, and slowed down long enough to take stock—to look at what in his life might help him realize his vision and what might get in the way. He engaged in a number of activities, quietly and with little fanfare. He found a coach . . . The regular meetings and conversations provided a structure within which

Roberto could begin to grapple with his hopes for the future and his current reality. All in all, Roberto spent several months talking through issues, deciding which strengths to leverage and what he needed to change. He developed a learning agenda and began to implement it.

This is the third step in intentional change: development of an agenda and focusing on moving toward the desired future. While performance at work or happiness in life may be the eventual consequence of our efforts, a learning agenda focuses on the *process* of development itself. It focuses our energy on learning first, outcomes second. The orientation to learning arouses a positive belief in one's capability and the hope of improvement.[11]

A major threat to effective goal setting and planning is that we are already busy and cannot add anything else to our lives. We can only succeed in the change process, then, if we determine when to say "no" and stop some current activities in our lives to make room for new activities.

Another potential challenge or threat is the development of a plan that calls for people to engage in activities at odds with their preferred learning style and therefore difficult to adopt. When this occurs, a person becomes demotivated and often stops the activities, or becomes impatient and decides that the goals are not worth the effort.[12]

When engaging in any personal change process, it is a good idea to choose only a few key things to work on. Ellen focused on understanding what others were feeling. For Roberto, the challenge was clear: if he was going to have more positive impact on the people around him, he needed to temper his desire for action and novelty as well as his impatience. He needed to channel his energy more effectively and in a healthier way.

Step 4: Experimentation—and Practice, Practice, Practice

Once your agenda or plan points you in the right direction, you have to practice sufficiently to go beyond comfort to mastery of the new habits. That is what worked for both Ellen and Roberto. The new attitudes and behaviors have to become unconscious responses. Early wins spark hope—which in turn engenders energy and commitment to the process. Then, the fourth step in the intentional change process is to experiment with and practice desired changes. Acting on your plan and moving toward your goals involves numerous activities and experimenting with new behavior. To develop or learn new behavior, you must find ways to learn more from current or ongoing experiences. That is, the experimentation and practice does not always require attending courses or engaging in a new activity. It may involve trying something different in a current setting, reflecting on what occurs, and experimenting further in this setting. Sometimes, this part of the process requires finding and using opportunities to learn and change.

Interestingly, people often downplay experimentation and may not even think they have changed until they have tried new behavior in work or other real-world settings.[13] Because of this, we often rush to try new behaviors in "hot" settings, like work. It is easy to become discouraged if we do this, however, because it is not necessarily safe to try new ways of being in settings where performance is constantly measured. In fact, experimentation and practice are most effective if they are done in conditions in which we feel safe. This sense of psychological safety creates an atmosphere in which we can try new behavior, perceptions, and thoughts with relatively low risk of shame, embarrassment, or serious consequences of failure.[14] This is probably part of the reason that executive coaching can be so helpful. A good coach can provide perspective, feedback, guidance, and confrontation, all within the confines of a safe and confidential environment. Also, a good coach can coax and goad you to continue the practice in the same way a fitness instructor will push you for "five more" repetitions of an exercise.

Hopefully, *following* a period of experimentation in a safe setting (such as with a coach or in personal activities), you will want to practice the new behaviors in the actual settings within which you wish to use them, such as at work or at home. During this part of the process, intentional change and learning begins to look like a continuous improvement process.

For Ellen and Roberto, practicing new behaviors at work and then making them a way of life were crucial steps in their development. Although they were faced with different issues, both practiced becoming attuned to people by simply paying more conscious attention to what was going on around them. We saw how Ellen practiced her visualization of others' feelings and responses over and over. In Roberto's case, he watched people a lot more carefully to see their reactions to him. He focused on how his actions and mood affected others as a way to understand himself and to help him know how to better manage himself. This was something he had done before; it was part of the reason he had been so successful. But now, he began to consciously monitor his habitual responses and thought patterns—noticing more, assuming less, and not taking his first assumptions about individuals or groups for granted. He questioned his quick judgments and automatic responses. He worked hard to avoid the trap of his own perceptions—to understand individuals' experiences from their points of view, rather than his. He schooled himself to draw conclusions based on what he actually saw, thought, and felt rather than habitual patterns of thought and action. In essence, Roberto was transforming his newfound self-awareness into a new level of social awareness that in turn enabled him to manage his own actions more effectively. So, to build social awareness, he worked heavily on his self-management emotional intelligence competencies.[15]

Step 5: Don't Try This Alone

As you begin to engage in intentional change, you need to involve other people—connection is essential. For both Roberto and Ellen, their bosses, a coach, their spouses, and a few close friends were essential to their transformation. Sometimes, this is really the first discovery—finding a coach or a good friend or perhaps a colleague who is on a similar quest. The next step: talking to such people, checking your reality with theirs, and opening yourself to their views. Honest dialogue can spark our own creativity, new ways of understanding self and others, and help us stay the course. This takes courage and persistence. Just as it is difficult to really look at oneself, it is not easy to seek others' opinions, expertise, and help. By involving others, you turn up the heat. It is a lot harder to stop the process of developing yourself when you have other people invested in helping you change.

Our relationships are an essential part of our environment and are key to sustaining personal transformation. The most crucial relationships are often within groups that have particular importance to us. These relationships and groups give us a sense of identity. They guide us as to what is appropriate and good behavior, and provide feedback on our behavior.[16]

Based on theories of social identity, our social setting, our culture, our reference groups, and our relationships mediate and moderate our sense of who we are and who we want to be. We develop and elaborate our ideal selves from these contexts as well as label and interpret our real selves from these contexts. And we interpret and value strengths (things we consider to be part of our core and wish to preserve) and gaps (things we consider to be weaknesses or that we wish to change) from them.

In this sense, our relationships are mediators, moderators, interpreters, sources of feedback, and sources of support, and they give us permission to change and learn. They may also be the most important source of protection from relapses or returning to our earlier forms of behavior.[17]

Resonance Within Yourself = Resonance with Others

As we saw, Roberto went through a process of self-discovery that resulted in stepwise changes in his leadership. A gradual awakening to the desire for inner peace and more positive impact on people around him sparked him to enter into a process of envisioning his ideal future, his ideal self. He looked back over his life to see how his habits had developed, and he came to some conclusions about which patterns still served him and which did not. He began consciously monitoring his thoughts, feelings, and behavior, paying attention to what had been automatic responses.

The outcome of this process is that Roberto's internal state is healthier. He is calmer, more in control of his desires, and more content as a person. He now understands better the source of some of the tension that used to trouble him and others. He has learned to manage his intensity and creativity, and is no longer at the mercy of his own achievement drive. He now uses his desire for novelty to turn difficult situations into creative challenges, and is not on a constant quest for diversity of experience. He is more likely to slow down, metaphorically and actually, taking deep breaths and practicing mindful connection with people.

Roberto now manages himself much better around the people with whom he works. He restrains himself. He does not overwhelm people with new plans and projects when he sees that they are still grappling with what is happening in the moment. Roberto has learned to control his impulses, to manage his emotions and his strengths so his best ideas are presented to people when they are most ready. And when inevitably he falls into the old patterns, running too hard and too fast for the people around him, he can self-correct much earlier than before.

Similarly, Ellen's transformation from a hard-driving, results-driven leader to an engaging team leader was a journey of building resonance with others, which eventually led to resonance within herself.

Developing the capacity for renewal in these two somewhat different and yet similar journeys has enabled Roberto and Ellen to consciously manage their strengths to leverage their talent and energy to inspire passion and create resonance. This has been a powerful lesson. They each learned how to use their many talents consciously so their enthusiasm and passion did not become a liability, but a source of inspiration for others. In both cases, these leaders' reflection and intentional change impacted their organizations positively. In fact, Roberto found the process so relevant personally that he sponsored an organizationwide program for over 3,000 managers of UniCredit's retail division to help each of them begin their own process of leadership development.

In the next three chapters, we will explore how leaders developed their resonance and renewed themselves by cultivating mindfulness, hope, and compassion. And how, through resonant relationships, these qualities spread to others. Before proceeding, however, you may choose to explore your own process of intentional change by working through the exercises at the end of this chapter and in appendix B.

Exercise 1: Taking a Fantasy Job

THIS IS AN OPPORTUNITY to imagine yourself doing the kind of work or jobs that you sometimes fantasize, or wonder, "What would it be like if I were doing X?" Make believe the following three events have occurred:

1. You enter a new machine called a *neurophysiological remaker*. After a few minutes inside of the machine, genetic reengineering and virtual neural implants give you the body, knowledge, and capability to do any job—and do it well.

2. You are given the financial resources and certifications (i.e., licenses) based on your new capabilities.

3. For one year, you are free of all personal, social, and financial responsibilities in your current or desired life.

List five to ten jobs that you would love to do or try. Consider a wide variety of jobs—in sports, music, medicine, politics, agriculture, religion. Consider working in other countries. Consider jobs you have heard about or seen in the movies or on television.

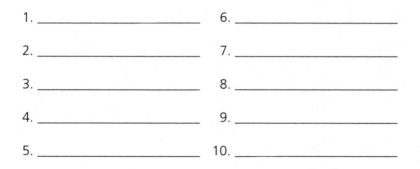

1. _____   6. _____

2. _____   7. _____

3. _____   8. _____

4. _____   9. _____

5. _____   10. _____

Choose the three jobs in your list that most interest you or seem the most exciting or rewarding. Describe each of them below, including what you will most enjoy or look forward to about each.

1. _____

_____

_____

_____

2. _____

_____

_____

_____

3. _____

_____

_____

_____

Sometimes people describe a "fantasy" job as one they really wish for and want to do. Other times, the job represents some interesting or exciting activities or conditions. In other words, sometimes it is not the job that is the fantasy but some aspect of it or condition under which the job is done. As you read your descriptions of the jobs you would most like to do or try, do you notice themes or patterns? How are these jobs similar? Are there activities (such as being outdoors) that are part of each? Are there conditions of work (such as working with a team) that are part of each? Are there consequences (such as being famous) that are a part of each? List those themes or patterns.

Exercise 2: My Legacy

WHAT WOULD YOU WISH to have as your legacy in life? In other words, what will remain or continue as a result of you having lived and worked all of these years?

Exercise 3: Developing Your Personal Vision

A PERSONAL VISION is the deepest expression of what we want in life. It is a description of our preferred future, not a prediction of what will be. In this sense, your personal vision should describe what you want out of life and work and what kind of person you want to be. Instead of a forecast of what you think might be likely in the future, your personal vision is a description of the future you dream about. Consider your responses to these exercises along with your answers to and reflections about the three exercises at the end of chapter 7. This will help you to identify the most important elements of your personal vision.

These exercises and questionnaires are best completed over a period of time. Do not try to complete them in one or two sittings.

Each should provoke somewhat different reflections, thoughts, and feelings. What are the overall themes you observe about your dreams and wishes? It is now time to pull together all of these reflections, thoughts, and ideas into a coherent statement of your desired future.

To write your personal vision: choose a year in the future (at least five years out and no more than fifteen) that has symbolic meaning to you. Imagine yourself, and your life, at that time. Write a vivid description of all aspects of your life—in the present tense. In other words, write your vision *as if* it is that particular date in the future.

If you are in a loving relationship, your personal vision is really part of a shared vision for the pair of you. If relevant and appropriate, try repeating the process with your partner or spouse to create a family shared vision.

SIX

Mindfulness

I T IS JUST PAST DAWN in London, long before most people are awake. If you are up early, walking in Hyde Park, you are likely to see John Studzinski running with three big dogs. He is moving fast, enjoying the crisp air and the sights along the way. He stops and smiles while the dogs quickly sniff the grass and flowers, reading the canine version of the morning paper.[1]

By this time in the morning, John (known to many people as Studs) will have spent time reading, writing, and meditating—an invigorating start to a very full day. By eight, he will attend a breakfast meeting then move on to ten or more hours of intense conversations, decisions, and action. Most evenings, you can find him sitting with friends and colleagues, all talking animatedly as they work together on important social issues: human rights, homelessness, poverty, even nurturing young artists.

John Studzinski is an intense, passionate, and successful businessman. He was at the helm during the years when Morgan Stanley Europe grew by a multiple of ten. Now he is CEO of the

Corporate Investment Banking and Markets Division of HSBC Bank and a member of the Group Management Board of HSBC. With his co-CEO, Stuart Gulliver, he has led dramatic change in the division. Some say these changes could define the industry in the coming years. In the meantime, the effort has resulted in noticeable and profitable improvements.

John is also known as a leader in the arts. He is a trustee of the Tate Gallery and the Sir John Soane Museum in London. As if this is not enough, John's real passion, some would say his real work, is social activism. He is the Vice Chair of Human Rights Watch, supports several local organizations in London and was granted Knight of the Order of St. Gregory by Pope John Paul II for his work with the homeless.[2]

John accomplishes more in one day than many people do in a week. So how does he do it? One thing that stands out is his acute self-awareness and keen insight about people and the world around him. He knows what is important to him, and why. He has figured out how to live his beliefs and values. He sees other people and situations *very* clearly. He notices what is happening inside him and around him. John is awake, aware, and actively attentive to himself, people, and situations. And he *uses* what he sees.

We call this mindfulness. Let us look now at exactly what mindfulness is, what it looks like, and how effective leaders cultivate it to manage the inevitable cycle of sacrifice and renewal—and to sustain their resonance.

Minding the Medicine Wheel

Mindfulness is the capacity to be fully aware of all that one experiences *inside the self*—body, mind, heart, spirit—and to pay full attention to what is happening *around us*—people, the natural world, our surroundings, and events.

In defining mindfulness we draw on two traditions: cognitive psychology and Buddhist philosophy. Ellen Langer, a Harvard professor, uses the word *mindfulness* to describe a healthy state of cognitive openness, curiosity, and awareness.[3] Jon Kabat-Zinn of the University of Massachusetts comes at mindfulness from a slightly different perspective. Basing his work on ancient Buddhist traditions as well as modern psychology, neurophysiology, and medicine, he and his colleagues define mindfulness as ". . . moment-to-moment awareness."[4] In bringing these two schools of thought together, we are able to apply what can be a somewhat abstract concept to the actual *practice* of leadership.

In fact, mindfulness enables us to counter the effects of the Sacrifice Syndrome and is a first, and crucial, step in renewal. Awareness of one's self enables us to notice the detrimental effects of power stress (and then, we can do something about it before it becomes a big problem). Attending to ourselves also enables us to stay the course—living healthily and in accordance with our values even when the pressure is on.

Living mindfully means that we are constantly and consciously in tune with ourselves—listening carefully to our bodies, minds, hearts, and spirits. The best among us consciously develop the capacity for deep self-awareness, noting and building on our understanding of our inner experiences. Attending to ourselves like this enables us to be very clear about what is most important to us; it allows us to engage our passion and build on positive emotional states. Attending carefully enables us to recognize early on when we are heading down the wrong path—toward allowing a slight compromise in our values, making a wrong decision, or ignoring our health. People who live mindfully catch problems before they become serious, because they pay attention to their inner voice: a voice that includes intuition, wisdom, and a subtle but very sophisticated analysis of what is going on in the world. Mindfulness means using all the clues available—our emotions, thoughts, physical sensations, in-the-moment reactions, and sense of right, wrong, justice, and injustice. Subtle, fleeting emotions as well as small, seemingly unimportant ideas are often terribly important, as is listening to our bodies.

People like John Studzinski do this on a daily basis—in part by making sure they create quiet moments in their day to really tune in to what is going on *inside* as well as around them, and to then attend to those sensations, feelings, and thoughts.

It takes some effort to train oneself to be mindful. Some people, like John, deliberately organize their lives to include practices that help hone the skills of awareness, attention, and reflection. There is no one way to do this—meditation, prayer, listening to music, aerobic exercise, and being in nature all provide opportunities for openness to one's quiet inner voice. One thing is certain, though— to develop your capacity for mindfulness, you must, as John says, "be comfortable with your own company." You need to focus on yourself, and you need to spend time *alone*, as well as learning with others. If you are interested in exploring some of these prac- tices now, you may want to turn to the exercises at the end of this chapter and in appendix B.

The importance of living life mindfully is not news—we have just forgotten some of the wisdom of the ages. Almost every cul- ture around the world has some sort of scheme that helps people to focus on themselves holistically, in order to find peace within, create harmony in their communities and balance in their envi- ronments. In some native North American tribes, this scheme takes a compass-like form called a *medicine wheel*, in which each of the four compass points represents one of our essential elements: the rational, intellectual mind; physical body; emotions (heart); and spirit.[5]

What we are talking about, then, is both ancient wisdom and common sense: a deep understanding of ourselves allows us to act in ways that are not only meaningful to us but inspiring to others. Contrary to popular belief, cultivating the capacity for mindful- ness is not just a nice-to-have or something to be done for private reasons: it is actually essential for sustaining good leadership. It can be one of the most important things we do, resulting in a step- wise change in our effectiveness as leaders. Maybe most impor- tant, when we attend to ourselves by developing our minds, taking care of our bodies, understanding and using the power of our emotions, and attending to our spirituality, however we choose to do so, we can begin to reach our full potential as *people*.

So mindfulness starts with attending to one's self holistically. To be mindful, we must first wake up to our inner experience and attend consciously to these insights. But it doesn't stop there—mindfulness includes paying attention to *what is happening around us*; that is, being acutely aware and seeking deep understanding of people, our surroundings, the natural world, and events.[6] Then, we must *do* something with our perceptions, feelings, and thoughts. John Studzinski does this through his work in human rights and homelessness, but also in the attentive, mindful way that he connects with the people he works with at HSBC.

John is acutely aware of the people in his world—coworkers at HSBC, clients, and colleagues in the arts and the social networks he leads. In fact, we believe a good bit of his success is due to his ability to tune in to the needs of others. Take clients, for example. John spends at least half his time reaching out to his key clients. He gets to know them as people, and he tunes in to their real business needs, constantly pushing himself to look beyond the obvious or the current situation. Surely, you might say, this is just common sense? Maybe so, but it is far less common in practice. In fact, many organizational cultures (maybe even society today) drive people to action, rather than reflection, which means that *real* listening is actually quite rare.

So for John and other mindful leaders, it is not just a matter of meeting with clients. It is a matter of connecting authentically with them, listening deeply to them, to the point that they can read and understand their clients' subtle messages, even their unformed hopes. Reading between the lines—while in an authentic and trusting relationship with people—is behavior that defines mindfulness. And for leaders, it brings effectiveness and success.

When we attend to ourselves holistically, and become more fully engaged with people, our communities, and our environment, it becomes much less likely that we will do harm and more likely that we will do good. Why? Because we are attending to balance, both inside ourselves and in the world around us.

Some people make mindfulness a way of life. It doesn't take a disaster or a radical change to get them refocused on what they believe in or what they want to do in their lives. They live with their eyes open—able to adjust their behavior gradually, adapting to new circumstances while staying true to their core beliefs and working toward their goals and vision.

Awake, Aware, and Attentive

Let's look at how John Studzinski cultivates and maintains mindfulness. As we have said, mindfulness means being awake, aware, and attentive. So, first of all, John takes mindfulness seriously by staying "awake" in every sense of the word: He takes *time* to observe, listen, and learn. And he focuses on his inner world as a way to get clear about what is important to him. He builds in time each day for reflection. He reads widely and spends time with political, social, spiritual, and business leaders. He spends some weekends working in a homeless center. The result: on a daily basis, at work and in life, he does not have to spend much time figuring out what is right and what is wrong. He is clear about who he is, what is important to him, what he cares about and about his beliefs.

Sometimes, people who are this clear about their beliefs become rigid. Not John. As he said to us in a recent conversation, "Never assume the status quo is right, especially when it comes to people and human dignity." In other words, never let yourself get boxed in by ideas—your own or others'. That is where awareness comes in—an approach that John applies to the wider environment. He not only watches trends in his business, he also constantly seeks to understand what is new, what is different in the environment *around* the business. He seeks out people who are different from himself and opinions that are different from his. He goes out of his way to work with and befriend people of all ages, enabling him to learn from the multiple perspectives that different generations bring to conversations. In essence, he not only seeks newness and variety, he considers it, notices what is relevant, and adapts himself to constantly changing situations.

As John puts it, "No two situations are the same, no matter how similar they may appear. It is easy to assume that because things look more or less the same, they are indeed the same. You have to see how and when things, and people, have changed. If you were to direct the same play twice, and the actors changed, you'd actually have a different play. It is no different in business— to deal with the new play you need to observe people and the context very, very carefully, looking for those subtle signals that let you know what people are thinking and feeling, what is happening in the wider environment. Then, you have to take what you see and interpret it in the context of this new environment."

In business, this is easier said than done. It is difficult to stay focused and attentive to your "inner voice" or the wider environment when you have, say, lost a contract or disappointed a client. And even in day-to-day life and work, very little is crystal clear; things just move too fast to be totally predictable. John's point, however, is that these are exactly the situations that most require attention and openness. In other words, they require you to truly "attend" to them. Those moments when you feel pressed for time or vulnerable, angry, or baffled are exactly when you need to be most receptive, exploring what happened, who did or did not do what to whom, and the subtle impact on the wider environment. Oddly, it is often the quiet, subtle, disturbing feelings that are the messages we need to listen to most closely. This, too, is hard— when we have that nagging sense that something needs to be done, changed, or understood differently, we often discount our intuition, especially if the facts don't add up or the messages we are sensing make us uncomfortable.

Being open to learning, especially learning from failures, requires courage. And living mindfully requires resilience. As we saw in chapter 3, shutting down, becoming defensive, and creating dissonance can be the default response to the pressures of a leader's role. Mindfulness, then, is both an antidote to shutting down (and creating dissonance) and also a necessary condition for resonance.

So how do leaders really *use* mindfulness in practice? What are the ways in which mindfulness can be used to help us renew ourselves and counterbalance our natural tendency toward continual self-sacrifice? How does mindfulness help us maintain resonance?

Let us examine two situations that leaders commonly face and in which mindfulness can play a critical role. One of our examples depicts the importance of being highly vigilant when you are navigating in unknown territory. The other shows that mindfulness is crucial when you need to understand the particular environment in which you are working and those with whom you are working.

Navigating the Unknown

When dealing with a crisis or the unknown, we simply cannot predict what is to come. It takes confidence and optimism to let go of preconceived notions while also studiously opening oneself to new information and solutions. The process of opening up can make us feel vulnerable, even afraid. Many leaders simply shut down in order to avoid this kind of uneasiness. Many shut down to prove to people around them that they are decisive and know what to do (even when they do not). Avoiding openness—and vulnerability—results in a narrow focus and can ultimately cause you to slip into mindlessness.

Most of us experience times when it seems easier to give up what we believe, step away from our principles and go along with the status quo. Sometimes, behaving in the politically correct way is a lot easier than staying true to ourselves. Then it becomes all too easy for people to demonstrate values only when someone is watching them or it is convenient. Sometimes we feel vulnerable simply because no one seems to see things as we do, and no one else seems to have the courage to stick it out and do the right thing. When we feel like this, it is easy to lose confidence in ourselves, to question whether in fact we are doing the right thing or just being stubborn. Knowing where your personal line is, and also having people around you who share your values, whom you can trust and talk to, makes a huge difference.

Dan Sontag, vice president and head of the Advisory Business at Merrill Lynch, stepped onto what he referred to as "Wisconsin spring ice" when he began managing the private client business at Merrill Lynch. Why spring ice? Well, the landscape looked solid and safe, but in fact the surface was perilous, and just underneath the waters were raging. He was managing people who had just yesterday been peers, and he was doing it at time when the industry and the company were in turmoil. At Merrill, the new top team had defined a radically different strategy. Many of the old guard had left, and the web of relationships that had been the mechanism for influencing decisions was disrupted. Certain key aspects of the company's culture were not standing the test of time. A new culture had not yet emerged, so those rules that guide behavior in small and large ways in a business were simply not as clear as they had been in the past.

When faced with this kind of turbulence, mindfulness becomes even more important. You need more, rather than less, information, and it is generally more difficult to get. You need to leverage your strengths and find those people who are succeeding despite the disruptions. You need to stay calm.

Dan's response? He told us that he got very, very clear about those few core beliefs that had always guided his decisions and behavior, even in the midst of confusion and change. He also held onto the following tenets:

- Build trust through clarity and consistency.
- Make sure you *never* profess beliefs when people are watching, only to act differently when the temperature rises and the pressure is on.
- Know that you will feel uncomfortable, even vulnerable, because in the midst of real change around you, the rules are not clear and politically expedient behavior is very tempting.

It takes courage to stand on fragile spring ice, carefully choosing each step based on conviction. In high-pressure situations like Dan's, many people point outward: they find reasons for their problems outside of themselves. They blame others or the situation and they look for excuses. Good leaders point inward: they take personal responsibility for what is happening and what needs to be done, even when circumstances play a definitive role. Dan Sontag routinely asks himself, "What is my part in creating this situation and what do I, personally, need to do about it?"

Mindfulness starts with *self-awareness*: knowing yourself enables you to make choices about how you respond to people and situations. Deep knowledge about yourself enables you to be consistent, to present yourself authentically, as you are. We trust—and follow—people who are real, who are consistent, whose behavior, values, and beliefs are aligned. We trust people whom we do not constantly have to second-guess.

Honing the skills of mindful attention to oneself enables us to make better choices because we recognize and deal with our internal state—thoughts, physical sensations, and emotions. We are then better able to make sense of people and situations around us. Our perceptions are clear, not clouded by our own filters, biases, and unexplored or unacknowledged feelings.[7] Through purposeful, conscious direction of our attention, we are able to see things that might normally pass right by us, giving us access to deeper insight, wisdom, and choices.

Understanding Your Environment and the People Around You

For a leader, each conversation and exchange is an opportunity to gather valuable information about people, groups, and cultures, while building relationships and resonance. Attending carefully to our human environment and our relationships enables us to see details we may have missed and generate more accurate ideas about what is really going on. We notice subtle patterns in people's behavior, group dynamics, organizational processes, and even worldwide events. When we are mindful, we are more in control of ourselves and situations simply because we see reality more clearly.

Judi Johansen, president and CEO of PacifiCorp, an investor-owned utility company in the western United States, sees mindfulness as a way of life and a necessary baseline for success as a leader of a complex business.[8] Some years ago, when she was still practicing law, Judi represented the "Lilliputians" in a case that would determine who would determine electric rates in one part of the country. At the low point, Judi's clients were not even at the negotiating table, much less influencing decisions. Judi describes reading the situation this way: "I saw that the path they were going down was not going to get them where they wanted to go. I saw disunity in the group." She saw that the one hundred or so representatives of the small companies did not share an agenda and as such could not possibly fight the big guys.

It would have been easy to attend to the loudest, most powerful voices in her client group, or to attempt to hammer out a common position by herself (she did know what she was doing, after all). But Judi was paying attention to the dance between people and groups. By listening to their conversations, watching how they interacted, and noting what they hinted about one another in one-on-one discussions with her, she saw subtle signs of competition and mistrust among the members of the group. She also noticed the opposing side's quiet satisfaction in the face of this situation.

And Judi acted on what she saw. One memorable day, she managed to pull all one hundred-plus clients together in the parking lot of a hotel. Microphone in hand, she recounted what she had seen: the disunity, how it was not serving them, how their opponents loved every minute of it. She pointed out how obvious it was—to everyone except themselves. She called on them to reach across the competitive boundaries and join together as one voice.

It worked. Judi's mindful approach to both the environment in which she was operating and the people with whom she was dealing—her careful awareness and attentiveness to this delicate situation—resulted in the group members putting their competitiveness aside, getting a seat at the negotiating table, and ultimately achieving their aims.

Some years later, Judi found herself in yet another situation in which her mindful approach to the environment and people would be crucial: she was appointed as the first female administrator at Bonneville Power Administration, a federal agency selling electricity and setting energy policy affecting four states, fifty-two Native American tribes, investor-owned utilities, public utilities, numerous commissions, and various state and local governments. Talk about complexity: Judi's job was to create the blueprints for and then to build commitment to plans for allocation of finite resources across multiple constituencies with insatiable needs.

To succeed, Judi *had* to scan her environment. It was not enough to rely on the institutional folks whose job it was to monitor information and opinion. She had to get personally involved. She needed to be up close and personal—talking to people, listening to what was said as well as what was *not* said. Judi constantly assesses how people perceive things, noticing everything that goes on. She watches individuals and the dynamics between people. She tracks body language as carefully as what is said, noticing everything—even people's annoying habits at meetings, which can impart valuable information about their level of anxiety, competitiveness, acceptance or rejection of ideas and the like. She has trained herself to interpret—accurately—the conversation that goes on *behind* the words. When she studies people, she generates hypotheses about their underlying feelings, motives, relationships, etc. She tests her perception subtly, and when she is that much surer she really understands what is going on, she can act based on this deeper understanding.

In the end, she has succeeded time and again, managing to support the creation of numerous plans that optimize resources and that have not only met the needs of constituents but have also enabled them to make the necessary trade-offs at critical junctures.

Today, Judi's mindful attention to people and to her environment gives her the ability to truly understand the needs of her organization and its constituencies. As she puts it, "Mindfulness is a way of life. This is what I do."

Talking Without Words

Our subtle emotional and physiological responses are an important source of data, and at any given moment we are communicating a vast amount of information to one another about how we feel.[9] Through infinitesimal changes in musculature and then facial expressions, we signal to others our true emotions, giving them clues about how to respond to us.

This communication is critical in facilitating social interaction. Paul Ekman, formerly a professor of psychology at the University of California San Francisco, has studied the emotions and facial expressions of people all over the world. He concludes that by attending carefully (we would say mindfully) to others we effectively minimize distortion. Rather than understanding people's experiences through our filters, we see their feelings more clearly and we can more accurately interpret their thoughts and perspectives. When we do this, we are better able to relate to people because we are more in tune with *their* experience.

Leaders who read their world this way can more easily avoid uninformed, bad decisions and have a much better chance of successfully joining the dance and influencing complex group and organizational dynamics. Robert Polet understands this truth. When he accepted his new job as president and CEO of the Gucci Group, he turned his commitment to mindfulness into a powerful tool for resonance. One month after joining the company, he scheduled visits to nearly half of Gucci's stores and offices, personally visiting more than twenty-five hundred people in a little less than four weeks' time. Simply by showing up, listening, and sharing food and good conversation, he was able to convey who he was as a leader, thereby addressing the natural anxiety people feel as a result of a major leadership change. Equally as important, he took the opportunity to really watch individuals and groups—noting the level of self-confidence and genuineness, whether people were "natural or acting" (his own words), and the degree to which they "owned" the business and approached it with passion.

The outcomes of this kind of scanning are at once obvious and subtle. Surely Robert's people now know he will be a hands-on leader, deeply interested in their experience and the day-to-day reality of the business. Many of them also know him as a person. He is no longer the faceless, maybe scary, new CEO. They have shared food and conversation and laughter, and have seen that he is a real person who cares about them, and who wants to discuss their ideas about the business.

On a more subtle level, Robert quickly gained a sense of the *emotional reality* of his organization and the differences among the brand groups and across regions.[10] He watched how people responded to leadership (his own and local managers') and saw how best to use power effectively as he began to make some changes. Reading the environment like this enabled him to make early, and sometimes surprising, decisions about people. In fact, he found some of the best people in unlikely places and jobs and was able to rapidly involve them in his new organization. An organization chart would never have afforded him this highly accurate picture of who was who and what individuals could really do. Robert also gained a sense of collective values and history that are rooted in his observations, not just in what he has been told by those who hired him. He saw cultural norms in action, and was better able to adjust his own behavior quickly to build relationships in the organization. He is more likely to be able to avoid the cultural and relational landmines that exist in any organization, and is also more likely to capitalize on individuals' and teams' strengths. Additionally, he has found allies in unexpected places.

As Robert knows, watching the emotional dance among people gives you an edge. It gives you clues about what you are dealing with, and how to manage a situation. You can more easily decide when and how you interact to influence and guide people. This is equally true when we look at groups and cultures. Although more abstract, and therefore harder to see and understand, these larger manifestations of the human system also dance: groups rely on other groups for information, decisions, and actions; cultures come together in harmony or clash inside organizations, as well as across geographic regions and the boundaries of belief.

Mindfulness, then, as people like John, Dan, Judi, and Robert have discovered, gives us an edge. But it is not something we are born with; it is something we learn, and something we can lose. If only it were easy to see when we are becoming mindless. Over the years, we have spoken with countless managers who, when things finally fall apart, sit bewildered and confused. They look around, find that they have plateaued, or maybe been laid off or cast aside. How did it happen? they wonder. What went wrong? Why didn't I see what was coming?

In chapter 4, we discussed wake-up calls. These are often the only prompt for action that some people recognize, and for many people they come late in the game—after problems have occurred and chances have been missed. Other people wake up but do not stay alert. Over time, they slip back into habits of inattentiveness, reawakening only if they experience another crisis. Becoming numb, or mindless, is often a slow, steady decline in awareness. The subtle messages that tell us something is not right can become mere whispers, and it may take years before we recognize that we are in trouble. Let us look at how this slow slide into mindlessness happens—and why.

Slipping into Mindlessness

"Steve" was a smart, dedicated executive who near the pinnacle of his career found himself cut off from the powerful team at the top of his organization. He had been doing the right thing for years, delivering results in a single-minded, no-holds-barred manner. He was proud of what he had accomplished. But over the years, he had slowly lost touch with the real goals of his organization. Like so many highly driven people, his personal ambition took over. He slowly adopted patterns of behavior that irritated colleagues and clients alike, without even realizing how obvious his motives were. By the time he moved into senior management, the pattern was set: he was most often in a self-protective mode, and largely focused on his personal success. In this mode, he was intolerant of anyone who questioned him or expected him to open up to new ways of seeing or doing things. Steve had become clueless. He saw the world through his own, increasingly limited, perspective. He had slowly shut himself off from others and from awareness of the changing nature of his organization. He did not do this deliberately—he had become caught in the Sacrifice Syndrome and had not cultivated the capacity for mindfulness or renewal over the years. Nevertheless, Steve's mindless behavior was *the* reason he was not invited to join the team at the top.

Steve's story is common, and sad. What a waste of talent. Clearly, mindlessness is a problem on the job. But the problem does not stop at work. One of the saddest things we ever heard was a fifty-something executive talking with a younger colleague, encouraging him to pay attention to his children. He said, "I have completely missed out on my daughter's youth. She's twelve now, and I do not know what she likes to do, or what she thinks. I definitely don't know how she feels about much of anything. Except me. I do know how she feels about me. She doesn't like me much. She will not talk with me, does not want to spend time with me, does not have much good to say. I've asked her why, and all she says is 'You haven't been here all these years, why bother now?'"

How does this happen? How do some of us find ourselves waking up to a derailed career or an unhappy, distant family? In our work with leaders, we have tried to identify exactly what pushes good people into mindlessness and becoming trapped in the Sacrifice Syndrome.

There are several reasons leaders can easily lose their edge and slip into mindlessness, as Steve did. First, the pressures of the job are such that sometimes it is easy to get tunnel vision—natural cognitive processes coupled with the pressures of the job cause us to over-focus on some things to the exclusion of others. Second, many of us find ourselves on the path of "should dos" rather than carefully attending to our deepest held beliefs and desires. And finally, because leaders are vulnerable and facing huge business risks daily, many people choose coping strategies that cause them to shut down.

Tunnel Vision and Multitasking: Gift or Curse?

People who are good at doing several complex tasks at once (reading an e-mail while talking on the phone while thinking about how to open the team meeting while weighing the pros and cons of the new strategy) are often valued in our organizations. They accomplish a lot. Multitasking is valued even more at the executive level. Leaders need to stay focused and efficient for months, sometimes years, on end. They have to keep lots of big ideas at the top of their mind, concurrently, including a huge amount of detail and information about their increasingly complex environment.

Many executives feel that mega-multitasking becomes a badge of honor. They consider distraction or even their secret desire for a break to be a sign of weakness. In fact, as advisers we are often asked for tips on how leaders can stay alert and avoid losing concentration over the long hours and months of unrelenting hard work. These executives skip vacations and don't even spend weekends away from e-mail, cell phone, and PDA. While becoming better and better at accomplishing more and more, many executives overdevelop skills associated with efficiency, which is then confused with effectiveness. Let us look at why this happens.

Keeping ourselves constantly focused is difficult; in fact, it is unnatural. Research has shown that the ability to stay intensely focused *declines over time.* That is why so many studies have been done regarding work-shift lengths in jobs that require absolute concentration, such as airport flight control.[11] Nevertheless, focus is valued and valuable, and many executives become exceedingly good at narrowing their attention and sustaining focus for protracted periods. The price of this effort, however, is that we literally train our minds *not* to notice what is going on around us.

When focusing too narrowly, people have little tolerance (or mental space) for unrelated thoughts. We ignore extraneous data, including internal thoughts and feelings and external information. The result, of course, is that we miss a great deal. We may not see subtle patterns, may not pay attention to the anomalies that can point us in a new direction or give early warning about problems. In essence, we can develop tunnel vision—seeing only what we need to see to reach the goal. This, of course, means we miss information that tells us that the goal (or the target, or the strategy) might need to change. We also miss new opportunities, or subtle signs that we need to reexamine our choices and paths in our professional roles as well as personal lives.

Unexamined, intensive focus can cause problems and can lead to mindlessness. But the desire to organize and prioritize information is natural, and we can improve how we do this—so we can focus without becoming mindless.[12] Our brains deal with the complexity of the world around us by filtering and categorizing information as it comes in. In an effort to simplify our experience and to make events more predictable we create mental categories that help us to process information—we label things, feelings, and experiences, even people. This cognitive process enables us to make distinctions easily, predict outcomes, and make "sense" of our experience. This cognitive process allows us to live in a complex world. Think about it. If we had to take in every bit of information discretely, all day long, we would be concurrently processing billions of sights, sounds, smells, tastes, sensations, feelings, thoughts, and then trying to link these with millions of memories, past experiences, etc. We would be paralyzed.

We now know that one of the first organizing structures in the brain is an emotional response to what our senses tell us. This response occurs as some of the "older" brain structures, such as the amygdala, process information and draw on emotional memories. Then, the information is guided to the appropriate segment of our neocortex for further analysis. At each step along the neurological pathways, our brains make choices about what we believe we have experienced.[13]

A simple example: Walking down the street, you see a large dog coming toward you. Your amygdala may react to the large animal quickly: fear pulses through you, your breathing rate increases, blood surges to your large muscles. In less than a nanosecond, however, the size and shape of the animal is processed by your neocortex, and you label the animal "dog." If your past experience of dogs has been frightening, your blood pressure might go up. But if you have loved large dogs, your emotional arousal may be the exact opposite and you begin to experience caring and compassion. In either case, information processing continues as you take in other information: the leash that keeps the dog safely at a distance, the friendly person walking the dog, the fact that the person is your neighbor, the dog is familiar, you know the dog likes to play with your dogs. All of this happens almost completely below the surface of your awareness, and in less time than it takes to draw a deep breath.[14]

The process of assimilating information and categorizing it is thus a natural and largely unconscious process. So, what is the problem? This natural cognitive process can easily backfire. Mental patterns of analysis and interpretation are often habitual, and can be unrelated to real information.

A humorous example: Our young friend, Lucas—eighteen months old at the time—had recently learned lots of new words for common—and not so common—animals. "Cat" and "dog" were favorites—he could finally call to the beloved household pets. "Bear" was also a favorite word, but a bit scary, given some of the pictures he had seen. One day, his Aunt Abby visited, bringing her dog—named "Bear." Imagine Luke's dismay: he had finally mastered categories, and words to go with them, for dogs and bears, and here was this confusing situation. For a while, he simply refused to call the dog by name. Lucas is a very bright little boy, however, so with some coaxing he came to understand a new category—names! With this new category, he could accept a dog named Bear.

Even smart, rational adults can fall prey to outdated categories. In fact it is surprising how often our categories do not fit reality, and how often we see what we think, rather than think about what we see. And if the two do not match we are confused. Some people (unlike Lucas) will actually try to force-fit the information they take in, making it fit their categories. This is a process called assimilation and though natural to a point, when overused it becomes the source of stereotypes and mindless interactions between people.

Let us look at how this plays out at work. We see it happen often on teams, especially teams that have worked together for some time. Over time, team members begin to form a shorthand way of interpreting one another's behavior and end up using this shorthand in a somewhat unconscious way. Team members might think, for example, "Oh, of course Scott would see the issue *that* way. He's a finance guy." Or, "Susan always supports Scott; we know what she will say, so let's not even attempt to bring her in." Or, "Mike always speaks first, thinks later." While any of these descriptions may be somewhat true, they are also stereotypes—automatic, fairly rigid prejudgments that limit our ability to see what is really happening.

Furthermore, we often see what we are looking for, and nothing more than that. This means that for the team in the example, Scott's opinion on the numbers will be heard, while his thoughtful comment on a succession issue is likely to be missed. When Susan sits next to Scott, it will be interpreted as support—even if she takes the last chair in the room. Mike's contribution will likely be discounted much of the time, and no one will notice the times he is fully prepared, thoughtful, and reflective.

On the other hand, mindful attention to how we make sense of the facts around us lets us make better judgments about what is truth, what is perception, and what is somewhere in between. But even those of us who remain open to new thoughts and ideas have often learned to overuse one source of "data": that which can be rationally explained. This is a result of over-focusing on data we process intellectually, as opposed to data related to our emotions or our bodies. Many of our educational and work organizations encourage this tendency in the quest for increased specialization.

But in the process, we lose sight of other important clues and real information.

Devoting greater mindshare to one aspect of our life or work may leave less room available for others. In our effort to be efficient, we are blind to anything unrelated to our focus. We often completely miss the creative solution; the new way of doing something; even the glaringly obvious, but novel, way of responding to a situation. When mindlessly concentrating, there is little room for subtlety. Slowly, over time, narrow focus and constant multitasking cause exhaustion: our mental processes are truncated and our emotional responses become unpredictable.

Patrick Cescau, CEO of Unilever, is about as intensely focused as they come.[15] He manages the downside well, however, because of his absolute passion for learning. As he puts it, "Learning causes your world to open up, so you can see things a little bit differently." But learning requires openness, opportunity, and time. Patrick hones the skill of learning by deliberately seeking new experiences and by consciously using life as a laboratory. He is passionate about exploration. Patrick applies this curiosity to the study of people. He watches people very carefully—their expressions and body language, what they say and how they say it. Then he tries to make sense of it: what they are feeling, what they are doing, and why they are doing it. He challenges himself to resist the urge to make quick judgments or assumptions about what people intend or want. He deliberately seeks multiple interpretations for people's behavior, weighing his interpretations against what he actually sees, not what he wants to see. In other words, he consciously manages how he takes in information, how he interprets it, and how he reacts.

As Patrick will testify, this practice enables us to avoid the pitfalls of mindlessness and attend carefully to what is really going on in ourselves and around us. And we can learn how to do this better; it just takes conscious attention to our habitual thought patterns, curiosity, and discipline. As we do this, however, it is important to pay attention to other forces that can also push us into mindlessness.

Let us look now at a second way that people allow mindlessness to take over.

When "Shoulds" Lead to Compromises

"Justin" was a star. He whizzed through school, jumped through all of the hoops in his early career, and marched all the way to the CFO role by his mid-forties. In his company, this job had always been a stepping stone to the CEO position. However, to his great surprise, when his CEO retired, the board hired an outside candidate. Not only did he not get the job, the person who did was not interested in keeping Justin around. Justin was shocked. How could this have happened? He thought he was the perfect candidate. The board's answer: "It's a different world, now, and we need a different kind of CEO." What did this mean?

Justin had created himself in the image of the ideal CEO: perfect career history, good results, normal family life. He even looked the part—handsome, well-groomed, a bit stern. Many years later, Justin recognizes the "shoulds" and "oughts" that drove him as he diligently went about building his career.[16] He had done all the right things in school, courted a very nice young woman, driven himself to achieve goals at work, married, and started a family. He had good intentions, was doing the "right" things, and was living up to his own and others' expectations. Surely there is nothing wrong with that. But like many driven and talented people, Justin was treating life's big decisions almost as if they were on a checklist of to-dos that could be ignored once they were completed:

✓ University

✓ Find a mate

✓ Prove myself at work

✓ Have children

✓ Move up the ladder

But the problem is that learning does not (or at least should not) stop after school, and in fact our world requires that we constantly change and adjust to new and radically different circumstances. And, after we get married and have children, inattention to these relationships and neglecting the hard work it takes to keep them vibrant causes a lot of suffering. We see it all the time: people become more distant rather than closer over the years of marriage, communication becomes mostly instrumental—who needs to go where, what needs to be done in the house, that sort of thing. Children do not really know their parents, and parents are too busy to understand their kids. Relationships become sadly empty as making the right career moves and achievement for achievement's sake become our primary goals.

The worst thing about this kind of lock-step life is that we can begin to lose touch with ourselves and our understanding of what truly matters. Our noble purpose disappears and we wake up one day to find that we have little to ground and guide us.[17]

It is not that others' expectations and our responsibilities toward others are not important. They are. But when they preclude awareness of our own beliefs and desires, then we cannot attend to ourselves and we spend all of our energy and time fulfilling others' needs and wants. When this happens, we have essentially begun to close down, and, out of necessity, we develop defensive routines to help us get by.

We can become a shadow of the person we once were, playing roles rather than living authentically. Oddly, when this happens people often become strongly attached to ideas—even empty rhetoric—about roles, values, and principles while their real-life actions are far from ideal. Maybe they hold on to bad marriages because of a belief in the institution, while they quietly seek love and connection somewhere else. Or maybe on the surface they lead a life of integrity and publicly stand up for good causes, while cutting corners in their businesses and actually causing harm. Or maybe they just push on, pretending to be strong when inside they are crumbling.

So it was for Justin. During the years leading up to Justin's derailment, he had gradually felt less fulfilled at work, and home life was too much routine, offering too little excitement. Like many strong people, though, Justin felt he could handle his situation and he worked hard to avoid dealing with the truth: trouble at work and trouble at home. He did not know where to start. Maybe he was scared. Many of us are, for when we begin to realize that something is very wrong and that we must change, we often resist the inevitable. More defensive routines kick in: we get angry, we feel sorry for ourselves, we fight or we freeze. We become paralyzed by our own emotions. In these situations, we may, like Justin, slip into mindless seeking, going through life's checklist without thinking or feeling clearly. As we shut down, we often overlook key opportunities in life or work. We fail to spot the clues that tell us we need to pay attention, or change—as Justin missed the early messages from colleagues and the board that his behavior was out of synch with where the organization was going.

Fragile Self-Esteem and the Imposter Syndrome

For successful people one of the most common defenses is to take a key strength—self-confidence—and use it as a shield. For some, this means becoming brittle and self-protective. For others, it means living with a sense that one day they will be found out and people will finally see that they are not as good as they seemed. That was the case with "Nicole." Nicole was the SVP of Research and Development for a large pharmaceutical company. She had started her career as a physician, but had quickly moved into the corporate world, seeing opportunities and the chance to make a difference on a broader scale. Over the years as a senior executive, she had faced many challenges—not the least of which were the constant reminders that she was the only woman on the senior team. Nicole adopted a defensive stance, deliberately overachieving while relying on her talent, strong personality, track record, and a somewhat brittle exterior to keep threats at bay. This kind of self-protectiveness takes a lot of energy and depletes our reserves. And having to prove oneself over and over can lead to chronic uneasiness—Can I overcome the next hurdle? Will we win the next battle?

As time went on it became harder and harder for Nicole to get things done. She was always ready for battle. The intricate relationships at the top of her organization required constant vigilance, attention, and even a kind of intimacy between people. Making the most difficult decisions required open dialogue and some vulnerability as team members made the hard trade-offs the business required. According to colleagues, Nicole's self-confidence and strength always seemed to get in the way of these conversations. Gradually, both she and her team members simply got tired of fighting and started avoiding each other. Then the catch-22 set in: the less contact she had, the less influence she could wield. And with less influence came more insecurity, more attempts to defend herself and more friction.

Whenever we encounter people who seem to need to prove their worth, even when their position or accomplishments actually speak for themselves, we begin to suspect that we might be dealing with someone who is quite insecure and overwhelmed. So Nicole's very evident confidence and brittle interpersonal style were clues: she was protecting herself.

In fact, it is often the case that people who seem most self-confident, whose self-esteem may even seem over the top, are the people who are actually the most fragile. Michael Kernis and his colleagues note that contrary to popular belief, unrelenting high self-esteem is not really an indicator of optimal self-esteem, and may in fact be "fragile high self-esteem."[18] When people must continually protect an image of themselves, this is a clue that in fact they do not have a strong sense of self, and that they are delicate and even insecure, trying to hide from a threatening world.

We suspect that for many professionals, fragile high self-esteem can also be a byproduct of success. People who excel at school, and then in the workplace, often get a tremendous amount of positive feedback—more, maybe, than they think they deserve. Leaders may find themselves waiting for the other shoe to drop, thinking that somehow people will figure out that they are really not all that great and the game will be over.

In our talks with executives, they often mention this "imposter syndrome"—that nagging sense that we are not really as good as everyone thinks we are.[19] The more mindful leaders recognize the imposter syndrome for what it is and do not let insecurity drive them to bad behavior. But some people respond to the fear of being found out by developing superficial bravado and using over-the-top self-confidence as a shield. They ignore or hide their own weaknesses. They avoid putting strong people who might show them up on their teams and try constantly to get everyone to pay attention to how fabulous they are. Others build a wall; it is just too risky to let people in.

But mindfulness *requires* connection with other people. You cannot really understand others unless you are in contact with them. Many leaders find themselves deliberately shying away from close connection and relationships at work. They fear they will be found out or believe they will lose objectivity. Or they simply do not take the time. Or people just will not let them get close. For many reasons, building close relationships with people just seems wrong. It is tempting (and typical) for leaders to throw up their hands and give up on connecting. It is just too hard.

So it is easy to slip into mindlessness. The pressure of a leader's role, coupled with internal messages about what we should do and our attempts to deal with stress, vulnerability, and insecurity cause us to shut down. Unfortunately, that response—shutting down—is exactly the opposite of what we must do in order to sustain effectiveness and maintain resonance in ourselves and with others. We need to be open, not closed—constantly exploring ourselves, others, and our environment. This enables us to stay centered and calm, even when the pressure is on, and to see what we must do in order to stay true to ourselves. Attending to others and the environment means we have more and more accurate information and can make better decisions. Mindfulness enables us to counter the effects of the Sacrifice Syndrome, propelling us into renewal.

Defining Your Practice:
Cultivating Mindfulness

But becoming mindful and maintaining that state does not happen by accident. We are asked occasionally whether the development of mindfulness has a place in the business world. We answer with an enthusiastic, "Yes!" Mindfulness is the practical application of self-awareness, self-management, and social awareness; in short, developing mindfulness means developing emotional intelligence. What has been known and practiced for thousands of years in the world's great religious and philosophical traditions is only now becoming known in the Western study of management and leadership. Self-awareness really does matter, and so does consciously managing our habitual thoughts, feelings, and responses.

As we have pointed out in this book and in other writings, self-awareness is a fundamental component of emotional intelligence that has a positive impact not only on our personal development and well-being, but on the bottom line as well. So, mindfulness is not just a nice-to-have—it makes a difference in performance.

Assuming we have a desire to develop our capacity for mindfulness, what can we actually *do*? We know from our practice and that of our colleagues that there are many paths to mindfulness, from purely cognitive "training" to Buddhist meditation practices to corporate programs such as working with a coach. We recommend a combination of reflection, practice, and supportive relationships. Adjusting one's thought patterns is usually necessary, since most of us have developed automatic, habitual cognitive processes that do not serve us well. This means that most of us have to engage in a process of intentional change. At the end of this chapter and in appendix B we have included some reflections and practices that will help you develop mindfulness intentionally. Let us go back to Patrick Cescau of Unilever and look at how this very successful leader cultivates mindfulness as a way of life.

Reflection

When he talked to us about how he maintains mindfulness in everyday work situations, Patrick Cescau told us that finding a corner of peace and quiet in the mind, a place of stillness, is absolutely essential for leaders. That means finding some way to systematically reflect, whether through meditation, spiritual practice, walking in natural, beautiful surroundings, or writing one's personal thoughts and feelings in a journal.

Why is reflection so important? It takes a lot of self-control to manage the inevitable stress and power dynamics inherent in leadership. If you do not have time for yourself, to reflect, to find peace, you will become lost. And if you do not have time for yourself, you will not be good for anyone else. Reflection is one way to build a path to renewal into your life. This includes finding opportunities to stay calm and centered. When you are resonant within yourself, you can create resonance with others. It is not possible to become mindful if we do allow our mind, body, heart, and spirit to speak to us, and it is very hard to hear those quiet voices in the noisy, busy world we live in.

Patrick also recognizes that the pressures—and the loneliness—of leadership can make it very difficult to remain open and mindful, attending holistically to one's self and others. That is why over the years he has deliberately incorporated practices into his life that help him cultivate mindfulness. He is one of those people who loves to learn—which helps when it comes to mindfulness. He reads often and widely—fiction, poetry, autobiography, anything—and he finds like-minded souls with whom to discuss new ideas. He finds time to engage in activities that bring him peace, often very simple things like an evening at home with his family, a joke and a good laugh with friends, and quiet moments alone.

Another tool that Patrick uses is to take time during his day to stop and take himself to a soothing mental space—a place in the mind where he finds serenity and reflection. For Patrick, a place that actually brings him a sense of peace and well being is the desert. He often refers to the wisdom of favorite old Arabic sayings, "Allah created the desert as his garden, from which he removed all life so that he could take walks in peace and quietness." And as the caravan drivers tell it, "Allah has removed from the Sahara all that is unnecessary so human beings grasp the essence of things."[20]

Patrick actually goes to the desert whenever he can—a place for renewal and rejuvenation. But of course, like most of us, he can not pick up and go away at will, and we need to find other ways to reconnect with the peace we feel in special settings. This has led him to learn how to calm his mind through imagery.

During reflective times he will simply take half an hour, close his eyes, and imagine he is in those special places in the world that he loves. He will see the desert in his mind, feel the wind, smell the rich scent of hot earth. Using this kind of mental imagery can be a powerful tool indeed. In fact, research has shown how simply imagining a peaceful scene can actually change our physiology, calming us down.[21]

How else can reflection help us become more mindful? Rather than simply using it to look inward, at the self, Patrick often practices reflecting about the people around him and with whom he works. He describes the process this way: "I watch people very carefully. Then, I 'speak to myself' about what I see. Am I interpreting correctly? Are my own ideas getting in the way? Am I seeing the whole picture?"

This played out in an interesting way a few years ago. One year, as a leader of one of Unilever's businesses, Patrick realized that he and his team could not raise salaries for everyone, as they had done in the past. They worked out a system of meritocracy, based on a performance appraisal that they believed would allow them to fairly determine how they could selectively raise salaries. Patrick was very proud of the solution and the system.

Of course, Patrick knew his team would be challenged by the system, but he was ready for that. He believed that the system was so fair, it would be easy to defend. Inevitably, a man who was not getting a raise came to him. Patrick was ready, and they went through his performance appraisal together. The outcome was of course the same, and Patrick asked the man if he thought the results were different. He did not disagree; in fact he agreed with the evaluation. Then, however, the man said something Patrick never expected: "But you have missed something in this system. I have given everything to this company, I have done the very best that I could. I have worked as hard as I could, been as committed as I could, and done absolutely everything I could. I have been loyal, dedicated, and true, and used all my talents and I have inspired the people around me to better performance. I have given my *heart*."

Patrick realized that in fact, the man was right, and he told him so. He said, "You have a point. In fact, our system might not measure everything that is important. But you see, if I change this decision for you, we will lose face (an important issue in that culture). But I tell you this—if, at the end of next year, you can tell me that you have given everything you could, and been committed, and can show me how this has impacted results, you will get a raise. In the meantime we, as a team, will examine our system and consider how best to measure these more subtle aspects of performance that you so rightly point out."

What Patrick did in this instance was to use a situation to *develop* mindfulness, not only practice it. Patrick used his experiences as a way to push the boundaries of his own thinking. After the incident, he reviewed the underlying assumptions—both his own and others'—that drove the specifics of the performance system. In doing so, he noticed that certain things were missing, like how to measure commitment and loyalty and how these impacted the overall climate and team results. He and his team were able to make adjustments and change their system over time.

We cannot leave this discussion without saying something about how authentic relationships can also provoke mindfulness. Authentic connection to our loved ones and friends provides us with two things critical in developing mindfulness: safety and an accurate reflection of how others see us and we see them. We can learn a tremendous amount from the image that others reflect. In our most intimate relationships—with wives, husbands, partners, children, and dear friends—we learn about who we are, about how on track we are in living our professed values. And we can see what we are not, and learn from this, too. This brings us to how we can use our relationships as a way of attaining mindfulness.

Supportive Relationships

Reflection, contemplation, meditation, cognitive training: however you choose to explore your inner world, these things are all critical to developing mindfulness. But even they are not enough. In addition to attending to yourself, you need to pay attention to the other side of the equation, and learn how to attend consciously to other people and the world around you. This is very difficult (if not impossible) to do by yourself. How can you be sure if you are reading other people right if you never check it out with them, or with others? How will you know if you have considered all possibilities regarding a specific situation if you do not engage in dialogue with others? How will you even know if your view of yourself is accurate?

Learning mindfulness includes attending to how and what other people think, feel, and do. This gives you information about the world around you, certainly, but it also gives you information about yourself. It is a lesson that Josie Harper, director of athletics and recreation at Dartmouth College, learned a few years ago when she found herself in the difficult situation of having to shut down one of her athletic programs. It was a last resort, and naturally not a popular decision. But Josie knew that absorbing another budget cut and having every program suffer, across the board, was not the direction she was willing to take. Past budget cuts had caused many of the programs to be lean and at risk of slipping backwards. As difficult as the decision was, and after much consideration, she decided to recommend dropping one sport—men's and women's swimming and diving. She realized this would be viewed as a risk and perceived as a radical step—one that would be very unpopular with constituents. Certainly the people that concerned Josie the most were the student athletes.

And, not surprisingly, student athletes, parents, and alumni alike were unhappy with her. She was barraged with phone calls, e-mails, and even tearful pleas in the hallways and at meetings. Amid all of the tumult, in a situation in which many people would be tempted to put up a wall around themselves, or at least a "Do Not Disturb" sign on their doors, Josie stayed close and attentive; she stayed in relationship with people. Even during those weeks when people actually hated what she was doing—and maybe hated her—she continued to reach out, to connect, to talk. She made sure she had all her facts straight and, as importantly, that she truly understood the emotions and opinions of the people affected by her decision. She met as many people as possible—personally and without time limits. She listened, she talked, she stayed centered, grounded, and connected even during the most difficult conversations. With help from others in administration, her approach worked: in the end, students, parents, and alumni pulled together in a phenomenal way, and the program was actually saved.

Josie tells us that these "fifty days from hell" were one of the greatest learning experiences of her life. "Other people's observations, their comments to me during a difficult time, have been a source of my discovering who I am to them, what they see in me. They have given me a sound sense of the impact I have on people."[22] Beyond the learning, Josie came out of this situation with *better* relationships, even though what she had to do was terribly hard on everyone.

You do not get that kind of outcome unless you are in *contact* with people—unless you are open, available, and willing to engage in the give and take of relationship. Paul McDermott, assistant regional administrator of the U.S. government's General Services Administration, has put that kind of real contact into practice in his organization, as a way to continually develop

mindfulness and to strengthen the "glue" that holds people together.[23] He starts with the premise that emotionally intelligent
behavior is a baseline for healthy relationships at work. He acts
on this personally and holds team members accountable for doing
the same. More than that, however, he carefully defines his relationship with people. Work in many governments is difficult
because of the long-standing network among civil servants, many
of whom have been in the division for years and years. Long-
standing alliances, old slights, and the everlasting competition for
resources are antithetical to transparency and trust, both foundations for healthy relationships. Paul has taken the stance that he
needs to continually challenge himself to develop mindfulness—
to read people constantly, and to recognize what they are trying
to tell him.

For Paul and the team, the focus on *how* they work together
pays off. Their results are consistently good, and they are known
as one of the least bureaucratic, most effective organizations
within the government. In fact, as Paul puts it, "During a period
of intense challenges, mindfulness, compassion, and resiliency
have allowed us to excel in the face of adversity. Mindfulness and
emotional intelligence have created an environment where you
can truly come to work and do something great, and be with caring friends while you achieve excellence." These are powerful
statements—backed up by powerful results. During this period,
well known and valid measures of customer satisfaction and employee engagement are up. And, no coincidence, we believe, revenue is up dramatically as well.[24]

As advisers for many years to leaders of some of the most
powerful organizations in the world, we have become convinced
that being awake, aware, and attentive to self, others, and the environment is a key to effective leadership (not to mention a much
more fulfilling life). It is definitely worth spending time and energy
developing the capacity to live mindfully. We personally have engaged in mindful practices over the years and know from our own
experiences and from working with great leaders that in fact being

more aware, moment to moment, of all that we experience enables us to live more fully—and, yes, be more successful in the work that we do.

A caution, however: We have also learned that some people actually turn mindfulness into the end goal. And the peculiar trap of turning ourselves into a project is one of which we all must beware. Nothing is as annoying as people who continually recount their personal journey, telling anyone who will listen what they do to develop themselves, how hard it is, how rewarding, etc. Leaders who navigate around that trap, we have seen, do so by simply holding onto a noble goal that is beyond themselves, their needs, or their wants—so that mindfulness does not turn into self-centeredness.

Once a person is mindful, what does he or she do with this insight and attentiveness? We believe the great leaders turn to hope and to compassion, as we will explore in the following chapters.

Look, Listen, and Ask

This series of activities will enable you to practice mindfulness. The first exercise focuses on you, and your attunement to yourself. The second and third activities are focused on your ability to tune in to other people, to understand them and to accurately interpret what they are feeling and why they behave in certain ways. Try this series of skill-building tasks for a week or two, as well as those in appendix B, and see what happens in the way you relate to yourself and others.

Exercise 1: Name That Feeling

THREE TIMES a day for a week, stop what you are doing, close your eyes and concentrate on how you are feeling. Put a word to the feeling or feelings you are experiencing. Do not analyze, just name. At first, this might take as long as five minutes, and you might notice that the words you choose to name your feelings are simple, not nuanced. For example, you may describe your feelings with words like "stressed" or "pressured" or "happy." As you practice, however, you will find that you are able to name your feelings much more quickly and with more accuracy. For example, "stressed" becomes "frustrated and a little bit anxious"; "happy" becomes "happy and proud of myself" or "grateful to my team."

Exercise 2: Watch, Look, and Listen

I N THIS EXERCISE, you will attempt to surface your own almost unconscious "sense making" about others' thoughts and feelings. This is difficult and will take discipline, as most of us make sense of people and situations automatically and somewhat unconsciously.

First, select two or three people with whom you meet face-to-face regularly, and spend twenty minutes or so writing some notes about what you think their typical reactions to you are. Remember their words, their actions, their facial expressions, tone of voice, and body language. Do not analyze—just name the emotional reactions you think you get from them and what you guess they think. You might want to simplify this by thinking specifically about an incident or two when you were engaged in something together.

Then, for a week or so, discipline yourself to watch these individuals very carefully when you are together. Try not to be obvious; you might scare them. Look at their eyes, their faces. Note their posture, hand movements, and overall body motion when you are together. In this state of heightened awareness, pay attention to the "invisible clues" they give to what they are thinking and feeling.

Finally, at least once or twice a day, for each of the people you are studying, take five minutes to write notes for yourself about what you have seen. At first, you might simply write observations—what they did, what you saw. Later on, as you get better at observing subtle clues, attempt to name the emotions you believe you have seen. Try not to over interpret what you have seen, and be careful not to confuse your emotions with theirs.

Exercise 3: Check It Out

A FTER A WEEK or so of observing and attempting to understand people's emotions and related thoughts, you can begin to test your assumptions. Depending on your relationship with the person/people you have been studying you may either be quite open, fully describing what you are doing and why (for your own learning and to improve your relationship with them). Or, if this is a bit too direct, simply begin to naturally introduce statements and questions into conversation that focus on what the other person is actually feeling. Do not name it for them—this causes defensiveness. Rather, try combining simple observations with naming your own feelings and light interpretation, such as, "I noticed just now that we've lost eye contact with each other, and I'm a bit uncomfortable. Seems like you might be too. What happened?" Or, "This conversation is great! You seem as excited as I am about what we are planning." Alternatively, you can, in your search for understanding and developing your ability to interpret others' reactions, simply ask a question: "How do you feel right now about that?" Check their answers with your interpretation.

If you want to take this learning process to the next level, start carefully watching what is happening among people in groups. Notice the interaction and play of emotions between people, not just what happens to an individual at a given moment. Notice how the mood of a group is distinct from the moods of the individuals involved. The art of reading group behavior is extremely sophisticated; mastering it will enable you to be incredibly effective in managing people's energy toward a vision or goal.

SEVEN

Hope

WALK ONTO THE GROUNDS of the Nkomo Primary School in the province of KwaZuluNatal, South Africa, and you will see children running, laughing, and playing games in the warm sun. Elsewhere on the grounds, boys and girls sit on rows of benches, leaning eagerly forward as their teacher explains the lesson written on a blackboard propped against a large shade tree. From other classrooms—shelters made of sticks and reeds— you can hear the sound of children singing, reciting their lessons in delightful harmony.

Clearly, this is a place of genuine learning—yet it has not always been that way. Just a few short years ago, this school did not exist. The province had too few schools, especially in deep rural areas, and many children simply did not have access to education. One local woman wanted to see things change. More than simply seeing a need, however, she saw in the faces of the province's children tangible, living potential that was being wasted.

Mrs. Zikhali, now the headmistress of the Nkomo Primary School, had hope and a dream. Where there was no school at all, she imagined a vibrant learning community, filled with teachers and children, good classrooms, and resources. She imagined young, eager minds learning about their Zulu culture and the world beyond South Africa. She wanted young people to grow up to be strong, powerful citizens of the new democracy. She had profound hope for the future of the children and her country.

It was hope that drove her to dream, to envision what could be. In our work with leaders, we have learned that having such hopes and dreams is indeed the first step to creating any reality that may initially appear unattainable, as Mrs. Zikhali's dream certainly did. She started small: in 1998 she had only some land, a reed hut, makeshift classrooms under trees, and whatever materials she could find. Sixty hopeful and eager children came to the school. For some people, this would have been enough—surely it was better than nothing. But Mrs. Zikhali knew there were more children in the community who were not in school, and she had to get more teachers. She also knew the government of South Africa assigned teachers to a school only when there were actual classrooms for them. So she had to build more. In the early days, things were rough. When a visitor parked his car under a tree to avoid the midday sun, one of the young boys approached him and said, "Please Sir, remove your car from my classroom."

How did she do it? Mrs. Zikhali's vision for a better future drove her to action. She decided to raise money to build classrooms quickly, and in a way that involved the community. She worked with the government, of course, but she went far beyond the typical funding sources. First, she wrote to the heads of large corporations in South Africa, explaining the situation and her dream. They listened and responded. Surely hers was not the only such request, but something about how she conveyed her message caught people's attention.

Then she took a good look at her community—asking herself where, in this poor community, were the resources that could support her school? Where was there interest in educating the people of the region? The answer was close at hand: one of the key features of the region is its game reserves. Because the reserves cater to wealthy people, they operate on an economic scale vastly different from typical South African community businesses. The reserves have a vested interest in building the capabilities of the region's people, since they are neighbors, workers, managers, and supporters. With the help of Isaac Tembe, Field Officer of the Africa Foundation, and Jason King, the general manager of the Phinda Game Reserve at the time, Mrs. Zikhali created a plan to share her dream with the Reserve and its visitors, creatively connecting the school with the resources needed for growth. Now she regularly invites visitors from the Reserve to visit the school. They love it, and many even insist on donating money, materials, or their time.

Today more than seven hundred and sixty children attend the school, which has eleven classrooms and two teachers' rooms. Children leave the school to go on to high school and, in some cases, to technical schools and college. All of them have hope and dreams, and because they received a solid educational beginning at the Nkomo School, they have a way to make their dreams come true.

The little room that was once the entire school just a few years ago now serves as the teachers' office, library, and resource center. Mrs. Zikhali's desk sits in that room amid stacks of books, but she rarely sits down. On the wall near her desk is the school's vision statement. What is most striking about it is that the words, which are not unique, are so *alive*. "The Nkomo Primary School's vision is to . . . provide quality education that will develop the full potential of every learner. . . . We are dedicated to transforming education in order to build a firm foundation. In doing this, we will insure that our school provides a relevant and quality learning experience to learners and all stakeholders in the school community."

These words are alive because they are *lived* by Mrs. Zikhali and by the teachers, children, parents, and community members who are so vitally involved in the school's success. Mrs. Zikhali's hope and passion are contagious, jumping off the page of that vision statement. And when teachers enter the room each day, they see the vision statement there on the wall—among the books, students' drawings, and classroom supplies—reminding them about their purpose. They think about how they are creating dreams in the children, their families, and the community.

We can only imagine the physical and emotional sacrifices Mrs. Zikhali made as she led the initiative to start and then grow this wonderful school. She is a resonant leader—creating a positive emotional tone within the school itself and between the school and its stakeholders.[1]

As we have said, the overall positive emotional tone crafted by resonant leaders is characterized by a sense of hope. That is why it feels exciting and often fun to be with resonant leaders and part of their organizations. In these settings, people do not necessarily feel happy or satisfied all the time, but they are challenged and feel hopeful about the future. They are more open-minded, creative, interested in their work, and motivated to do whatever is needed to accomplish individual and group goals.[2]

Despite the inevitable challenges of leading an institution such as the Nkomo Primary School, the climate is very positive, marked by excitement, passion, and hope for the future. This is the kind of climate that all effective leaders create. They do so in part by stimulating others to think about the possibilities and to look ahead. They and the people around them are pulled to the future. We believe that this kind of hope is key not only in creating resonance, but also in enabling leaders to stay the course, renewing themselves in body, mind, heart, and spirit.

Before we delve into how leaders can actually cultivate hope, however, let us examine what we mean by the word.

What Is This Thing Called Hope?

Hope is a hot topic these days. There have been three books on recent best-seller lists in the United States about hope or a closely related subject. In one of these books, *The Anatomy of Hope: How People Prevail in the Face of Illness*, Harvard professor Jerome Groopman writes about the role hope plays in helping people to heal from and survive cancer or, when they cannot, to live through their last days with dignity and love.[3] Aspects of hope, in particular the feelings of elation and happiness and sense of some control over one's destiny, spark renewal, as we have explained in chapter 4. In a hopeful state, we have more physiological as well as emotional resiliency, and we are mentally and physically prepared to deal with challenges.[4]

Renewal through hope works like this: when Mrs. Zikhali, perhaps in the middle of a telephone conversation with a parent or calming a frustrated teacher, glances at the vision statement on the wall, she remembers the dream. The return of that momentary sensation engages a different part of her brain than the part she is using to discuss someone's problem. This in turn sets renewal into motion. Her body resets itself. A slight smile and sense of confidence about her purpose return. She is nourishing her body, rekindling the passion that drives her. At the same time, the person she is dealing with begins to catch her mood, becoming calmer, more open, and more willing to engage with her to solve the problem.[5]

Indeed, hope has been shown to lead to other positive emotions, more positive thoughts, superior coping abilities, and less depression—even in people with serious physical conditions such as spinal cord injuries. To use another example: adolescent burn survivors who report hopeful feelings exhibit less harmful behavior to themselves and others and more positive interactions with caregivers and friends.[6] Hope has also been shown to predict higher grades in college students, as well as account for 56 percent of actual track performance in college athletes.[7]

These examples are part of a growing body of literature on the impact of positive emotions on our behavior, including how effectively we reason and think, how we interact with other people, and what we are capable of doing.[8] Specifically, positive emotions impact our openness and cognitive flexibility, problem-solving abilities, empathy, willingness to seek variety, and persistence.[9]

But what, exactly, is hope?[10] Social science has given us a definition of hope that goes beyond the philosophy of human nature and virtue. One of the better articulated theories is put forth by C. R. Snyder and his colleagues, who write about hopeful thought as a combination of clearly articulating goals, believing that one can attain those goals, charting a course of action or a path, and arriving at the goal while experiencing a sense of well-being as a result of the process.[11]

When we experience hope, then, we feel elated about a future that seems feasible.[12] Hope is an emotional state accompanied by clear thoughts about what the future can be and how to get there.[13] So not only does Mrs. Zikhali feel excitement and happiness on a regular basis, she also *knows* that the children of her Zulu community can learn in her school and that they will have different lives than they likely would have without education. She feels optimistic, believing that she and her community can make the dream come true, and she intends to keep trying to make it happen. That is why leaders like Mrs. Zikhali, who have a hopeful outlook, are able to create both resonant relationships among their people and an exciting organization in which to work.

But what does it take to actually cultivate the kind of hope that leads to renewal and ultimately to sustainable resonance? Our experience in working with leaders who demonstrate the power of hope every day has led us to three key lessons:

- The leader needs to have dreams and aspirations, but also be in touch with those of the people around him or her. This helps to form the desired image of the future.

- The leader needs to be optimistic and believe in his or her ability to make change.

- The leader must see the desired future as realistic and feasible.

Having a Dream

Ole Einar Bjoerndalen, a Norwegian biathlete, won his fourth gold medal in the 2002 Winter Olympics. The biathlon is a grueling event: the athlete skis 7.5 kilometers, stops to shoot a rifle at a small target fifty meters distant, slings the rifle back on his shoulder, then skis another 7.5 kilometers to the next target. And all of this is done at an altitude at which the air is thin and it is hard to breathe, making physical exertion even more difficult. Yet Ole became the first person to ever win the biathlon grand slam—and he did so after falling on a downhill ski run and missing three shots as a result.

Before he started his winning streak, Ole was a good, but not great, biathlete by Olympic standards. What was his bridge to greatness? Positive thinking. His coach, who happened to be a vacuum cleaner salesmen, had developed techniques to motivate himself and other salesmen. They would positively visualize their conversation with a potential customer. Even if it did not work out at first, they continually envisioned and engaged the hope that the next conversation would lead to a sale. These same techniques helped Ole to literally see his wins and stay focused on triumphing—even when he fell.[14]

Indeed, many world-class athletes use visualization techniques and positive thought. They spend a great deal of time envisioning their moves in detail, using hope to bring about their victories.[15]

We can all apply visualization to cultivate hope in our lives.[16] Besides triggering mindfulness and a sense of renewal, such exercises can help guide our decisions and future actions. The key is that the vision should evoke in your mind a specific, clear mental picture of the future—one that you find inspiring and that you believe can happen. A sense of purpose or meaning in your work often follows naturally from such images. And the positive emotions that are generated as you think about your desired future are actually powerful drivers of behavior. Let's look at how this works.

The Effect of Having a Dream: Positive and Negative Emotional Attractors

Our friend and colleague Daniel Goleman had the privilege of moderating dialogues among His Holiness the Dalai Lama, Buddhist monks, and western scholars and philosophers as part of Adam Engle's Mind and Life Institute meeting in March 2000.[17]

One outcome of these meetings was the book *Destructive Emotions*, which we believe is one of the best summaries of the science, philosophy, and spirituality of emotions to date.[18] Western and Buddhist thought, while clearly not always aligned, are surprisingly similar in the assessment of the power of emotions and their effect on individual behavior, groups, and society. Specifically, there is agreement that destructive emotions such as hatred, greed, and jealousy have a negative physiological as well as psychological impact on the person experiencing them, and can also harm relationships and cause dissonance.[19]

On the other hand, positive emotions such as compassion, confidence, and generosity have a decidedly constructive effect on neurological functioning, psychological well-being, physical health, and personal relationships. Hope, then—as an umbrella for a number of positive emotions—is good for us and our relationships. Additionally, as we discussed in chapter 5, it is a key component of intentional change—a central element in the development of the ideal self and one's personal vision. Therefore, it is an essential foundation for our own development.[20]

Hope acts as a magnet—an "attractor" in the terminology of complexity theory.[21] Like other positive emotions such as excitement, amusement, elation, and happiness, hope has a positive impact on our brains and hormones. It affects our perceptions of the events around us, so that we tend to see things in general more positively. In this way, the attractor catalyzes a self-perpetuating sequence, or self-organizing system. As the positive emotional attractor, then, hope allows you to consider your strengths, your dreams, and desired vision for the future. Such contemplation then slows your breathing, lowers your blood pressure, strengthens your immune system, and engages your parasympathetic nervous system. You feel calm, elated, happy, amused, and optimistic. You are up for the challenges ahead, energized, and prepared to act on your strengths to make your vision become reality.

In contrast, when you invoke the negative emotional attractor such as jealousy or resentment, you focus on weaknesses, fear, and a distorted sense of what is realistic (read: pessimistic) or you dwell on past events and what went wrong. You feel nervous, anxious, depressed, cynical, or filled with despair. Your sympathetic nervous system is activated—your blood pressure increases, as does your breathing. Your facial muscles tighten. Your body prepares for threat or injury, and in doing so elicits the stress response. In other words, you get set to defend yourself, preparing for fight or flight by sending blood to large muscle groups and closing off neural circuits not necessary to survival, as described in chapter 3 and appendix A.

At work, the stress response often shows up as abrupt, thoughtless treatment of people, "ready-fire-aim" decisions, and cynicism. Cynicism is one of the most destructive manifestations of negativity and dissonance. It causes people to focus solely on what is most wrong with a person, group, or an organization, with little or no call on individuals to take responsibility for making positive change. Cynicism is self-perpetuating, breeding frustration and despair—even hopelessness—which in turn breed more cynicism. In this state, there can be little, if any, movement toward a constructive vision of the future.

The negative emotional attractor such as resentment pushes you to focus all your energy on things that are wrong. Have you ever wondered why it is so hard to lose weight? We believe it is because the concept of "losing weight" is in and of itself a negatively conceived goal that arouses defensiveness, stress, and the sympathetic nervous system. So, the negative emotional attractor makes you work too hard for the wrong reasons, and may actually divert you from your desired future. If, however, you are motivated to feel vibrant and look good—and losing weight is part of this goal, your parasympathetic nervous system can be aroused and provide energy for action.

But, in their efforts to change themselves or help others, many people want to focus on and explain weaknesses. They want to diagnose and fix the problem. This is a common mistake. Once people become firmly focused on their weaknesses, they are pulled to the negative emotional attractor and have a hard time visualizing positive outcomes—and a hard time achieving those outcomes.

The focus on negativity is common in our organizations, and many leaders are deeply involved in creating and perpetuating the negative emotional attractor. They are worried about shortfalls: not meeting quarterly goals, resource scarcity, personnel problems, and a myriad of other problems. And they insist that they need to stay focused on these things. They refuse to turn their attention to more hopeful aspects of the environment, because they feel it just is not realistic.

The way you approach others also reflects which emotional attractor is pulling you. When it is the negative emotional attractor, you may fall into the negative spiral of expectations that Jean François Manzoni of IMD calls the "set-up-to-fail" syndrome. You see a person as failing and focus on monitoring him. In the process of close monitoring, you make him feel threatened and pressured. He may stumble or deliver, but you see the performance as a half-empty glass. At that point, there is almost nothing that person can do to reverse the downward spiral of expectations and performance.[22]

On the other hand, the positive emotional attractor such as hope allows you to move toward your aspirations while opening yourself, others, and your organization to new possibilities. In the Zikhali and Bjoerndalen examples above, you can see how you— the leader—can choose to spark energy for change in other people by focusing on what they are doing right, rather than on their shortcomings.

In fact, to make a sustainable change in habits or behavior, a person needs to *start* with the positive emotional attractor. With the energy generated from positive emotions we can move smoothly, without becoming trapped, through the negative emotional attractor. A leader conveying hope and associated positive emotions will stimulate the energy and creativity troubled employees need to deal with the real performance issues. That is because when a person experiences the powerful drive of hope and excitement—*and also the realistic grounding of reasonable doubt and concern*—energy is mobilized in a positive direction, rather than turning to defensiveness. Moving back and forth between these poles ensures continuous energy and reasonable shifts in direction and adjustment of plans. To engage intentionally in personal change, therefore, we need to spend more time, in particular emotional time, in the positive emotional attractor.

Probably the single most common argument against creating a positive, hopeful, resonant climate is that leaders must deal daily with unpleasant situations where no solutions will leave everyone feeling great. It just is not realistic to think that everything will feel good all the time, so rather than deal with the difficult emotional issues that arise in these situations, many leaders simply leave this "soft stuff" by the wayside. They concentrate on results and often slip into mindlessness, as discussed in chapter 6. They take a deep breath when they have to deal with common, painful problems (like layoffs or firing someone for poor performance) and generally ignore the emotional realm as much as possible. In other words, they default to the negative emotional attractor. Our argument: research in the fields of neurophysiology, psychology, sociology, and management indicates clearly and quite conclusively that it is precisely engaging in the soft stuff—rather than maintaining a negative orientation and focus—that leads to positive expectations, positive emotions, and hope, and thus the ability to envision and achieve goals.[23]

Consider, for example, the case of one doctor and his family who were thrust into a life-altering situation, and how they used the power of hope, and specifically a vivid dream of the future, to attract to themselves a positive outcome indeed.

Dr. Ghannoum and His Dream

When Dr. Mahmoud Ghannoum took his family on holiday to England from their home in Kuwait, little did he know that his world was about to change dramatically. Early one morning, his oldest son awakened Mahmoud and his wife. "You won't believe what happened!" he said. Turning on the television, Mahmoud discovered that Saddam Hussein's armies had just invaded Kuwait. As reporters repeated the story, the fog of shock and confusion slowly gave way to a clear realization: "Oh my God," he thought. "My job, the university—our whole way of life—is gone."

Mahmoud had recently been promoted to full professor of Microbial Physiology at Kuwait University. His wife was assistant to the Chief Engineer of Public Works. They had three children; their youngest son was only four months old. Mahmoud told us that his thoughts seemed to come in waves. Clearly, he and his family would not be returning home after this vacation. His children needed to go to school: what would happen? Most of their worldly possessions were lost: how would they replace them? Their jobs were gone: what would they do for money? Where would they live?

During the next two days, as the disbelief wore off and the reality set in, Mahmoud and his wife made a conscious decision: rather than dwelling on the past and their losses right now, they would focus on the present and the future. They would focus on hope. They were safe in England. They were talented professionals and they vowed to rebuild their life.

Then Mahmoud had another thought. He remembered a dream that he and his wife had long kept in their hearts: to live and work in the United States. Maybe, he told his wife, this was the time to try to make that dream happen. After all, they truly had nothing left to lose. Mahmoud and his wife began talking more about that dream, remembering the details they had once envisioned, and they slowly began to form a new vision of what their lives might look like in the future.

That dream kept them going through the first two months after the invasion. To give themselves time to decide what they wanted to do, they found creative ways to take care of the essentials. Within two weeks they got two of their children enrolled in an English school. Mahmoud got a part-time job teaching at a local college where he would have flexibility to look toward the future. He went to the library and collected as many of his published writings as he could. For the first time, he created a résumé for a new and different culture. He called colleagues while his wife, who had also taken temporary work, contacted friends and relatives. Soon the contacts paid off: Mahmoud was invited to give a talk at a conference in Washington, D.C. He and his wife started to feel the possibility of a future they would want, even if tragedy had forced them into it. Mahmoud's emotional intelligence helped him to stay in touch with his wife's feelings and ensure that they both kept talking about the family's future. It was as if the two of them fed off of each other's moments of hope.

When in Washington, Mahmoud called on the future president of the Infectious Disease Society, who at the time was the head of a major program in the National Institutes of Health. After hearing Mahmoud's story and about his hopes for the future, he gave him an office and his Rolodex. He told Mahmoud about another meeting in Washington the following week, suggesting it would be a good opportunity to meet other colleagues. Mahmoud did not have the money to stay in the United States so he took a risk and called friends to ask for help. They immediately responded, inviting him to stay in their homes and even circulating his résumé.

Mahmoud's easy smile and affable nature presented a striking distinction from the usual intellectual intensity and nerdiness of most people in the field. People who knew him wanted to spend more time with him. People who met him wanted to do more for him. By the end of the second conference, Mahmoud had two offers for full-time teaching and research positions. After consulting his wife, he took a job at UCLA.

Mahmoud and his wife's passion, commitment, and hope drove them into an exciting life. Their wake-up call was obvious and unavoidable—but they could easily have chosen a less positive future or become trapped in mourning the past and in trying to find a way to get back to Kuwait, rather than revitalizing and realizing a long-held dream. Instead, they consciously managed the stress of the change, focusing on the future, their children, and their relationship. During the entire process, they remained open to one another, mindful of their feelings and their relationship.

They talked often and deeply to stay in touch with each other. The quality of their relationship helped them weave their way through the confusing emotions and practical challenges of the transition. Throughout, their hope and compassion were contagious, and whenever they reached out, friends and colleagues responded warmly.

Since he has come to the United States, Mahmoud's career has taken off. Today, he is director of the Center for Medical Mycology at the University Hospitals in Cleveland and a professor at Case Western Reserve University. His vision is to develop the Center into the most advanced center for research on the study of fungus, his specialty. His colleagues share his enthusiasm and excitement about the future. His ability to build resonant relationships with people in his lab, colleagues in the field, and donors has inspired passionate interest in his work and the Center's potential. He has published hundreds of articles and five books, and in 2004, he was awarded a prestigious grant from Bristol-Myers Squibb.

Mahmoud has exceeded even his own hopes in terms of impact in his field, and he believes that this would not have happened had he been in Kuwait. His relationship with his wife continues to be a source of joy for them both, and his children have grown into successful young adults.

Even Bad News Can Spark a Dream

Clearly, learning that his country had been invaded could be called the epitome of bad news for Mahmoud. Let us now look at another example of how people's sense of hope can be tested by a very different kind of bad news: poor performance in a company.

How do you inspire hope in an organization when performance is poor? Or, more to the point, should you use valuable time and energy to create a resonant environment when problems are mounting and results are not forthcoming? In many conversations with executives, we hear a litany of arguments against stimulating a positive mood when things are tough. Under such conditions, many executives argue for getting down to business and for leaving the soft stuff (like building resonance) for later. Images of "Chainsaw Al" Dunlap and similar "specialists" in downsizing, cost cutting, right-sizing, and otherwise bringing discipline to an organization come to mind. These individuals, who clearly did not spark resonance, might say that when there is tough work to do, even a salute to building resonance is a distraction and misleading.

Yet, as we have seen, when an environment is dissonant (as it can so easily become when things are tough) people do not perform their best. So, just when things are most difficult, good leaders find a way to deal with problems and performance issues *while concurrently sparking resonance.*

Belmiro Azevedo, founder of Sonae, an influential Portuguese company, has a unique and inspirational way of moving people out of key management positions when performance has been poor. Belmiro is a compassionate and yet a driven builder of companies. In 1984, he bought a small family-run furniture business, which by 2001 had become the largest non-bank private employer in Portugal. Along with the furniture business, Sonae now boasts large construction and IT consulting divisions, as well as a tourism division comprising resorts, hotels, and spas.

Whatever the ups and downs of the business may be at any given moment, people feel excited to be a part of Sonae. Belmiro's passion for growth is understood by everyone, and they feel part of it. We asked him how he handles the problems that inevitably arise with such growth; for example a division's general manager who did just fine when his business turned over 5 million euros a year, but began to stumble consistently once the business grew past 100 million euros.

Belmiro's answer? In the face of poor performance, he tries to help his people develop. "I offer training, consultants, and coaches," he said. And when that doesn't work? "Well, if I have decided that despite attempts to help there is no progress or hope that the manager can improve, I change strategy," he told us. "At one of our monthly lunches, after discussing the manager's division, I ask, 'If you had unlimited funds, what business would you develop for today's market? What is needed?' And then I listen. Almost everyone comes back to me with one or two ideas for businesses. If any of the ideas makes sense to me, I make them an offer by the end of the lunch: if they develop a plan for this new business that I approve, I will provide the venture capital for 49 percent of the stock." He smiled and added, "It doesn't work all the time, but you would be surprised how often they come up with a great business plan, and we go into business together. Meanwhile, I am free to place a different executive in charge of the division."

What Belmiro is doing, essentially, is offering his people a chance to dream—to hope—even when they have been performing poorly. In fact, he sees this as a way to help them *out* of a performance rut. That is how Belmiro uses hope and excitement about the future to renew his business, his executives who are stumbling, and himself. Of course, most leaders cannot set up poor performers in a new business, but those who follow the principle of renewal through hope almost always have good results. These leaders use creativity—and emotional intelligence—to inspire hope in even the most difficult situations.

This brings us to a final point about crafting a vision and a dream to inspire hope. Personal vision—an individual's hopes and dreams for the future—is a powerful driver of individual change. But it is not enough to spark *collective* change. Resonant leaders go beyond the individual level—they inspire hope and craft meaningful visions at the larger, collective level of an entire organization.

Dreams at the Collective Level: When "Vision" Isn't

Your personal vision consists in part of your dreams for the future. Your deep beliefs, values, and philosophy are part of your personal vision. This vision is a meaningful concept that inspires hope: it stirs you. Similarly, the path to hope in organizations is often through vision and values.

We are not talking here about the "vision thing" extolled by posters or lobby art. To most people the ideas they push are meaningless because they are not shared throughout the organization or are full of platitudes, uninspiring numbers goals, or vague aspirations such as "be the best." These kinds of visions do not spark images of the collective dream. A shared vision truly inspires an organization to hopefulness and success. It is the kind of vision that interrupts the hustle and hectic activities of people's individual busy schedules. It brings you back to your purpose and brings your body back to renewal. Remember Mrs. Zikhali? Her school's vision, like other *real* collective visions, is a shared reflection of values and dreams, aspirations and hope. Mrs. Zikhali's vision was personal at first, but it fast became the teachers' and the community's as well—*their* vision. A shared vision reminds us of the meaning of our work.

All too often, however, organizational vision statements sound like something made up by a marketing department or public relations person. Here is a story of one such situation, and what was done to correct it. Schalon Newton, a former executive and now a strategy consultant, was trying to help top management of a prominent multinational communicate its vision throughout the organization. But the campaign felt consummately flat; it lacked energy. Why, Schalon wondered, did no one seem able to get excited about the company's vision, much less translate it to the wider organization? He knew from conversations with executives and others throughout the company that the vision as stated was indeed dry and cold. No one could make it come alive, even though the executives he spoke with seemed to believe in it. What was wrong?

Schalon decided to start by asking questions. He asked the executives if it was reasonable to assume that their subordinates expected them to be committed to the vision, to understand it and to reflect it in their actions. They said "yes." Schalon then challenged them to see how well they actually knew what the vision embodied.

He took the thirty-plus words in the actual vision statement and added several others from the longer mission statement, as well as an assortment of commonly used phrases from other corporate mission statements. He placed each word or phrase on a card. He handed the nine executives the deck and gave them fifteen minutes to assemble the words and phrases into their actual vision statement.

After ten minutes of frustration with no consensus on the words or the proper order, he started giving the executives hints—filling in some of the words for them and leaving spaces for others. When after ten more minutes the executives still had only ten of the words in place, they all sat down, frustrated, a bit humbled, and ready to talk about how to create *a living and inspirational vision.*

Schalon's point was simple but critical: You cannot inspire others about a vision if you yourself cannot articulate it. To feel the passion and hope that a vision should invoke, you have to know it so well that it is something you do not have to read to remember—not just a poster on a wall. Only then can leaders begin to inspire hope through a shared dream. Only then will collective vision serve to renew leaders and reinvigorate everyone around them.

Believing the Dream: a Primer on Optimism and Efficacy

So far in this chapter we have talked about developing a vision and a dream as a first step to cultivating hope—and ultimately renewal and sustainable resonance. What is the next step? You must actually *believe in your dream.* Hope is driven, we believe, in part by the belief that the desired image of the future (the dream) is possible. Our sense of optimism has a primary effect on this belief. Martin Seligman is a professor at the University of Pennsylvania who has devoted his life to studying optimism. He describes optimism as part trait, part learned. Because optimism and pessimism are in part traits—we are born with a tendency toward one or the other—they can be considered part of one's personality, present over time and in all sorts of situations. In this they are unlike feelings, which are fleeting and not part of one's personality.[24]

Traits are also fairly steady over time—they are the basis for our feelings or experience in any given situation. For example, the trait we call optimism is an underlying state of mind that makes it more likely that we will interpret problems as temporary and fix-able. Its opposite, pessimism, leads us to interpret the exact same problems as long-lasting, and impossible to fix. But optimism and pessimism are not only relatively stable traits that may seem to have been inherited—they are the result of our experiences and what we have learned as well.[25]

Optimism is a way of looking at life. We all know people who truly see the glass as half full most of the time. Maybe you are one of those people. This outlook actually influences how you feel and what you think about things that happen to you and around you. Optimistic people tend to believe that good things will happen, and when bad things do happen, that the situation is bound to change for the better fairly quickly.[26]

The interesting thing is that there are specific *leadership actions* associated with optimism, such as seeking opportunities and deliberately overcoming obstacles to a goal, as well as overtly expecting the best from people and situations.[27] These actions are key to emotional intelligence, and people who are generally optimistic are happier, more resilient, and more productive; they live longer; recover from illnesses faster; and are more likely to create resonance and lead effectively.[28] Moreover, optimism contributes to a general feeling of well-being, which in turn contributes to renewal, helping leaders cope with the challenges and disappointments inherent in their work.

But if optimism is largely a stable part of your personality and a result of the sum of your past experiences, what about people who are not blessed with this outlook? What chance do they have of becoming resonant, emotionally intelligent leaders—of relying on hope to regularly renew themselves and those around them? This is where research on expectations, which can be consciously altered, helps us find some answers.

There are numerous studies in medicine and the social sciences indicating that whatever people believe will happen actually does happen quite often, regardless of whether it realistically should happen or not. For example, in one infamous study, teachers were given descriptions of students before the school year began, including assessment of their intellectual ability, curiosity, and other characteristics. They were told that some students were "high potential," and indeed by the end of the school year these students were performing exactly as had been predicted, and better than their peers. Why is this so surprising? Because the students' profiles were randomly assigned and had *nothing* to do with their actual abilities.[29] In a 2004 CNN television special on education in the United States, this same dynamic was considered with respect to the gap between white and black students' performance.[30] Of course, there are no differences in the two groups' IQ and other abilities, and yet in U.S. schools, black students consistently score lower on standardized tests and other measures of academic performance.[31] While some small part of the differences can be explained by things such as allocation of resources to schools, the lesson about a self-fulfilling prophecy is painfully clear: expectations can actually affect outcomes.[32]

I Think I Can

But what of the link between hope and the ability to achieve a desired outcome? Will and human volition are topics that have absorbed many philosophical and religious thinkers, including Aristotle, Buddha, Thomas Aquinas, Mohammed, Spinoza, and William James, for centuries.[33] Today social scientists study what they call "self-efficacy": our sense of what we can do, impact, and control.[34] Many psychologists believe that self-efficacy is one of the most important predictors of what people will actually do and how successful they will be in accomplishing their goals.

Like optimism and pessimism, self-efficacy is also considered a combination of inherited tendency and learned behavior and similarly linked to one's approach to life.[35] This set of beliefs about one's general competence can be altered or changed through personal effort, other people's actions and beliefs, and one's successes or failures in life.[36] Believing that you have some control over your fate is an important aspect in determining your attitudes and expectations about the future—hopefulness or despair—and also your behavior.

So, self-efficacy is an important addition to hope—the belief (or faith) in a possible outcome plus one's sense of power in affecting outcomes *do* affect the actual reality and ultimate results. And linking belief, efficacy, and hope is not necessarily an individual endeavor. There are limits to what individuals can do alone, and in today's complex world we can argue that almost nothing of substance can be accomplished by a single individual, no matter how great, how powerful, how talented.

In addition to self-efficacy, therefore, we need to develop *collective efficacy*: the belief of its members that a group—a family, a team, an organization, a nation—can come together to have impact on and exert some control over events.[37] Witness recent events in South Asia in early 2005. Following devastating earthquakes and the resulting tsunami, thousands of people lost everything. And yet communities and nations came together in hope and with a collective belief in their ability to rebuild their lives. Similarly, worldwide movements to conserve energy, burn less fossil fuels, preserve rain forests, and natural habitats are driven, in part, by the collective belief that together we can make a difference in the health of our planet and the future of the natural environment we pass on to our children and grandchildren.

We cannot end our discussion of efficacy and its link to hope without mentioning religious or spiritual faith. People all over the world link hope, self-efficacy, and collective efficacy to a god, however defined—as a higher power, universal force, or spiritual guide.[38] We witness the importance of spirituality and religion as major driving social forces.[39] While this has also resulted in many conflicts, many people find hope through their spiritual practice. Scientists are studying the effects of prayer on the human brain, emotions, and health.[40] On the whole, it appears that people who regularly practice religious or spiritual activities experience lower blood pressure, better immune system function, lower levels of stress hormones, different neural patterns, and other positive physical effects.[41] We suspect these people use prayer or other practices such as meditation to engage the renewal we discussed at length in chapter 6.

Can Hope Hurt?

Much of what we have been arguing here reinforces our notion that optimism and efficacy—a belief in a dream, and confidence that your dream or vision will actually occur, and that you can do something to make it happen—are key for cultivating hope. But what about the argument that misplaced hope is really just delusion? There are certainly arguments *against* inspiring optimism and hope continuously in individuals and organizations.[42] These arguments hold that, by focusing only on positive outcomes, and looking at the glass half full, we do ignore the other side of reality—threats, problems, issues that need attending to. When this happens, some say people are likely to overestimate their—or their organizations'—capabilities, make decisions based on "what could be" rather than "what is," and take thoughtless risks.

Interestingly, research does not support this. Current studies of individuals and groups indicate that because we really do want to be able to predict the future as accurately as possible, we mentally put the brakes on delusional thoughts.[43] Because we want to understand what is currently happening, and to the best of our ability predict what will happen, we seek information, feedback, and knowledge to help us create a realistic picture.

We argue that positive emotions and hope do not spark delusion—they simply give us the strength to deal with our current reality while engaging our talents in moving toward the future.

That said, there is no denying that some leaders—and some societies—misuse hope, usually for selfish reasons. Throughout history, we have seen societies and leaders feed downtrodden groups with hope while continuing to mistreat or abuse them. Hope is given as an antidote to pain and to numb people to the current reality. Nobel Prize winner Elie Wiesel, a concentration camp survivor, summarized this misuse of hope by saying, "My hope should not be someone else's nightmare."[44]

Clearly, then, as leaders we also need to ask ourselves *why* we want to inspire hope: for the greater good or personal gain? This difference is typically the difference between resonant leaders and demagogues, as we described in *Primal Leadership*.[45]

There are manipulative leaders, even charismatic ones, who can create the illusion of hope. But it is not based on an overall positive emotional tone, but a negative one. Such leaders typically manipulate others into thinking they are doing good while they are advocating the destructions of others—what Dr. Wiesel referred to as someone else's nightmare. To be a resonant leader, the hope we feel and stimulate in others should enhance but not interfere with their hope. This is part of the larger responsibility of being a great leader.

Seeing the Dream as Feasible

As we have seen, a belief that something will happen can often make it so, and this goes for both good outcomes and bad. But beyond basic optimism, and one's belief in our ability to make change, our vision needs to be realistic rather than delusional, and we need to sense how it will come about. The last step for cultivating the kind of hope that leads to renewal is to see the hope as *feasible*—that is, the dream or image about which a person feels hope must seem possible. If our dreams seem too far-fetched, we do not feel hope and, therefore, do not experience the benefits of the renewal process.

Never is it more important for a leader to understand the concept of feasible hope than when dealing with a crisis that has affected the organization, such as a major product recall or sudden drop in the demand for its products and services. In such circumstances, more of the same is not enough. A crisis precipitates a condition of threat and fear, invoking people's stress response. An extreme crisis provokes extreme stress. And the combination of extreme threat and power stress often results in many of the psychological and physiological symptoms of chronic stress—leading ultimately to the Sacrifice Syndrome for those affected or close to a crisis. People often turn to others for assurance or interpretation of their feelings in such trying times.[46]

The physical presence of a positive and calm leader during a crisis is particularly reassuring. Similarly, demonstrating courage in the face of imminent danger or stress sets an example and inspires others to also serve with courage. That is what it means to use positive emotional contagion, and it is exactly what Kenneth Chenault, chairman and CEO of American Express, managed to do during the most trying days following the destruction of the World Trade Center.[47]

On that fateful morning of September 11, 2001, Ken Chenault happened to be visiting the Salt Lake City office. He was talking on the phone with a colleague in the New York headquarters when suddenly, the call was interrupted. A plane had just crashed into one of the Twin Towers, across the street from the company headquarters. Chenault asked to be transferred to security, and ordered the immediate evacuation of the more than four thousand employees.[48]

Although he had assumed leadership of the company only months before, Ken Chenault had already begun to receive accolades about his attributes as a leader.[49] Doug Lennick, an inspirational company senior vice president at the time who now writes about executive talent, told us that once he was back in New York, Ken Chenault wasted no time. He set up an office for himself in each of the six locations to which employees had been dispersed. He spent a few days in each one, making the rounds and getting to know his employees personally. Then, on September 20, he organized a town hall meeting of five thousand American Express employees at New York's Paramount Theater. While others had doubts about the timing and location of the meeting, this leader felt it was necessary. During the meeting, Ken Chenault expressed his feelings of despair, sadness, and anger; embracing upset employees, saying, "I represent the best company and best people in the world. You are my strength and I love you."[50]

During the discussion, he invoked hope in a time of uncertainty. Yet rather than offering empty promises or platitudes that would ring false, especially given the tragic situation, he made sure that the hope he offered was feasible and realistic. So in addition to being authentic and in touch with the emotions of his employees, he was also very practical: he recognized that people had needs above and beyond his ability to help. That is why he arranged for the company to provide a series of counseling services to ensure that employees' emotional and psychological needs were met. And indeed, in the chaotic days that followed the collapse of the Twin Towers, he made sure that American Express acted quickly on behalf of its customers as well. The company waived millions of dollars in delinquent fees, increased credit limits to people in need, and helped over half a million cardholders by chartering airplanes and buses and finding other creative ways to get people home.

Unfortunately, not all leadership inspires hope during fragile and sensitive times of extreme crisis. In fact, we have heard tales of how, in the aftermath of September 11, some company leaders took their already dissonant style to even greater extremes, even if they did not intend it. Particularly in times of crisis, where extreme emotions are aroused, leaders are at high risk for succumbing to power stress. They become trapped—quickly—in the Sacrifice Syndrome and may channel their negative emotions or even amplify them.

But Ken Chenault established a connection, turning the grief and shock into action. He created a sense of hope. Creating and managing an overall positive emotional tone in the environment requires being in an authentically positive state oneself. To inspire others, the leader must be in touch with his or her own emotions, and no matter how difficult the situation, must also engage hope personally. Then the leader needs to communicate this hopeful state and spread it, consciously and unconsciously, verbally and nonverbally. In times of crisis, the leader has to convey enormously difficult information, acknowledging the traumatic emotional realities of the day, and simultaneously reassuring people that things are moving in a positive direction—engendering hope, not fear; resilience and the sense of overcoming great odds, not confusion or paralysis.

One caution: it can be surprisingly challenging to inspire hope once the immediate crisis is over. Strangely, once an organization has come through a crisis, people often experience a crash—a kind of depression sets in. In the absence of the threat and the hopeful vision of the future, energy levels drop and people sometimes wish nostalgically for the good old days when things were tough and everyone pulled together around the challenge and the dream. What they are longing for, of course, is camaraderie and the clarity and specificity of a simple goal: survival. This is where some executives find it easy to let their organizations down: without a galvanizing crisis they cannot manage to keep the energy high, focus vision, and construct a compelling case for the future. This is where the development and nurturing of a shared vision and hope becomes critical. It is a positive alternative to creating urgency through a crisis. Using vision and hope as the driving force, rather than real or manufactured crisis, is a more powerful motivational force without many of the negative effects that stress and defensiveness have on learning, innovation, and adaptability.

As with mindfulness, hope is a source of personal renewal and a path to resonance. The third important component in establishing and maintaining resonance (and personal renewal) is the experience of compassion. In the next chapter, we will see how this works.

But first, we offer here (and in appendix B) a few exercises to stimulate your dreams and help you get in touch with your personal sense of hope.[51]

Exercise 1: My Hopes and Dreams

THINK ABOUT where you would be sitting and reading this book if it were ten to fifteen years from now and you were living your ideal life. What kinds of people would be around you? What does your environment look and feel like? What might you be doing during a typical day or week? Don't worry about the feasibility of creating this kind of ideal life. Let the image develop, and place yourself in the picture.

Try doing some "free writing" around this vision or else speak your vision into a tape recorder or talk about it with a trusted friend. When doing this exercise, many people report that they experience a release of energy, feeling more optimistic than they had even moments earlier. This kind of envisioning of an ideal future can be a powerful way to connect with the real possibilities for change in our lives.

Exercise 2: What I Want to Do at Some Point in the Future

NUMBER a sheet of paper 1 through 27. List all of the things you want to do or experience before you die. Don't worry about priorities or practicality—just write down whatever comes to you. Be as specific as you can. If you need more than 27 lines, add more.

Exercise 3: What Would I Do If . . . ?

YOU HAVE just been told that you've received a major, unexpected inheritance. It is such a large amount of money that you immediately know you have complete freedom from all financial concerns. In fact, the amount of money allows you to consider doing and having things that you never had thought were possible. How would your life and work change?

Exercise 4: Look for Themes

REVIEW YOUR ANSWERS to the above three exercises. What patterns of themes appear across the exercises? What are the items in each that stand out as the most important to you about your dream of the future?

EIGHT

Compassion

L ECHESA TSENOLI, a respected member of the South African Parliament, helped lead South Africa out of apartheid. Today he helps direct his country toward the future. His outstanding leadership and commitment to people enables him to stand up to the most difficult battles, including the continuing struggle for complete equality for all South Africans, overcoming poverty, and fighting the spread of HIV and AIDS. He is an admired leader (some say he is a hero), known for keen insights and a self-deprecating humor that enable him to engage people quickly and easily.[1]

Lechesa's journey has been long and hard indeed—and compassion has played a critical role in his success. In the early days of the fight against apartheid, he worked in the most difficult and exciting areas, visiting townships and organizing young people around issues of housing, poverty, and social justice. He and his fellow activists saw poverty the likes of which many of them could not have fathomed, and yet they found wisdom in the words of the people with whom they spoke. Though many of these people were not formally educated and struggled daily just to survive, Lechesa found that they truly understood the political issues of the day and in many cases knew what could be done about them. This touched Lechesa deeply. As he said in a recent conversation, "Any shred of arrogance about class was completely gone as a result of these experiences."

During the dangerous years that followed the early work, Lechesa was challenged to bridge even bigger gaps. Again and again, he found that when he was able to see and feel what others were experiencing, he could connect to them in a deep way that furthered his understanding of the situation. He would learn that his capacity for empathy and compassion were even more important during extreme crisis—and even when it came to dealing with his enemies.

Like thousands of others, Lechesa was detained for his anti-apartheid activities in the 1980s. He tells us, "In 1985, I got married, had my first child, and was detained for the first time. When my wife came to prison with my firstborn, there was glass between us and my little son could not understand why he could not touch me. That was one of the worst nights of my life." During the long months in detention, he and his fellow freedom fighters had no way of knowing what was going on out in the world. No information, no conversations, and carefully monitored family visits.

In situations like this, many people drift into hopelessness. Not Lechesa. Just as he had done in his anti-apartheid work, in detention he tapped into his compassion for others to build relationships that enabled him to endure captivity—and even to support the cause from the inside. How? By reaching out to his own jailors. Lechesa knew that if there was any chance of improving the situation for himself and his fellow detainees, he had to find a way to understand these guards. He could not accept that all of them were bad people, or oblivious to justice. He guessed they wanted some of the same things he did: a good life, a safe and happy family, love, freedom. He was curious about them. Over time, he talked to the guards about their families, their lives, what they cared about. As he put it, "This is where I really learned that you must never mistake your consciousness, your assumptions, for the experiences and beliefs of others. You must *listen*. The ability to really listen to and understand the experience of others first—and then make sense of it—is what you must do."

Lechesa made a *choice* to focus on these guards as people with feelings, beliefs, uncertainties, and fears. He made a choice to understand them and allow himself to experience the positive feelings that often accompany understanding of others. Despite the intense anger he felt at the guards at times, he observed each one as a separate person. He recalls, "I was interested in these guards, and I also had a goal—we needed information, and the guards had it. The days were long, even for them, and they would pass the time by talking with us. I found out that one of the guards had a sister who was in the Black Sash, the white women's organization that supported our cause. He did not agree with her, but I could tell that in his heart of hearts he understood our position. By this time, I really knew the man. I had engaged him, related to him, talked to him as one person to another. I cared about him, and he cared about me."

Lechesa believes that this one guard encouraged other guards to "ease up" in their treatment of the prisoners. It made an inhumane place seem more human. Ultimately, the guard was willing to break the law and give Lechesa a newspaper for a few hours each day. During those hours, he and each of his colleagues would take a part of the paper, read it and write a summary. At the end of the day, they could all read the news of the day. As Lechesa said, "Knowing what was going on outside gave us hope. It saved our lives." Lechesa told us that having the news to hold onto gave him strength to be able to look at his wife and his baby son on the other side of the prison glass without completely breaking down. Getting the news also alleviated some of the toxic effects of the stress of detainment. As he and other political detainees followed the progress of the movement in the news, sharing the joys of small victories that were reported, they maintained commitment and stayed connected to their cause.

Ultimately, Lechesa's knowledge that one guard, at least, saw him as a person—and Lechesa's own ability to see that guard as a fellow human caught in a horrible struggle—made the long hours of each day pass with an occasional positive feeling. It gave him hope, yes, but it also evoked something beyond hope: it stimulated compassion for the guards.

Feeling compassion for and building rapport with people who are different from ourselves is difficult, to say the least. But it was precisely that kind of care and concern for other people, in this case the enemy, that enabled Lechesa and his colleagues to endure a terrible situation. He led his guards by understanding them and their situation, and then engaging them so they could understand his experience. The result? Lechesa created resonance in the most trying circumstances.

We have spent much of this book illustrating how effective leaders have resonant *relationships*. In other words, they are leaders who are in touch with the people around them. Resonant relationships require people to *know* each other. To be resonant with others, you have to be in tune with them, something deeper than having a mental model or an intellectual insight about another person. Being in tune with others involves *caring* about them— and that is what evokes compassion. You feel curiosity, respect, and real empathy. Being in touch with others and feeling compassion has other benefits: it arouses renewal. So, compassion is a key to renewal, and to unlocking the chains of the Sacrifice Syndrome.

In this chapter we will explore more examples of the benefits of compassion, and we will look at ways to cultivate it in our lives and work.

Compassion Defined: Empathy in Action

Compassion is empathy and caring in action. Being open to others enables us to face tough times with creativity and resilience. Empathy enables us to connect with people. It helps us get things done, and to deal with power stress and the sacrifices inherent in leadership.

In order to be empathic, we must begin with curiosity about other people and their experiences. Most people are born with curiosity—we only have to look at the bright eyes of a healthy four-year-old to see it in its pure form. At that age, the world is a miraculous place full of mysteries to explore. Sadly, as we age we often lose the ability to see things—and people—through a clear lens. We end up seeing the world through a filter of our own beliefs. Much miscommunication happens because people's ability to take in information from each other is seriously curtailed by their pre-judgments. Carried to the extreme, a relationship can be ruled by prejudices and stereotypes, with very little real information passing between people, never mind actual connection and understanding.

It is impossible to be free of all prejudgment—we simply could not live in the world without some assumptions. However, effective leaders are able to suspend automatic judgment, and can work to understand other people without filters. Effective leaders care enough to want to learn about other people, to feel what they feel and see the world the way they do. And then they do something with what they've learned.

We define compassion as having three components:

- Understanding and empathy for others' feelings and experiences
- Caring for others
- Willingness to act on those feelings of care and empathy[2]

When experiencing compassion, a person does not assume or expect reciprocity or an equal exchange. Compassion means giving selflessly. This goes beyond the common definition of compassion in the West and within Buddhist philosophy; both traditions tend to link compassion with empathy and caring for others who are in pain. We believe compassion incorporates the desire to reach out and help others whether or not their condition is based on suffering and pain. Our definition of compassion, then, is closer to that of Confucian philosophy: compassion is the emotional expression of the virtue of benevolence.[3]

People often confuse sympathy, that is, feeling sorry for someone, with caring about someone and feeling compassion. Some of this confusion is the fault of the field of psychology and a limited view of what has been called "need for affiliation." For decades, wanting to be close to others was viewed as trying to fill a need. This view of relationships is based on a deficiency model—and assumes that a need for affiliation is aroused because of a gap in a person's current life. Freud and others fueled this perspective. At a deeper level, the model assumes that a desire for closeness is based on the fears or anxiety of being rejected. Even today, some of the widely used measures of this desire look at how people use it in an attempt to avoid rejection, rather than experiencing and expressing their non-anxious desire and enjoyment of being close with others.[4]

So people aroused by a *need* for affiliation look for evidence that their loved ones or close friends really care about them. They value proof such as frequent declarations of affection, frequent calls, visits, chances to spend time together, and even some degree of exclusivity. For example, wanting to know you are someone's best friend might be seen as evidence that the person is less likely to reject you.

At the opposite end of the spectrum lies what we consider to be a more positive, non-anxious form of intimacy or desire to be close to others. It is not based on reciprocity or the need for declarations of any kind, and does not require proof of affection. Rather, we are looking at the drive for relationship and regard from a glass-half-full perspective: our desire for contact and intimacy are natural and we derive great satisfaction and pleasure from compassionate relationships. From this perspective, we simply enjoy being with certain other people. When we come together, it is as if we have not been apart, even if years have intervened. We can comfortably pick up the relationship where we left off and not feel as if something was missing. It is this form of the affiliation drive that is the basis for the experience of compassion.

So compassion is empathy in action. It is based on a wholesome desire to connect with others and to meet their needs. The best way to understand what compassion is, however, is to see how it actually leads, in practice, to renewal of both leaders and those around them, and ultimately to sustainable resonance and results.

Compassion in Action

As managing partner and COO for Morgan Lewis Bockius, one of the the largest law firms in the United States, Tom Sharbaugh is responsible for ensuring that the firm's operations run smoothly—including human resources, information technology, and finance.[5] Just try to imagine what running a large, successful law firm like Tom's might entail. To begin with, there is the fact that the most successful people (like the lawyers Tom works with) are also the most *un*manageable. They are independent, achievement oriented, and focused outward on clients, not inward on firm issues. In other words, most lawyers could not care less about the business operations of the firm. They are interested in plying their trade.

The problem is that attorneys nevertheless are in fact responsible for the most important operations issues, such as billing and collecting fees. All too often, however, this work slips to the bottom of the list. Tom's challenge? To get the lawyers in his charge to care enough to make this part of the job a priority too.

Tom is a lawyer himself, and he understands how lawyers think and what they care about. He feels real empathy for the daily struggles, pressures, drives, and highs and lows of the profession. He shares his fellow attorneys' frustrations and their passion. He can get inside their hearts and minds; he knows what drives them, he knows what makes them crazy, and he cares about them. He knew, therefore, that he couldn't simply order the lawyers to cooperate; that method doesn't work with people who are driven primarily by a desire for excellence and individual success.

This is a story, then, about how Tom used his empathy in action—his compassion for the lawyers in his firm—to motivate them toward the greater good of the firm, simultaneously sparking renewal in the lawyers and in himself as a leader. He relied on a method that many managers who lead very successful people must use: influencing people through ambiguous authority.[6] That means getting people to do things by making sure they *want* to do them.

Tom's solution was simple and effective. He organized all the attorneys into teams, taking care to put people together with others they would actually see during the normal course of the workday. Then he set revenue collection targets for the teams, publicized them widely, and organized an open competition. He set up contests, including prizes: umbrellas, golf shirts, vouchers for restaurants and movies, even $100 bills. To his utter amazement, these lawyers—who really, really did not need these tokens (certainly not the money)—became totally engrossed in the contests, dramatically improving the revenue collection cycle in the firm.

Why did this work? In a word, it worked because Tom Sharbaugh has compassion for lawyers, he understands and cares about them. In setting up the competition, he acted in concert with their feelings—he created a system that spoke to the achievement motive and autonomy drives that are often very high in lawyers. He managed the process publicly, so that winners got public acclaim (also something many attorneys like). On the other hand, contest losers were not punished. Tom understood that he needed to spark *resonance* in these teams, not dissonance. He had to avoid demotivating people. He knew that if there were serious financial consequences tied to the results, individuals would be furious—not a tone he wanted to set.

Tom used compassion on a collective level, and it moved an entire firm. None of this would have worked had Tom not gone about it in a way that was mindful of others' feelings and motivations. He tells us that long ago, through the actions of a mentor, he learned that punishing people for what they do wrong is not the way to spark resonance, loyalty, or commitment. Rather, long-term success comes when people care about each other and act together in the service of the greater good.

Tom moves people. He uses emotional intelligence and compassion to tap into people's desires. He guides people's behavior primarily through ensuring that he is in tune with what they need, want, and will do. An added benefit: in addition to sparking resonance, Tom's stance—emotionally intelligent and compassionate—keeps him in renewal. He's quick to reflect and engage mindfully with people, and he holds a hopeful vision in ways that people can relate to. His actions and their results are deeply satisfying, and this enables him to stay the course and even avoid the Sacrifice Syndrome in difficult times.

Consider yet another story of compassion, which we witnessed at an airport one rainy night in Cleveland. This story highlights how the contagious nature of compassion can spark an almost immediate sense of renewal, shifting a negative environment to a positive one. The flight for Boston was slated to leave at 7:30 p.m., but the plane was already delayed by an hour. Then came a second announcement: the plane would be yet another forty-five minutes late. The waiting area was getting crowded. Some passengers had come from connecting flights and were tired and hungry. Others were just annoyed because they suspected that the flight would be delayed even longer and might not leave at all because of the rain. Everyone was getting irritated, and it was evident that the fatigue and heat were building toward frustration.

Most of us have been in these situations. Passengers start to talk to the airline personnel with barely suppressed anger and sometimes outright rudeness. This often spreads as people get annoyed at each other taking up too much room in the crowded area. Then people start giving dirty looks to others who are discarding their paper cups and newspapers on the floor, and the tension mounts steadily.

Suddenly one of the waiting passengers pulled several balloons from her bag and blew them up. She shaped them into a rabbit and handed the balloon animal to a man sitting next to her. She noticed someone near her smiling and asked what animal she liked. "Dogs," she said. The woman pulled out more balloons, blew them up and shaped them into a dachshund. That led to more smiles from more people sitting around her. Within ten minutes, people were watching her and smiling at each other. After thirty minutes, the passengers were talking and laughing with each other. Even one of the airline counter clerks came over and said, "I know by now you probably don't even want to talk to me. But can I have a rabbit?" The crowd warmed even to her.

The passenger creating the balloon animals made a helicopter and gave it to the flight crew, who were sitting in the same area—and feeling frustrated as well. By the time we boarded the flight, two hours and fifteen minutes late, it was like a family reunion. People were laughing and joking, carrying balloons. This one woman making balloon animals had managed to change the mood of almost everyone on the flight. Her social awareness and compassion started a contagion of curiosity and then moved it into laughter. She turned a potentially hostile situation into a pleasant, social event. Her acts of compassion led to others, and then a new norm was born. (By the way, it turned out she was a professional clown on the way to a clown convention!)

The Business Case for Compassion

As we have said throughout this book, leaders experience stress as part of their daily life. Because of their responsibilities, they are under what can be described as power stress. But to function effectively, leaders need the opportunity to recover from the effects of chronic stress and renew themselves—mind, body, heart, and spirit.

Fortunately, compassion—for self and others—can aid this process, and as a result it actually can be good for business. Why? First, since compassion—like mindfulness and hope—works as a renewing agent for leaders, it decreases stress levels and improves leaders' overall effectiveness, among other things. All of the renewing physiological effects of positive emotions discussed in the earlier chapters are engaged with the experience of compassion (see appendix A for a refresher of the details).

Second, in an organization an approach to culture that is not founded on understanding and caring usually backfires. Negative techniques or strategies designed to drive favorable performance results, like creating a crisis to spur urgency or focusing on bad budget numbers to emphasize how dire things are, rarely engage leaders or the people around them. A positive, compassionate stance like Tom Sharbaugh's can lead to much better results.[7]

Leading with compassion can favorably impact the bottom line while enabling leaders to sustain their effectiveness for longer periods of time. This is a novel argument for compassion. It is not only that compassion is a virtue (a spiritual argument); it is. It is not only that the use of compassion leads to important organizational results, such as development of more people as leaders, higher commitment, responsiveness to customers, and a sense of shared community and social responsibility—which it will. The most compelling argument for compassion may be this: to sustain one's effectiveness as a leader, manager, or professional, the experience of compassion will set in motion restorative mental, emotional, and physiological processes. And all of this leads to a more positive environment in an organization, which research has shown affects how that organization actually performs, as we discussed in chapter 4. Consider the following example of how compassion fostered multiple benefits for one leader and the people and organizations he involved in his compassionate endeavor.

Visit Mark Scott at his office and he will proudly show you a photograph of himself with Mark Richt, coach of the University of Georgia's famous football team, the Georgia Bulldogs. Though Mark did not play football when he was at the university years ago, he and Coach Richt are nevertheless linked—and their relationship grew from an act of compassion.

As the Atlanta-based Vice President of Public Relations for HomeBanc, a publicly traded mortgage banking company, Mark had worked for the Atlanta Neighborhood Development Project, a not-for-profit company that rebuilt neighborhoods in the city in the past. Having been personally involved in helping people obtain housing that they never thought possible, Mark understood both the need for more such housing—as well as the ripple effects created when people help others realize the American dream of owning a home. Neighborhoods improve, which decreases crime and attracts businesses there, which generates more jobs and income for those neighborhoods and therefore the entire city. And the individuals who create such housing benefit as well: they experience a feeling of connection to something larger than themselves, compassion, and renewal on a deep level.

All of this led Mark to start thinking about how he could involve more people in creating the housing that Atlanta needed for its low-income population. In 2001, he came up with a plan with one of the mortgage company's loan officers, who happened to have played for the Bulldogs. The plan involved helping those in need while simultaneously giving college football players the opportunity to learn lessons in humility and service to others. Mark Scott's pitch to Coach Richt was simple: help the players develop some social skills and the value of serving others through building low-income housing, while getting the team some positive press.

It worked like a wonder. Since 2002, one house per year has been built by the Bulldogs. National and local newspapers as well as television stations have broadcast these events.[8] The excitement spread, and Mark was asked to develop a similar program for the football teams at Georgia Tech and Florida Atlantic University. Each is busy building at least one home each year for a family in need.

In the press, the football players and coaches from these teams expressed their deep appreciation for what Mark Scott and Home-Banc did to get them involved in community work. As Reuben Houston, junior quarterback for the Georgia Tech Yellow Jackets said, "Once you get out there, you realize that you're helping somebody who has not been privileged to have a home, and it's a good feeling."[9] In addition, these projects enhanced HomeBanc's participation in the Habitat for Humanity projects in both Georgia and Florida.

Interestingly (and possibly related), Mark Richt was a new coach in 2001 and in his first season the team's record was just okay—eight wins, four losses. His records for 2003 and 2004 jumped to 13-1 and 11-3, respectively. For those readers who know a bit about American football, seasons like these impact alumni decisions to donate to the university—a very important aspect of the school's bottom line.[10]

What effect has this compassionate endeavor had on Mark Scott and HomeBanc? Mark was voted one of the top twenty PR executives in the United States in *PR Week* magazine in November 2003.[11] He says he feels good about how the company is contributing more than just money to important social causes. Moreover, the program has helped the visibility of HomeBanc dramatically— good publicity indeed for a home mortgage company. The act of compassion became something much more—it spread a feeling of contributing to the community and, we believe, the renewal effects on those involved.

Cultivating Compassion: It Starts with Listening

We have seen in this chapter some examples of what happens when leaders experience and show compassion. But how do they actually *do* this? How can we cultivate compassion in everyday leadership?

As we saw in our opening example of Lechesa Tsenoli, listening played a key role in his ability to begin to feel compassion for his captors. Over time, in his conversations with his guards, Lechesa really listened to what they were trying to tell him about their daily lives and their concerns. And that listening led to understanding, sparking his compassion.

Similarly, when Pedro Riveros took over as the country manager in Brazil for the chemical division of a *Fortune* 500 company, his success depended on how well he would learn to listen— though he did not know this at the time. Only thirty-three years old, he was responsible for sales operations in all of South America. In a culture that values age and social stature, he had neither.

Because Pedro had just spent time in a company-sponsored program on leadership, however, he was able to benefit from a

360-degree feedback process. He learned that his boss, peers, and former subordinates from his old job in the North American division believed that he was a quick study, showed a bias for action, and was outstanding in building new relationships. But they also scored him low on his ability to show compassion when leading others.

Having grown up in São Paulo, Pedro knew that what had been a problem in his assignment in North America would be a real disaster in his new South American assignment, a culture in which intangibles such as demonstrating understanding and compassion are valued even more openly. Pedro knew too that most of his new reports were older than he was, some were close to his father's age, and that the situation would be sensitive indeed. He decided the only way to gain their respect and cooperation was to make it clear that he valued their ideas and views.

But how to do this? Partly as a result of the feedback and partly as a result of examining some past mistakes; Pedro realized that simply listening better would greatly improve his management and even his leadership. When all else fails, listening usually brings one closer to real understanding. So during the early meetings in his new assignment, he asked a lot of questions and he listened. He showed interest in each of his reports and got to know them personally, building a sense of shared understanding and compassion. When he proposed ideas, he solicited people's reactions. Building on the strengths he had shown earlier, Pedro developed a new style based on listening and actively soliciting others' ideas. He was using a variety of his emotional intelligence competencies to know when and how to engage in these actions.

The result: gaining a sense of compassion, through listening, for those with whom he worked made Pedro a better leader. And the effect soon became clear: within two years of his appointment, his region posted the largest growth figures within the world-wide/global chemicals division, and he was commended by the international VP of the company.

Pedro and Lechesa Tsenoli discovered that deep listening can eventually lead to mutual understanding, a manifestation of compassion. Such understanding can take a leader down very different paths than he might otherwise have walked. Often, for instance, it can move people—and entire organizations—to service of various kinds, which becomes a vehicle for further compassion and opportunities for renewal. Compassion can infiltrate whole organizations—increasing everyone's capacity for renewal and resonance.

Growing a Culture of Compassion

Cultivating compassion in a way that makes it spread throughout the organization begins with establishing compassion as a norm. If the leader emphasizes compassion in an organization, emotional contagion alone will likely help it spread, and it will eventually become a norm, with the result of increased feelings of commitment to the organization.[12] Moreover, people in such an organizational culture report feeling more supported in their personal and career development.[13]

Leaders can help grow a culture of compassion in many ways, and one is by fostering compassion through personal example. Another is by crafting a vision in which compassion is a central tenet.

That was the approach taken by Thomas Strauss, President and CEO of Summa Health Systems in Akron, Ohio. After all, where more than in a hospital is compassion needed if the organization has any hope of succeeding? To help his hospital system develop a new level of compassion, therefore, Thomas used focus groups, interviews, and a series of discussions among staff to develop what they wanted in a compelling vision and powerful statement of their beliefs about themselves and the organization. They found one that reflected their values, beliefs, and hope. Everyone who works at Summa carries this wallet-size card with them.[14] It reads:

You Are Summa. You are what people see when they arrive here. Yours are the eyes they look into when they're frightened and lonely. Yours are the voices people hear when they ride the elevators and when they try to sleep and when they try to forget their problems. You are what they hear on their way to appointments that could affect their destinies. And what they hear after they leave those appointments. Yours are the comments people hear when you think they can't. Yours is the intelligence and caring that people hope they find here.

If you're noisy, so is the hospital. If you're rude, so is the hospital. And if you're wonderful, so is the hospital. No visitors, no patients, no physicians or coworkers can ever know the real you, the you that you know is there—unless you let them see it. All they can know is what they see and hear and experience.

And so we have a stake in your attitude and in the collective attitudes of everyone who works at the hospital. We are judged by your performance. We are the care you give, the attention you pay, the courtesies you extend.

Thank you for all you're doing.

The result of this one vehicle for spreading a norm of compassion? Interviews with current physicians and nursing staff as well as former staff have shown a dramatic increase in commitment of the staff and the reputation of Summa within the health care community as well as the patient community it serves.[15]

One benefit of making Summa's vision come alive in the form of this powerful statement was that it focused people's attention on caring for, helping, and coaching others. These behaviors soon became expectations people had for one another and a way to hold people accountable for being more emotionally intelligent. It was a way to remind people about what is considered important and valuable in the organization, and to help both newcomers and long-time employees adopt and maintain behaviors that dramatically affected the quality of service—and the resonance in the climate.

Leaders' ability to foster compassionate behavior throughout their organizations directly affects the bottom-line performance during difficult times.[16] Apart from formal, written vision statements, leaders can establish a new norm of compassion through their personal example. Former New York mayor Rudolph W.

Giuliani was able to do just that in the midst of enormous crisis— fostering a new norm for an entire city.

In his years in office before September 11, 2001, Rudy Giuliani was the subject of countless negative headlines. Because of his reactions to allegations of police brutality, he had been accused of fueling racial tensions in the city. His private life had become daily tabloid fodder in the latter years of his mayoralty. Yet in New York's darkest days, Giuliani transformed into a resonant leader. Shortly after the second plane struck the World Trade Center, he arrived at the scene. He set up a command center in a nearby building and then nearly got trapped there, emerging ash-covered but still retaining his composure.[17]

Throughout the day and night of September 11, Giuliani was on radio and television, and making visits to hospitals. At a late-afternoon press conference, he warned that feelings of anger and hatred were responsible for the tragedy, and he urged everyone to rise above it: "It's going to be a very difficult time," he said. "I don't think we yet know the pain we're going to feel. But the thing we have to focus on now is getting the city through this and surviving and being stronger for it. New York is still here . . . Tomorrow New York is going to be here. And we're going to rebuild, and we're going to be stronger than we were before."[18]

Even as he opened that door to hope, he also consistently urged the public to compassion: "We ask all New Yorkers to cooperate and to try to help each other. There are going to be a lot of people today who need help and need assistance," he said at the press conference. "If you could comfort them, help them and assist them, that might be a way in which all New Yorkers could lend a hand."[19]

All the while, the mayor was dealing with his own personal loss of many friends and colleagues. He was a whirlwind of activity, never forgetting that the dominant emotion he and others were feeling was grief and how quickly that can turn to anger. Instead, through his actions and words, he turned the grief into compassionate action—and in the process managed to create a new standard of behavior in the city. To this day, New Yorkers treat each other differently in the streets than they ever did before September 11. Indeed, in a city known for its brusqueness, a new level of courtesy has become the norm.[20]

We have just looked at several ways to cultivate compassion on both the individual and organizational levels. We will now turn to a final method of turning compassion into action in an organization: coaching.

Coaching Your Way to Compassion

Our work with leaders has shown us that one way compassion can spark renewal is through coaching. Coaching is one of the fastest-growing professions in the world. In 2002, approximately ten thousand professional coaches were practicing worldwide, and an estimated 59 percent of organizations were offering coaching or developmental counseling to their managers and executives.[21]

The first and foremost benefit of (good) coaching is the development of a steady stream of effective leaders from within the organization. The benefits are clear: hiring too many leaders from the outside can pose significant costs, including the demoralization of employees who have worked their way up through the ranks and felt a commitment to the organization. Hiring outsiders also means you will have new people within your ranks who may or may not be sensitive to the organization's markets, technology, or culture. And when the work of an outside hire ends in failure, it can cost the company well over six figures for executive search fees alone.[22]

Many organizations today, therefore, prefer hiring from within. That means developing people to become leaders—and that means coaching. Research on how effective leaders develop continues to point to mentors, coaches, or others who helped them along the way.[23]

Coaching differs from mentoring and teaching. Often, mentors are people higher in the organization who open doors and help with networking. Coaches, too, often provide mentoring, and teach leadership and even management skills. But they also provide guidance, support, and counseling on a wide variety of issues. The nature of the coaching relationship is complicated. At its best, coaching is a combination of deep understanding of the other person's hopes and dreams as well as the reality of their current situation. In this context, and with the support of clear ethical boundaries, the coach can provide support and advice, share expertise, and enable a person to engage in a process that will result in significant personal and professional development.

Clearly, then, coaching has many benefits for the person being coached. But we'd like to focus on the positive effects it provides *the person who is the coach*. Think about it: someone coaching another person—essentially giving of him- or herself to help develop someone else—is exhibiting a high form of compassion indeed.

Coaching and the Leader: A Win-Win Proposition

Coaching with compassion is likely to develop more effective leaders for the organization *and* enable the renewal of the leader who coaches. When leaders practice coaching with compassion and encourage it throughout their companies, three major benefits result:

- Leaders are less focused on themselves
- They are more open and in touch with people and issues around them, thereby avoiding isolation and CEO disease
- They experience regular renewal, which they need to sustain themselves and their effectiveness, and to stem the effects of the Sacrifice Syndrome

In coaching others for their development, the leader cannot help but experience compassion. But here we must make an important distinction: coaching people *for their development* is different than coaching others strictly for the organization's benefit. The latter is an instrumental perspective in approaching others.

Herminia Ibarra, a professor at INSEAD, has made the distinction between instrumental and social functions of a relationship. Her research has shown that the social function of relationships enhances an individual's sense of competence, identity, and effectiveness in a professional role.[24] She explains that these benefits came more from the social nature of the relationship than instrumental functions such as providing management exposure or advocacy for promotion.

Coaching for a specific instrumental, organizational purpose (such as teaching a necessary skill), then, rarely involves real compassion and therefore would not likely invoke renewal. Furthermore, some leaders try to coach their subordinates to fit into the organization's culture or serve the needs of the company. When this is done without sincere regard for the person being coached, it is an exercise in influence—for that leader's, or the organization's purpose. The leader's primary purpose is not to develop a person, but simply to shape or change that person for the organization's or his or her own benefit. This is likely to arouse power stress and the Sacrifice Syndrome because it is engaging the leader in an attempt to influence the other person.[25]

Coaching merely for the purpose of getting someone into a position or filling an organizational need can also result in what Kathy Kram, a professor at Boston University and her colleague Monica Higgins, from Harvard, describe as "weak ties." Their research shows that weak ties result in less effective mentoring relationships.[26] Coaching others where the primary concern is achieving organizational goals arouses instrumentality. This may or may not contribute to increased stress, but clearly it will not arouse renewal.

What we are talking about, then, is coaching with compassion, which we define as "helping others in their intentional change process."[27] As we discussed in chapter 5, sustainable changes in people's behavior or habits occur only when they want to change. Therefore, we define coaching as helping people engage their passion in pursuit of *their* dreams and aspirations. To do this, leaders who coach must thus be less focused on themselves.

Another benefit of coaching with compassion is that leaders will be more open to others and to the information around them. This kind of openness means the leader is less likely to succumb to CEO disease. As we have mentioned before, this term describes the likelihood that those around a leader will avoid supplying the leader with important information if it is negative or likely to displease. Leaders therefore become blocked off from criticism and disconfirming information about their strategy, vision, or personal style. They receive instead only positive feedback. Naturally, when this happens, it can easily result in a preoccupation with the self, escalating egocentrism, and even narcissism.

Coaching others with compassion can be an antidote to narcissism because the leader is genuinely focused on others. This decrease in self-preoccupation can help alleviate some of the tendency towards self-aggrandizement that comes along with the power of leadership. At the same time, the improved quality of the leader's relationships makes other people more willing to provide important negative or even critical reactions. Put in a more positive way, the openness to others and their ideas that coaching with compassion creates could result in moving you—the leader—into a relational world in which you get feedback and have to look at it. And because coaching helps you stay connected to others, you will avoid some aspects of the loneliness of the leadership role and the sense of isolation that occurs once someone has been a leader for a few years—and which has been shown to lead to many forms of stress-related illnesses.[28]

Now that we have looked at the benefits of coaching through compassion, how do leaders foster this crucial skill?

Becoming a Great Coach

To be *effective*, a coach, like a leader, needs to *build resonant relationships* with others. That means finding ways to stimulate mindfulness, hope, and compassion in oneself, first. Otherwise, there is absolutely no chance of inspiring those qualities and experiences in the people you coach. Emotional intelligence competencies help, and certain ones are key. One research study showed that self-awareness, social awareness, and a cognitive competency called pattern recognition were necessary for effectiveness in coaching relationships.[29]

Emotional self-awareness helps us keep appropriate boundaries in the coaching relationship. One of the most common mistakes we see in coaching is collusion—this is when care, compassion, and a lack of boundaries between the coach and the other person results in the coach taking on the other person's feelings and reactions as if they were her own. In contrast, a coach who understands herself well can recognize strong emotions in herself and be clear about what's hers, what is the coachee's, and what is shared. The self-aware coach, then, is able to maintain compassionate but objective support without sliding down the slippery slope of collusion.

Social awareness, and in particular empathy and organizational awareness, enable the coach to understand the other person deeply, and to also understand the subtle patterns of thought, behavior, politics, and culture in the organization as well. This understanding enables the coach to support creative—and effective—diagnoses and problem solving when it comes to organizational dilemmas.

Pattern recognition is making sense of seemingly random information. When helping another, effective coaches notice a wide variety of things about the person and how others react to him, and the person's situation—essentially making sense of these many observations through recognizing patterns.

In *Primal Leadership*, we told the story of Juan Trebino, the marketing director of a major oil company. Juan aspired to be the CEO or general manager of a major multinational, and at the age of forty, he was well on his way. But after receiving 360-degree feedback from others in his company, he discovered that his subordinates did not see him helping or coaching them—something that would be key for promotion and reaching his career goals. Although a charming and socially skillful manager, Juan agreed that he did not seem able to help people the way he wanted to. He guessed that his engineering training had made him too problem focused.

Juan was not unusual; indeed, we have noticed that when people first start coaching others, they often focus on the problem that the person presents. As Juan said, "Because of my training as an engineer, when people come to me with a problem, I see the problem, not the person." In this sense, Juan was typical of many others who see people coming to them for help as "problem-bearing platforms." Practice and training in coaching often helps people shift their focus to the interpersonal process and the coaching plan. While helpful, this also tends to preoccupy or distract the coach. Experienced coaches, therefore, go beyond the problem or the process they are using, and focus on the *person* they are trying to help. This evolution from focusing on the problem to the process to the person can be advanced with some coaching on coaching, which leaders can find through many training centers, including the coaching programs the authors conduct with clients.

Juan's path to change began with a plan to coach his son's soccer team for six months. He figured (rightly) that such work would be a good way to learn about coaching people on the job with compassion. It was easy for Juan to get in touch with compassion when it came to his son: he immediately thought of how much he loved him and how he felt as a soccer-team member. He wanted to help him develop with a minimum of frustration and disappointment. That was where we left Juan in our earlier book.

A few years after that coaching experience, Juan went to work for an international consulting firm. Being from Caracas, he was encouraged by corporate management to move into the South American operations. He headed the São Paulo office for three years. During that time, as we were told by one of the consultants working there, the junior consultants and new partners saw him as the most desirable mentor in all of their South American offices. He was popular because he went beyond the role of mentor to establish a coaching relationship. At one point, he was a coach/mentor to over twenty people in the company—besides doing his regular job. It made him feel great and added another dimension to how he was contributing to the success of the company—and to his own resilience. Today Juan reports that he feels better about his work than he ever has before, and his transformation from problem solver to compassionate coach helps him stay regularly renewed as a leader.

Compassion is a word not often heard in the boardroom or at management meetings. But, as we've shown in this chapter, the experience of compassion is key to renewal. And norms of compassion lead to a resonant climate and results.

In the next and final chapter, we offer a summary of the book's main ideas and some concluding thoughts about becoming a resonant leader. But first let us end this chapter with some exercises for exploring compassion. Perhaps the easiest way to find people and role models for coaching with compassion is to look at the people who have helped you. In workshops and courses, we have begun to ask people to reflect on their own experiences to discover some guiding principles of what works. The three reflective exercises that follow seem to help people develop this image of what compassion looks and feels like. Try them.

Exercise 1: Who Helped Me? A Three-Part Exercise

Part A

Think of the people who helped you the most in your life and career. Think of the people about whom you would say, "Without this person, I could not have accomplished or achieved as much as I have. Without this person, I would not be the person I am today."

Write their names on a sheet of paper. Next to each name, describe moments you remember with them that had a lasting impact on you. What did they say or do? Next to your description of those moments, write what you learned or took away from them.

Part B

Now think of the people who have tried to help, manage, or coach you over the last two years. Think of people who conducted performance reviews with you or gave you feedback in any aspect of your life or work. Think of the moments with them. What did they say or do?

Part C

As you consider what each person in these two reflections said or did and how it affected you, what were the differences?

Analysis of Your Reflections

When managers, executives, and advanced professionals do this exercise, they have warm, emotional reactions to the memories of the people who helped them. The feelings come back strongly as they remember moments that may have been tender or challenging, but had a lasting impact. When we recorded these reflections and coded them for which aspect of the change process was primarily involved, we discovered that 80 percent of the moments people recalled involved someone helping them extend their dreams, reach for new aspirations, or consider what it means to be successful or a good person. In other words, these people helped us re-create a new ideal self or personal vision, worked on our sense of hope, endorsed our strengths and capability in areas we doubted or never considered, and improved our mindfulness. Most, if not all, of these remembered moments were part of resonant relationships in which the person helping you was using compassion. The experiences may not have always felt good at the time (although many did), but they were always in the context of a trusting, caring relationship.

In contrast, most of the moments (over 50 percent) people recalled of others trying to help them in the last year or two involved someone giving them feedback and focusing on what they needed to do to improve; that is, focusing on their weaknesses. The application of the business practice of "gap analysis" was rampant as the tactic most used to help someone else work on their "development or performance improvement plan."

It is no wonder many people do not change. We are often doing the wrong things to encourage and support the exploration of a change. In fact, we are often doing the opposite to what has worked so well for most of us.

More importantly, the moments and people who helped us involved resonant relationships and often invoked compassion, even in the memory and telling of the stories to others years later. People who have tried to help us but focused on "data feedback" or "gap analysis" are often trying to engineer a more efficient human resource or help us solve a problem. In either case, we don't respond with the same feelings, and these sessions rarely evoke compassion in the other person.

The way people who helped us talked and what they did create a fascinating set of guidelines for how we might consider acting with others to elicit compassion and move us toward more resonant relationships. It can help leaders consider a way to make themselves more effective in developing others, but also engage the Cycle of Sacrifice and Renewal through compassion in helping others.

Exercise 2: Compassion Practice: Imagine Someone Else's Day

PICK SOMEONE with whom you work or live. Close your eyes and imagine their day from when they get up in the morning until when they go to bed at night. Imagine what they see, hear, think, and feel. What are their hopes and concerns as they go through their day? Who are the people that they see and care about? What are their stressors and worries? What is important to them? Be as specific as you can as you imagine their day, as if you were watching a videotape.

What did you notice from this exercise? What surprised you? What things did you wonder about, or notice that you really didn't know or couldn't imagine? How might you seek this information from them?

NINE

"Be the Change You Wish to See in the World"

P EOPLE WHO THINK they can be truly great leaders without personal transformation are fooling themselves. You cannot inspire others and create the resonant relationships that ignite greatness in your families, organizations, or communities without feeling inspired yourself, and working to be the best person you can be. You must "be the change you wish to see." *

The trouble is that personal transformation is not easy. Facing our own shortcomings is hard work indeed. Honesty with ourselves breeds vulnerability. When we see who we really are and do not like it much, it hurts. Contrary to popular belief, it is not change itself that is so hard; what is hard is being honest with ourselves, looking at ourselves with no filters and admitting that we need to change. Many of us shy away from this honesty, just to

*The title of this chapter is a quote by Mahatma Ghandi.

avoid the vulnerability and, yes, the pain that comes with seeing that we are not all that we might have thought, and in fact not all that we want. Self-discovery is really hard work. Maybe that is why so few people do it, and why so few people are really great human beings and great leaders.

And then there is the other difficulty that the job of being a leader itself actually creates many of the obstacles to becoming a *great* leader. Leadership is tough. It sometimes calls for the kinds of sacrifices described in the many stories of leaders throughout this book. And even for people who manage the role well, and even during good times, the heavy responsibilities, isolation, and looming threats take their toll, day in and day out. Leaders give of themselves almost constantly, often ignoring personal needs and desires—and can soon find themselves in the grips of that special brand of stress that accompanies the job of being the person in charge.

All of this is why personal transformation is not easy, quick, or linear. For many of us, living through it is an experience of surprise or extraordinary contradictions that only make sense much later on. While on the journey, we can easily feel lost, isolated, or simply confused. In hindsight we can probably pinpoint the moment the journey began, yet it is often hard to identify exactly when we began to move away from the "old" life toward one that speaks to our dreams.

But one thing we know for sure: becoming a resonant leader does not happen by accident. Great leadership comes as a result of hard work and a bit of luck. It requires discovering our own noble purpose, living it every day, and being fully aware of ourselves and other people as human beings—mind, body, heart, and spirit. As we have tried to show in these pages, great leaders are resonant within themselves and attuned to others.

Resonant leaders live their values, and they truly care about people. They create a sense of hope about the future and excitement about the present, for themselves and for others.

So, how do you know if you are a resonant leader? Ask yourself these questions:

- Am I inspirational? *and*

- Do I create an overall positive emotional tone that is characterized by hope? *and*

- Am I in touch with others? Do I know what is in others' hearts and minds? Do I experience and demonstrate compassion? *and*

- Am I mindful—authentic and in tune with myself, others, and the environment?

In this book, we have shared stories of people who can answer "yes" to the questions above, and we have shared examples of people who either never had or lost the capacity for resonance. We've shared how the best leaders we know not only create resonance, they sustain it over time by managing the Cycle of Sacrifice and Renewal. The best among us know that almost all of us are susceptible to dissonance, and that personal dissonance spreads quickly to the individuals, teams, and organizations we are charged with leading.

So, great leadership requires attention to creating and sustaining resonance. But how can we do this? How can we sustain resonance, avoid dissonance, and manage the sacrifices and the stress of our leadership roles? The stories we have shared, as well as current research, indicate that it is possible to manage the Cycle of Sacrifice and Renewal through cultivating mindfulness, hope, and compassion in ourselves and others.

We have seen this in action, and it is impressive. We have seen great leaders attend to themselves holistically: they are attuned to themselves in body, mind, heart, and spirit. They are also in touch with and attuned to the people around them, while mindfully attending to the broader environment as well. These leaders are compassionate toward themselves and others. Mindfulness and compassion enable them to create resonance in their relationships while continually renewing themselves.

But perhaps it is hope, above all else, that may be the first real step on a path of healing and renewal. If we cannot envision a better future, how can we consciously make the choices that will get us there? That magical and life-giving quality called hope is more than just optimism. It is also the result of developing a combination of emotional intelligence, intellectual flexibility, the ability to read one's environment and see possibilities, and a basic belief in one's own and others' power to influence our lives.

And it all starts with you. Any kind of personal transformation that ultimately results in you becoming a more resonant leader—and sustaining that success—begins with some kind of a challenge to your mindfulness and a growing awareness of your passion, beliefs, duties, and your true calling. Maybe this realization is a wake-up call—one that will start you on the path of intentional change.

After all, change *is* possible. Despite the sacrifice of leadership, you *can* renew yourself. You can counter the Sacrifice Syndrome to create and sustain resonance. And your resonance will become contagious. People in your families, teams, organizations, communities, and countries will be able to accomplish things that only the human spirit, when inspired and uplifted, can do. So be inspired. Pursue for yourself increased mindfulness, hope, and compassion. The people around you will feel the power of your passion, and will be moved by your commitment to sustaining resonance. They will feel the inspirational power of resonance, see possibilities, and aspire to greatness in themselves, personally and professionally.

Make the choice to be a leader—to be a *great* leader. If we can learn from courageous leaders who have remade themselves, we too can renew ourselves and sustain resonance. The following quote from Goethe captures the hope that drives intentional change, and it provides the best words we can think of with which to conclude the thoughts we have shared with you in this book:[1]

> *What you can do,*
> *or dream you can,*
> *begin it.*
> *Boldness has genius,*
> *power, and magic*
> *in it.*

Power Stress,
the Sacrifice Syndrome,
and the Renewal Cycle

THIS APPENDIX describes the physiological basis for the Sacrifice Syndrome and the Cycle of Sacrifice and Renewal. It goes on to explain how the neural and endocrine processes affect and are affected by emotion, how these interactions influence perception and mood, and how all of this emerges as thoughts and behavior. We offer this explanation as a way to understand a holistic approach to leadership and how the body, as well as the mind, heart and spirit, contribute to resonant leadership.

Leadership and Power Stress

The unique demands of leadership typically trigger a pattern of power stress and the Sacrifice Syndrome. In resonant leaders, this destructive combination is transformed by engaging certain specific experiences—such as mindfulness, hope, and compassion—that result in renewal. In essence, then, leaders are able to sustain resonance through managing the Cycle of Sacrifice and Renewal.[1]

Leadership requires the exercise of influence or power.[2] It requires having an impact on others and making things happen. It involves responsibility for the organization. The higher a person is elevated in an organization, the more "power" is involved in his or her role.[3] Success and effectiveness in leadership positions have been shown to be predicted by a leader's power motivation when modified by unconscious and conscious self-control.[4] As a result of their roles, leaders experience a form of stress called "power stress."[5]

Being in situations that are perceived to be uncontrollable and those involving social evaluation (i.e., where others observe and judge) as well as commitment to reaching important or salient goals or tasks seem to provoke even more stress than that aroused by other types of situations.[6] And humans have what many consider a unique ability to create their own stress by merely anticipating the above, stress-inducing situations.[7] Leadership involves many such events and situations daily. As a result, leaders are under a continuous stream of pressure and arousal of stress. Because power and the exercise of it are central to their role, we can say that leaders experience a great deal of power stress. That is, *power stress is part of the experience that results from the exercise of influence and sense of responsibility felt in leadership positions.*

In addition, leadership effectiveness requires the regular exercise of self-control: placing the good of the organization above personal impulses and needs.[8] Whether or not influence is exercised at the same time, the exercise of self-control is also stressful.[9] In other words, to inhibit an impulse, deny an urge, or hold back from saying something requires conscious or unconscious exertion of energy. A person must take attention from other thoughts or functions to focus on controlling a thought, feeling, or action. Sustaining one's self-control requires constant exercise of this focus and energy. Therefore, effective leadership invokes both power stress and stress resulting from the exercise of self-control.

Chronic Stress and the Sacrifice Syndrome

Arousal of power stress arouses the sympathetic nervous system (SNS), which initiates the classic fight or flight physical response.[10] Indeed, stress in most forms arouses the SNS.[11] Leaders are often in such situations. A major source of their stress involves having to influence others on whom they are dependent so that these others do their jobs; and these people in turn depend on others, and so forth until those actually doing direct work are reached. Meanwhile, the leader feels responsible for the collective effort and progress of the organization. This suggests that leaders are under a steady flow of stress related to the exercise of power and its responsibility. This could be labeled chronic stress, with episodes of acute stress (in the event of a crisis). This combination of types and degrees of stress is said to increase the "allostatic load," leading to a variety of deleterious consequences.[12]

Arousal of the sympathetic nervous system (SNS) results in increased secretion of multiple neurotransmitters including epinephrine and norepinephrine, which are associated with activation of the body through the hypothalamic-pituitary-adrenal (H-P-A) and the sympathetic-adrenal medullary axis, as shown in figure A-1.[13] Individuals experience an increase in systolic and diastolic blood pressure.[14] At the same time, blood flow is redirected to the large muscle groups.[15] Meanwhile, even neural circuitry is reallocated, in the sense that the brain appears to focus on those circuits deemed necessary to survival and there is activation of the right prefrontal cortex (RPFC) more so than on those in the left prefrontal cortex (LPFC).[16] Cortisol is secreted from the adrenal gland and causes dysregulation of inflammation in part by decreasing the body's ability to fight infection by suppressing cell-mediated immunity.[17] Cortisol has the additional impact of

The Sacrifice Syndrome

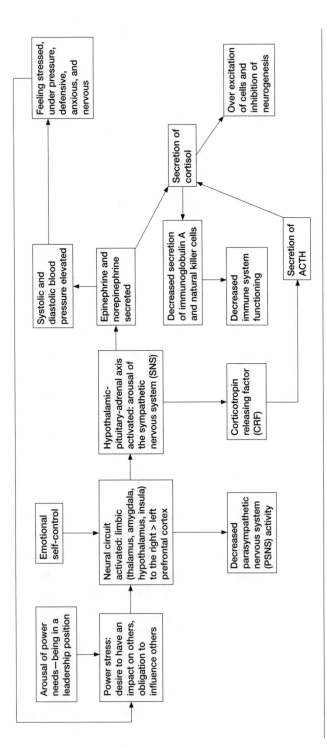

overexciting neurons and inhibiting the potential growth of neural tissue through normal neurogenesis.[18]

This arousal of the SNS and greater activation of the RFPC have been shown to be related to specific emotions, such as fear and disgust.[19] Other negative affect, such as feeling depressed or anxious and "unpleasant engagement with the environment" has been related to such neural circuits as well.[20]

The *chronic* release of glucocorticoids (e.g., cortisol) from the adrenal gland has immunosuppressive effects.[21] One study showed that people with the leadership motive pattern, i.e., high need for power, primacy of need for power over the need for affiliation, and high self-control, showed consistently lower levels of immunoglobulin A (S-IgA), an accepted indicator of immune system functioning.[22] However, it has also been shown that chronic stress may enhance immunoglobulin production, leading to an inappropriate antibody response, thereby increasing the possibility of autoimmune disorders, such as diabetes.[23]

Many common human diseases are attributed in part to over-activation of the SNS and heavy allostatic load, including hypertension, myocardial infarction, chronic infections, peptic ulcer disease, autoimmune disorders, obesity, cardiac arrhythmias, heart failure, diabetes, and susceptibility to cancer.[24] For example, hypertension in young adults is thought to be due to chronic stimulation of the SNS, activating norepinephrine pathways from the brain to the kidneys, skeletal muscle, and heart.[25] Peptic ulcer disease is caused, in part, by the presence of the bacteria *helicobacter pylori*. In this case stress decreases the body's ability to defend and heal from such infections and promotes the formation of ulcers.

Extensive studies of stress have shown that the body's reaction involves more than the stimulation of the SNS; it involves the abatement of the parasympathetic nervous systems (PSNS).[26] While the SNS is responsible for the body's ability to react quickly and effectively to physical or emotional provocation, the PSNS is responsible for recovery from such excitement and for keeping the body functioning at basal levels (i.e., at rest).[27]

The arousal of stress prepares individuals to deal with crisis in the short run. With chronic or repeated activation in the long run, it makes the body susceptible to gastro-intestinal distress, infection, and myocardial events, and as well as disturbing sleep patterns and other normal human functions.[28] Prolonged exposure to stress and arousal of the SNS does harm to the body, in effect draining one's energy and capability to function and innovate.[29] Studies of women suggest a slightly different response to stress, but one that still involves arousal of the SNS.[30] In his 1985 book *Motivation*, McClelland summarized a study suggesting that people high in "need for power" will not experience power stress to the same degree as others.[31] When in power-arousing situations or roles, they may experience sufficiently less power stress and therefore not show the same deleterious effects of power stress on the immune system. But the negative effects of chronic power stress, as that from being in a leadership role, have not been explored in this context.

Some scholars contend that genetic disposition determines why some people are more likely to experience stress and its negative effects than others.[32] While individual differences to stress are expected, as are differences in the severity of secretions emanating from arousal of the SNS, the dynamics of gene expression are believed to have more impact and may literally override inherited dispositions.[33] However, gene expression appears to be affected by environmental conditions, behavioral patterns, diet, and self-management activities.[34] Therefore, it is also now believed by medical researchers that genetic determination may have less impact on physiological processes than the summary of one's experiences and surrounding conditions.

Unchecked or unbalanced behavior in leadership positions, especially when people arouse their self-control in order to be effective, will result in damage over time. This may be labeled as burnout, burn-up, fatigue, an internal sense of restlessness or boredom, and other maladies and illnesses. In their review of the literature on job burnout, Professor Redford Williams and his colleagues highlighted the fact that, "empirical evidence suggests that job-related burnout has important dysfunctional ramifications, implying substantial costs to both organizations and individuals."[35]

The Cycle of Renewal

Renewal can come from several sources. Hope, the experience of compassion, and the practice of meditation leading to mindfulness evoke responses within the human body that arouse the PSNS, reversing the effects of the stress response and arousal of the SNS.[36] This can operate like an antidote to stress, as shown in figure A-2. We call it the renewal cycle.

Caring relationships are the key to arousal of the PSNS. In studies, caring relationships have been associated with lower blood pressure, enhanced immunity, and overall better health.[37] Social networks and social capital have both been found to decrease mortality rates in human population–based studies.[38] In primate studies it has been found that nurturing bonds between parents and their offspring increases the length of survival of the parent— both for males and females. In most primate species the female is the primary caregiver, and the females have a significant survival advantage. However, in owl monkeys, the father is the only parent to care for the offspring, and here the males have a strong survival advantage over their females.[39] Cardiac patients with pets to care for have greater survival rates and lower morbidity profiles than those without pets because of the decreased frequency of SNS activation.[40]

The PSNS helps maintain the body's status quo during times of quiescence, such as during sleeping and eating. It is also responsible for the coordinated response used to reverse the effects of the stimulated SNS after a stressful interaction.[41] Attachments cause a decrease in SNS reactivity via oxytocin and vasopressin's release from the hypothalamus.[42] Oxytocin decreases the hypothalamic-pituitary-adrenal axis and increases parasympathetic activity. The actions of oxytocin have been shown to reduce blood pressure, and reduce stress reactivity, reducing the chemical response elicited by stress and reversing its harmful effects on the body.[43] Social interactions (i.e., attachments) can therefore down-regulate an individual's SNS response to stress both in the presence and

The Cycle of Renewal

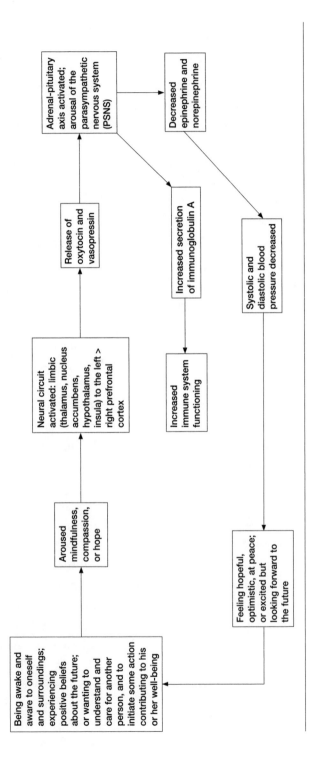

absence of the attachment figure by increasing the basal level activity of the PSNS.[44]

It is believed that during the experience of compassion, as well as hope and mindfulness, a person will more likely have a greater amount of neural activity through the LPFC than through the RPFC.[45] This activity comes from neural circuits that have been shown to relate to emotions such as happiness and amusement, and people experiencing such neural activity report feeling excited, enthusiastic, and interested— best characterized as sense of elation.[46] Such feelings are aroused through neural circuitry emanating from the positive equivalent of the amygdala, the nucleus accumbens.[47] Activation of these circuits evokes a mild sense of euphoria and well-being similar to the sense of hope associated with thought patterns predominating in part in the LPFC.[48] For example, viewing photographs of a person one loves results in relatively more activation of the LPFC and related areas than viewing photographs of friends.[49] In addition, the decreased functioning of the leader's immune system can be reversed by the arousal of the PSNS and other related processes.[50] Barbara Fredrickson and colleagues have shown that positive emotions like these are associated with greater openness of thought and attentiveness.[51]

Additional Exercises

Exercise 1: Insight into Your Operating Philosophy

OUR specific values do not always explain all of our actions. For example, two executives we met in a workshop recently both had "family" as their most important value. One chose to be an international VP of a large company and would fly to another city every Sunday night or Monday morning, returning to his home on Friday night or Saturday morning. The other was a plant manager of a chemical company who had turned down two promotions that were offered to him in the last year—one because it would involve a lot of travel and the other because it would have required his family to move. When asked how each of them could place "family" in the same position of importance and yet have such different life styles and choices, their answers raised another question.

The VP said that he provided for his family. His wife had the home she had always wanted and the freedom to pursue a job that did not pay much but allowed her to make what she felt was an important social contribution. His children could go to the best private schools, whose vision he and his wife trusted. The plant manager said that to him, family being the most important value meant, "That I get home for dinner with my family six nights a week. We spend time together doing whatever families do or, more importantly, what we want to do."

There were two possibilities to understand this dichotomy. One possibility was that one of them was not aware of his actions and its impact on others. For those that knew each of them well, that did not seem to be the case. The second possibility was that the difference was not in their most important value; it was in how they determined value. This we call a person's *operating philosophy*, because whatever philosophy rooted in a particular religion or ethical view of life as a grand scheme people may have, they convert it into a usable moral perceptual screen by making it operational.

In the following pages, we offer the Philosophical Orientation Questionnaire as an exercise you can use to understand aspects of your philosophy in action.[1] Answer the questions by indicating your current preference among the choices for each item by giving each a 1, 2, or 3.

- The option ranked "1" should be your first choice;

- The option ranked "2" should be your second choice;

- The option ranked "3" should be your last choice.

Some of the choices have multiple parts, separated by "OR." For each such item, select the most important part (i.e., the segment separated by an OR you most like), *underline it*, and assign the rank for that item (i.e., the rank reflecting your preference for the underlined word or phrase only, not the other parts of the item).

1. I think of my value, or worth, in terms of:

a. My relationships (e.g., family, friends)

b. My ideas OR ability to invent new concepts OR ability to analyze things

c. My financial net worth OR income

2. I feel most proud of organizations to which I belong when they:

   a. Have created new products/services

   b. Create financial worth for individuals (regardless of whether they are employees, investors, or partners) OR create jobs

   c. Have helped people live easier and healthier lives

3. When someone asks me to commit to spending time on a project, I ask myself:

   a. What can I learn from doing it?

   b. Will it help someone, or is someone counting on me to do it?

   c. Is it worth it to me?

4. Sometimes I will do something for no other reason than because:

   a. I want to figure out why something works the way it does

   b. It has to be done in order to do something else OR get something I want

   c. It will allow me to be with a person I care about OR it would please someone I care about

5. The way I can best contribute to others' lives is to:

   a. Help them find jobs OR develop financial security and independence

   b. Help them develop principles with which to guide their lives

   c. Help them build relationships with others or me OR help them feel better about themselves

6. I get most done when I am with someone I would describe as:

a. Pragmatic

b. Caring

c. Analytic

7. I consider my contribution to society in terms of:

a. Ideas, concepts, or products

b. Money

c. People and relationships

8. I define myself in terms of:

a. What I accomplish OR what I do (i.e., my activity/behavior)

b. My thoughts, values, and ideas

c. The people with whom I have relationships

9. I would describe myself as:

a. Analytic

b. Caring

c. Pragmatic

10. I consider the most important stakeholders of the organization for which I work to be:

a. The field or industry of which we are a part

b. Employees

c. Shareholders/investors OR customers/clients

11. When I read or listen to the news, I often think about:

a. Whether it gives me an idea as to how to make money OR seize an opportunity

b. The statement/s it makes about the nature of our society

c. The people in the stories (i.e., those affected by the events)

12. I believe many of society's problems could be resolved if more people were:

   a. Pragmatic

   b. Analytic

   c. Caring

13. When I have free time, I prefer to:

   a. Do things that need to be done (e.g. chores, duties)

   b. Figure out things OR think about what, why, and how things work and are the way they are

   c. Spend time talking or doing things with specific other people

14. The following are good principles to live by:

   a. Don't put off until tomorrow what you can do today.

   b. Do unto others as you would have others do unto you.

   c. To contemplate the meaning of life and events is an important activity.

15. I have the most fun, stimulation, or excitement when I am with someone I can describe as:

   a. Pragmatic

   b. Caring

   c. Analytic

16. I feel that an organization should contribute to society by:

   a. Providing a place for people to realize their dreams, develop, and contribute

   b. Creating ideas, products, or services

   c. Creating increased net worth (i.e., helping individuals build their net worth) OR creating jobs

17. People have spent a full life if they have:

    a. Cared for others and built relationships

    b. Made a million OR achieved financial security OR created jobs

    c. Developed ideas, products, or methods

18. Individuals should:

    a. Identify their goals and then work toward them, making sacrifices when necessary for their long-term goals

    b. Seek fulfillment through their relationships

    c. Understand themselves and why they do things

19. I will feel successful, if in ten years, I have:

    a. Written articles/books about OR taught people ideas or concepts OR invented new concepts, ideas, or products OR have figured a number of things out

    b. Known many people well OR a number of meaningful relationships

    c. A greater net worth than I do now OR financial security and freedom

20. My time is well spent in an activity if:

    a. I make friends OR meet interesting people

    b. I get interesting ideas OR observations from it

    c. I can make money from it

Scoring the Questionnaire

To calculate your scores on the Philosophical Orientation Questionnaire, copy the number you placed next to each item in the questionnaire (i.e., item 1a is the first item, item 20c is the last item above) to the right of that item on the chart on the next page. Add all of the items in each column for a column subtotal. Then, subtract the subtotal of each column from 60 to obtain a score for Pragmatic Value, Intellectual Value, and Human Value. Your highest score, after you subtract from 60, is the operating philosophy you use most frequently in making decisions, determining value and worth of things and activities.

Item	Pragmatic Value	Intellectual Value	Human Value
1	1.c _____	1.b _____	1.a _____
2	2.b _____	2.a _____	2.c _____
3	3.c _____	3.a _____	3.b _____
4	4.b _____	4.a _____	4.c _____
5	5.a _____	5.b _____	5.c _____
6	6.a _____	6.c _____	6.b _____
7	7.b _____	7.a _____	7.c _____
8	8.a _____	8.b _____	8.c _____
9	9.c _____	9.a _____	9.b _____
10	10.c _____	10.a _____	10.b _____
11	11.a _____	11.b _____	11.c _____
12	12.a _____	12.b _____	12.c _____
13	13.a _____	13.b _____	13.c _____
14	14.a _____	14.c _____	14.b _____
15	15.a _____	15.c _____	15.b _____
16	16.c _____	16.b _____	16.a _____
17	17.b _____	17.c _____	17.a _____
18	18.a _____	18.c _____	18.b _____
19	19.c _____	19.a _____	19.b _____
20	20.c _____	20.b _____	20.a _____
Add the scores			
Subtract from 60 for your TOTAL			

Interpretation

This questionnaire is designed to assist you in exploring your preferences regarding three basic operating philosophies; that of a *pragmatic philosophy*, an *intellectual philosophy*, and a *humanistic philosophy*. We see the worth, benefit, or goodness in ourselves, others, and organizations through the lens of our dominant operating philosophy. Our values are based on beliefs and determine our attitudes. A value typically includes an evaluation (i.e., good or bad designation) of an object or subject. Sets of values form proscriptions and prescriptions (i.e., statements of what *not* to do and what *to* do) that guide our daily life. Values also affect how we interpret and perceive things and events around us. An operating philosophy is a set of values that forms a way of perceiving and therefore determining value.

Pragmatic Philosophy

A pragmatic philosophy appears to be based in philosophies of utilitarianism, pragmatism, or consequentialism. With a dominant pragmatic philosophy, a person will tend to determine the worthiness of an activity in terms of its measurable utility toward desired ends or objectives. If the ends or objectives are not clear, or if their measurability is difficult, the activities will be less valued by someone with a dominant pragmatic philosophy. Although financial variables provide a convenient measure (i.e., in terms of dollars, or local currency), a dominant pragmatic philosophy does not imply that the person is focused or preoccupied with money. Money may merely be the measure used to assess the relative inputs and outputs.

Intellectual Philosophy

An intellectual philosophy appears to be based in a philosophy of rationalism, and possibly in the abstractions of mysticism. With a dominant intellectual philosophy, a person will tend to determine the worthiness of an activity in terms of its conceptual contribution to understanding something. Creating a cognitive map, or a framework describing what we know about something, is at the heart of this operating philosophy. There is a tendency to use abstract and symbolic variables to understand, describe, or explore a phenomenon.

Humanistic Philosophy

A humanistic philosophy appears to be based in philosophies of humanism and communitarianism. With a dominant humanistic philosophy, a person will tend to determine the worthiness of an activity in terms of its affect on specific other people and its impact on the quality of the relationship he/she has with specific others. Intimacy and friendship may be of primary importance to someone with a dominant humanistic philosophy, although the concern for others and relationships may occur in the context of work or other types of settings.

Philosophical Value Orientations

Each one of us believes in the three operating philosophies described above, but we give different weight to each. It is expected that many people will believe one of the three is more important than the others at any point in time in their lives. The relative weighting of the importance to us of these operating philosophies may change over time.

Begin your interpretation of your responses to this questionnaire by asking yourself if the Total scores (i.e., the relative raw scores at the bottom of the scoring sheet after you have subtracted them from 60) reflect your personal beliefs about the importance or ranking of these three philosophies. Just a reminder—because you ranked the most important item from each question with a "1," your scores had to be reversed (subtracted from a maximum score) to generate a number in which high means a stronger philosophy.

The gap between the various scores may reflect the degree to which your preference for any one of these values is closely related or not related. These scores, when close together, suggest that when making decisions in which the two or three philosophies are within, say 3 points, you will feel internally conflicted. You may even feel indecisive.

Another way to examine the meaning of the scores is through a percentile chart. On the following page, find the point on each of the three percentile graphs to place your Total score. Connect the three dots for a line.

The profile reflects a percentile distribution of your scores using the Total score against 1,320 managers, executives, and professionals. This sample has a range of ages from 17 to 63, with an averageage of 32. It is just over one-third female, and comes from U.S., European, South American, and Asian samples.

The raw scores and the percentile distribution are both helpful, but in different ways. The raw scores reflect how you answered each question. The percentile distribution shows your scores relative to the way in which others complete the instrument. The latter is said to adjust for the distortion in responding to questionnaires resulting from the social desirability or political correctness of certain answers. Since both the raw scores and the percentile graph provide slightly different information, you should analyze both pieces of information for insights into your philosophy.

For example, suppose your pragmatic philosophy score was 12, your intellectual philosophy score was 24, and your humanistic philosophy score was 24. Because the raw scores (again, after the subtraction from 60) of the intellectual and humanistic are close, it suggests that you may feel internal conflict at times when a situation involves people you care about and issues of justice, fairness, or following procedures. But when placed on the percentile chart, your percentile scores become pragmatic = 34th percentile, intellectual = 82nd percentile, and humanistic = 43rd percentile. This means that when others see how you act in many situations or over time, you would more frequently try to understand situations, create models or frameworks that explain what is going on rather than thinking about other's feelings (the humanistic philosophy) or calculating the costs and benefits of one versus another option (the pragmatic philosophy). It does not mean that you do not care about people, nor does it mean that you are not pragmatic. It is a *relative* weight. You may show this by which things you think about first, before other ways to look at a situation or problem.

Percentile	Pragmatic 30+	Intellectual 32+	Human 38+
100%			
	29	31	37
	28	30	35
	26	28	34
	24	27	
			33
90%			
	23	26	32
	22	25	
	21		
	20	24	31
80%			
			30
	19	23	
		22	
	18		29
70%			
	17	21	28
			27
60%			
	16	20	26
	15		
50%		19	25
	14		
		18	24
	13		
40%			
		17	23
	12		
		16	22
30%			21
	11	15	
			20
		14	
	10		19
20%	9		18
		13	
			17
	8	12	16
10%	7	11	15
		10	14
	6	9	12
	5	8	
0%			

Exercise 2: Responding to a Wake-up Call: Where Can I Open to My Vulnerability?

W HO in your world can you share your deepest worries and concerns with? Is there someone to whom you can show your vulnerable places, talk about your worst mistakes and your biggest hopes?

Who is this person? _____

When was the last time I had a conversation with him or her? Is it time for me to have another one? _____

If you can't identify a person in your life, would you be willing to seek an outside listener such as a coach or a counselor—some trusted advisor—who could listen and guide you through your thinking and your hopes or concerns? Take some time to talk to someone who has mentioned having such a relationship—what was helpful or not helpful about that relationship for them? Where could you seek such a relationship?

Exercise #3: Morning Mindfulness Check In (a ten-minute exercise)

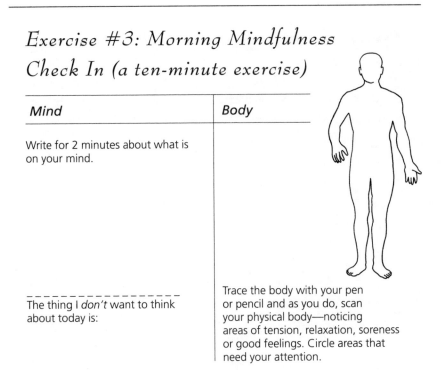

Mind	Body
Write for 2 minutes about what is on your mind.	
_ _ _ _ _ _ _ _ _ _ _ _ _ _ _ _ _ The thing I *don't* want to think about today is:	Trace the body with your pen or pencil and as you do, scan your physical body—noticing areas of tension, relaxation, soreness or good feelings. Circle areas that need your attention.

Heart	Mind
Name your current feeling: _____ Where do you notice it in your body? _____ What concrete action would support your continuing this feeling (if it is useful) or tending to it (if it is distressing)? Write below: _____ _____ _____ _____	Close your eyes and picture something or someone who inspires you. Sit with this feeling for a few deep breaths. Imagine yourself radiating this energy outwards during your day. What are you doing, saying, and feeling? What images came to mind during this exercise?

Exercise 4: Holistic Balance Exercise

IN THIS EXERCISE, use the following "medicine wheel" circle to indicate the various activities you currently engage in as per each category—mind, body, heart, and spirit.

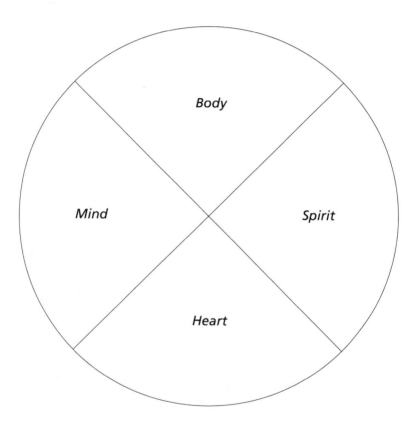

After doing so, reflect on how beneficial these activities are to you.

Write some notes about what you would change if you could.

Now consider your ideal, what activities would you—ideally—be engaging for you to achieve a balanced life (remember—*your* ideal of a balanced life, not someone else's).

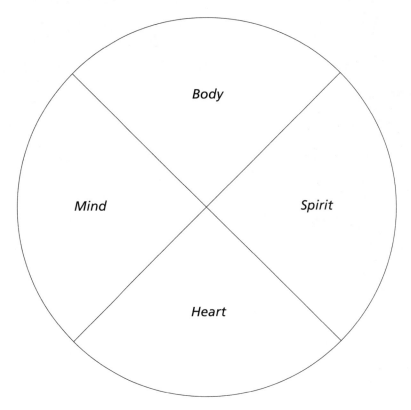

Reflect on the following questions:

What do you want more of in your life and what do you want less of? Do you need to simplify or intensify?

What skills, knowledge, learning, or change in limiting beliefs will help you progress toward the achievement of greater balance?

What must you give up, sacrifice, eliminate, or let go of in order to achieve the balance you want?

Exercise 5: Identifying Defensive Routines

W HEN WE ARE UNDER chronic power stress we have a tendency to turn to our habitual defensive routines to help us feel more in control. While we vary our responses to stress a bit, often we use many of the same strategies based on whether we tend to internalize or externalize problems, and whether we tend to approach or avoid stimuli. If you tend to *internalize* problems, it means you will tend to rely even more on yourself than usual. If you tend to *externalize* problems, you may either over rely on others, or distractions, or you may place blame for the problems outside yourself. If you tend to *approach* problems, you will rush to solve or respond; if you tend to *avoid* problems, you may wait too long to deal with things, or even ignore issues. Use the exercise below to help you identify your typical defensive routines and to assess how your habitual responses are affecting you and others.

> **Step 1: Which of these do you tend to do when under pressure?** Check all that apply to you. Then, choose the top five, and write them on the chart on the following page.

	Approach and Internalize
	I get to work earlier and stay at work later
	I continue to add new projects or take on more roles despite a realistic shortage of time or results
	I constantly remind myself of my own or other's high standards for me
	I expect everyone to perform at my high standards
	I can never say "no"

	Avoid and Internalize
	Move further inside: my office, my projects, my thoughts and concerns
	Become detached from relationships with colleagues, friends and family
	Communicate in short and direct statements about only "essential" information
	Only my mission and goals seem important
	I don't feel I need input from others
	Other people just get in the way

	Approach and Externalize
	I am the only one who knows the answer
	If anyone disagrees with me I will disregard them or make them sorry for disagreeing
	My closest friends and advisors always agree with me
	I never waiver on decisions

	Avoid and Externalize
	Focus on negative aspects of situation
	Wear anger and disappointment as a badge of honor
	Criticize or become cynical, with those who want things to change or have hope
	Blame my mood/circumstances on situation or someone else
	Gather and drink with like minded people and talk about what I think is wrong

Step 2: List your "top five" defensive routines: Note whether they are linked with approaching or avoiding issues or your feelings, and whether you tend to internalize or externalize your responses. Then, write some notes about how your routines affect you, your team/colleagues, and possibly your organization.

My Defensive Routines	Approach, Avoid, Internalize, Externalize	How this affects me: mind, body, heart, spirit	How this affects my team/close colleagues, family	How this affects the degree of resonance or dissonance in my environment

A first step in managing your defensive routines is to recognize what they are. In your list above, you have noted some of the ways you habitually respond, and how these patterns of behavior affect you and others. The next step is to ask yourself "Are these habits serving me, or others well?" While sometimes our defensive routines are in fact helpful, many times they are not. If you notice that your habits are not helping you or others, you will need to focus attention on your responses, monitoring when and how you respond to issues. Ideally, you will become more conscious of your choices, before you act.

Exercise 6: Watching the Dance

OBSERVING RELATIONSHIPS and groups is like watching a dance—there are rhythms, moves, tempos, times of leading, following, freestyle, and choreography. Mindful observance of the dance can give you important information—by framing interaction as a dance, it reminds us to pay attention to more than the conversation, but also to the movement, mirroring, tone, intensity, and cadences. It reminds us to pay attention to who is participating and how they show up. And it reminds us to pay attention to the process within us; what feelings and thoughts are evoked in us as we observe this dance?

Some reminders for "watching the dance":

- Who is participating?

- Who is leading?

- Who is following?

- Is the movement between participants rhythmic or discordant?

- What is the emotional tone?

- What is the emotional intensity?

- How does the dance shift over time?

- What emotions are evoked in me as I observe?

- What thoughts are evoked in me as I observe?

Chapter One

1. Emotional intelligence, resonance, and results: See Daniel Goleman, Richard Boyatzis, and Annie McKee, *Primal Leadership: Realizing the Power of Emotional Intelligence* (Boston: Harvard Business School Press, 2002).

2. Ibid.

Chapter Two

1. "Eduardo": Although a real person, we have used a pseudonym to protect the person from the embarrassing aspects of his story. Throughout the book, we will use a first name, in quotes the first time we mention him or her, to denote when a pseudonym is used.

2. Emotional reality: See Daniel Goleman, Richard Boyatzis, and Annie McKee, *Primal Leadership: Realizing the Power of Emotional Intelligence* (Boston: Harvard Business School Press, 2002). The concept has been expanded by Annie McKee and Fran Johnston in "The Impact and Opportunity of Emotion in Organizational Development" in *The NTL Handbook of Organizational Development and Change* (San Francisco: John Wiley & Sons/Pfeiffer, 2005).

3. Colleen Barrett and Southwest Airlines: Author conversation with Colleen Barrett, 2004. Much of the information about Colleen Barrett was gathered through author interviews and correspondence, 2004–2005.

4. Emotional intelligence and results: With Daniel Goleman, we have

presented numerous studies of the impact of EI and results in *Primal Leadership*. See also Benjamin Schneider and David Bowen, *Winning the Service Game* (Boston: Harvard Business School Press, 1995).

5. "The Most Powerful Women in Business," *Fortune*, October 13, 2003: 103–108.

6. Limbic contagion: Explained by Thomas Lewis, Fari Amini, and Richard Lannon in *A General Theory of Love* (New York: Random House, 2000). People do catch emotions from one another, and they catch them in particular from people they pay a lot of attention to, like leaders. For more on this, see Richard Petty, Leandre Fabriger, and Duane Wegener, "Emotional Factors in Attitudes and Persuasion," in *Handbook of Affective Sciences*, ed. Richard J. Davidson, Klaus R. Sherer, and H. Hill Goldsmith (New York: Oxford University Press, 2003), 752–772.

7. Contagion of emotions: See Elaine Hatfield, John Cacioppo, and Richard Rapson, *Emotional Contagion* (New York: Cambridge University Press, 1994); also see Paul Ekman, Joseph J. Campos, Richard J. Davidson, and Frans DeWaals, *Emotions Inside Out*, Annals of the New York Academy of Sciences, vol. 1000 (New York: New York Academy of Sciences, 2003); and Lyndall Strazdins, "Emotional Work and Emotional Contagion," in *Emotions in the Workplace: Research, Theory and Practice*, ed. Neal Ashkanasy, Wilfred Zerbe, and Charmine Hartel (Westport, CT: Quorum Books, 2000), 232–250.

8. Facial expression of emotion: See Paul Ekman, *Emotions Revealed: Recognizing Faces and Feelings to Improve Communication and Emotional Life* (New York: Henry Holt, 2004).

9. Emotions and communication: See Alfons O. Hamm, Harald T. Schupp, and Almut I. Weike, "Motivational Organization of Emotions: Autonomic Changes, Cortical Responses, and Reflex Modulation," in Davidson, Scherer, and Goldsmith, *Handbook of Affective Sciences*, 187–211.

10. Watching the leader's emotions: Ekman, *Emotions Revealed* (2004); for more on this see Daniel Goleman, *Destructive Emotions: How Can We Overcome Them? A Scientific Dialogue with the Dalai Lama* (New York: Bantam Books, 2003).

11. Catching the message even when it is nonverbal: See Thomas Lewis, Fari Amini, and Richard Lannon and their book *A General Theory of Love* (2000); Paul Ekman, "Should We Call It Expression or Communication?" in *Innovation in Social Science Research* 10, (1997): 333–344; and John Gottman, Robert Levenson, and Erica Woodin, "Facial Expression During Marital Conflict," in *Journal of Family Communication* 1, (2001): 37–57.

12. Reading the leader's mood: Anthony T. Pescosolido, "The Leader's Emotional Impact in Work Groups" (PhD diss., Case Western Reserve University, 2000).

13. Blood pressure rising when working for supervisors with negative styles: Nadia Wager, George Fieldman, and Trevor Hussey, "The Effect on Ambulatory Blood Pressure of Working Under Favorably and Unfavorably Perceived Supervisors," *Occupational Environmental Medicine* 60 (2003): 468–474.

14. Southwest's customer service relationships: Angela Vargo, Public Relations Specialist, Measurement and Evaluation, Southwest Airlines, was very helpful and insightful in our work with Southwest.

15. The link between emotions, attitudes, and behavior: For an overview on many studies linking emotions, attitude, and behavior, see Joseph P. Forgas, "Affective Influences on Attitudes and Judgments" in Davidson, Scherer, and Goldsmith, *Handbook of Affective Sciences*, 563–573.

16. Insulting offers and emotional response: Alan Sanfey, James Rilling, Jessica Aronson, Leigh Nystrom, and Jonathon Cohen, "The Neural Basis of Economic Decision-making in the Ultimatum Game," *Science* 300, no. 5626 (2003): 1755–1758.

17. Destructive emotions: Goleman, *Destructive Emotions*. In this book, renowned scientists and monks, including His Holiness the Dalai Lama, discussed the definition of destructive emotions. According to B. Alan Wallace, "Destructive emotions are those emotions that are harmful to oneself or others" (p. 53). Owen Flanagan posits that a western view of destructive states of mind includes ". . . low self-esteem, overconfidence, harboring negative emotions (e.g., anger, fear, jealousy and envy), lack of compassion, and an inability to have close interpersonal relations" (p. 67). Matthieu Ricard notes that from the Buddhist perspective, " . . . a destructive emotion—which is also referred to as an 'obscuring' or 'afflictive' mental factor—is something that prevents the mind from ascertaining reality as it is" (p. 75); he goes on to say that "Such emotional states impair one's judgment, the ability to make a correct assessment of things. . . . Thus, obscuring emotions impair one's freedom by chaining thoughts in a way that compels us to think, speak, and act in a biased way" (pp. 75–76).

18. Emotional intelligence and leadership competencies: The study of leadership competencies has a long and distinguished history, arguably beginning with David McClelland's early work (see David C. McClelland, "Testing for Competence Rather Than Intelligence," *American Psychologist*

28 (1973): 14–31). This work has been carried further by Richard Boyatzis, Lyle Spencer, Cary Cherniss, Daniel Goleman, and Annie McKee, as well as many other academic researchers and practitioners. See Richard Boyatzis, *The Competent Manager: A Model for Effective Performance* (New York: John Wiley & Sons, 1982); Lyle Spencer Jr. and Signe Spencer, *Competence at Work: Models for Superior Performance* (New York: John Wiley & Sons, 1993); and Cary Cherniss and Mitchel Adler, *Promoting Emotional Intelligence in Organizations: Make Training in Emotional Intelligence Effective* (Washington, DC: American Society of Training and Development, 2000). The foundational research has been extended considerably over the past ten years, and our work and the work of countless colleagues indicates that a set of competencies related to emotional intelligence are distinguishing factors in great leadership. See Daniel Goleman, *Working with Emotional Intelligence*, (New York: Bantam, 1998) for an early review of the theory and research and Goleman, Boyatzis, and McKee, *Primal Leadership*, for extension of the theory and more recent research.

19. Emotional intelligence, leadership style, and resonance: See Daniel Goleman, "What Makes a Leader?" *Harvard Business Review* (November–December 1998): 92–102; and Goleman, Boyatzis, and McKee, *Primal Leadership*. Also see Daniel Goleman, Richard Boyatzis, and Annie McKee, "Primal Leadership: The Hidden Driver of Great Performance," Harvard Business Review (December 2001): 42–51. For a discussion of clustering of these abilities or competencies, see Richard Boyatzis, Daniel Goleman, and Kenneth Rhee, "Clustering Competence in Emotional Intelligence: Insights from the Emotional Competence Inventory (ECI)," in *Handbook of Emotional Intelligence*, ed. Reuven Bar-On and James D. A. Parker (San Francisco: Jossey-Bass, 2000), 343–362.

20. Pattern recognition: This cognitive competency is, like competencies related to emotional intelligence, a defining factor in differentiating outstanding leaders from their more average peers. See Boyatzis, *The Competent Manager*; Spencer and Spencer, *Competence at Work*; Peter Senge, *The Fifth Discipline* (New York: Currency Doubleday, 1994); Richard Boyatzis, "Using Tipping Points of Emotional Intelligence and Cognitive Competencies to Predict Financial Performance of Leaders," *Psicothemia* (in press). See also Dominic Massaro, "A Pattern Recognition Account of Decision-making," in *Memory & Cognition* 22, (1994): 616–627

21. The link between emotion, cognition, and action: See Daniel Goleman, *Emotional Intelligence* (New York: Bantam, 1995), Goleman, Boyatzis, and McKee, *Primal Leadership*.

Chapter Three

1. Leadership requires the use of power: John Kotter, *Power in Management: How to Understand, Acquire, and Use It* (New York: AMACOM Press, 1979); John Kotter, *The General Managers* (New York: Free Press, 1982); David McClelland, *Power: The Inner Experience* (New York: Irvington Press, 1975); Gary A. Yukl, *Leadership in Organizations*, 5th edition (Upper Saddle River, NJ: Prentice Hall, 2001) and Gary A. Yukl and David Van Fleet, "Theory and Research on Leadership in Organizations," in *Handbook of Industrial and Organizational Psychology*, 2nd edition, vol. 3, ed. Marvin D. Dunnette and Leaetta M. Hough (Palo Alto, CA: Consulting Psychologists Press, 1990): 147–197. The early research on power stress was conducted by motivational psychologist David McClelland and his colleagues; see David McClelland, *Human Motivation* (Glenview, IL: Scott, Foresman & Co., 1985).

2. Defensive routines: Chris Argyris, *Strategy, Change & Defensive Routines* (Boston: Pitman Publishing, 1985).

3. Power stress: Alan F. Fontana, Roberta L. Rosenberg, Jonathan L. Marcus, and Robert D. Kerns, "Type A Behavior Pattern, Inhibited Power Motivation, and Activity Inhibition," *Journal of Personality and Social Psychology* 52 (1987): 177–183; John B. Jemmott III, "Psychosocial Stress, Social Motives and Disease Susceptibility," (PhD diss., Harvard University, 1982); David McClelland, *Human Motivation* (1985); David McClelland, Erik Floor, Richard Davidson, and Clifford Saron, "Stressed Power Motivation, Sympathetic Activation, Immune Function, and Illness," *Journal of Human Stress* 6, no. 2 (1980): 11–19; David McClelland and John B. Jemmott III, "Power Motivation, Stress, and Physical Illness," *Journal of Human Stress* 6, no. 4, no. 2 (1980): 6–15; David McClelland and Carol Kirshnit, "Effects of Motivational Arousal on Immune Function," (unpublished manuscript, Harvard University, 1982); and David McClelland, S. Locke, R. Williams, and M. Hurst, "Power Motivation, Distress and Immune Function," (unpublished manuscript, Harvard University, 1982); Richard Boyatzis, Melvin Smith, and Nancy Blaize, "Sustaining Leadership Effectiveness Through Coaching and Compassion: It's Not What You Think," *Academy of Management Learning and Education* (forthcoming); also see the references cited in note 1 for this chapter and appendix A.

4. Chronic stress and acute stress: Suzanne Segerstom and Gregory Miller, "Psychological Stress and the Human Immune System: A Meta-analytic Study of 30 Years of Inquiry," *Psychological Bulletin* 130, no. 4 (2004): 601–630.

5. Power arousal and leadership effectiveness: David McClelland, *Human Motivation* (1985); David McClelland and Richard Boyatzis, "The Leadership Motive Pattern and Long Term Success in Management," *Journal of Applied Psychology* 67 (1982): 737–743; Fontana et al., "Type A Behavior Pattern . . ."; Ruth L. Jacobs and David McClelland, "Moving Up the Corporate Ladder: A Longitudinal Study of the Leadership Motive Pattern and Managerial Success in Women and Men," *Consulting Psychology Journal: Practice and Research* 46 (1994): 32–41; and Sharon R. Jenkins, "Need for Power and Women's Careers over 14 Years: Structural Power, Job Satisfaction, and Motive Change," *Journal of Personality and Social Psychology*, 66 (1994): 155–165.

6. The brain and stress: This process is explained in more technical detail in appendix A.

7. Exercise of self-control is stressful: Roy Baumeister, Todd Heatherton, and Diane Tice, *Losing Control: How and Why People Fail at Self-Regulation* (New York: Academic Press, 1994); Roy Baumeister, "Ego Depletion and Self-regulation Failure: A Resource Model of Self-control," *Alcoholism: Clinical and Experimental Research* 27, no. 2 (2003): 281–284; Robert Sapolsky, "The Physiology and Pathophysiology of Unhappiness" in *Well-Being: The Foundation of Hedonic Psychology*, ed. Daniel Kahnemann, Edward Diener, and Norbert Schwarz (New York: Russell Sage Foundation, 1999), 453–469.

8. Stress, affect, and cognitive functioning: See Mustafa Al'Absi, Kenneth Hugdahl, and William Lovallo, "Adrenocortical Responses and Altered Working Memory Performance," *Psychophysiology* 39 (2002): 95–99; Hedva Braunstein-Bercovitz, Inbal Dimentman-Ashkenasi, and R. E. Lubow, "Stress Affects the Selection of Relevant from Irrelevant Stimuli," *Emotion* 1 (2001): 182–192; Michael Ennis, Kimberly Kelly, Mary K. Wingo, and Paul L. Lambert, "Cognitive Appraisal Mediates Adrenomedullary Activation to a Psychological Stressor," *Stress and Health* 17 (2001): 3–8; Peter Hancock and Paula A. Desmond, *Stress, Workload and Fatigue* (Mahwah, NJ: Lawrence Erlbaum, 2001).

9. Effects of cortisol: Sally S. Dickerson and Margaret Kemeny, "Acute Stressors and Cortisol Responses: A Theoretical Integration and Synthesis of Laboratory Research," *Psychological Bulletin* 130, no. 3 (2004): 355–391; Oakley Ray, "How the Mind Hurts and Heals the Body," *American Psychologist* 59, no.1 (2004): 29–40; Suzanne Segerstom and Gregory Miller, "Psychological Stress and the Human Immune System: A Meta-analytic Study of 30 Years of Inquiry," *Psychological Bulletin* 130, no. 4 (2004): 601–630; Gregory Miller, Sheldon Cohen, Sarah Pressman, Anita

Barkin, Bruce Rabin, and John Treanor, "Psychological Stress and Antibody Response to Influenza Vaccination: When Is the Critical Period for Stress, and How Does It Get Inside the Body?" *Psychosomatic Medicine* 66, no. 2 (2004): 215–223.

10.   Ibid.

11.   Process of neurogenesis; stem cells and the hippocampus: Peter S. Erikson, Ekaterina Perfilieva, Thomas Bjork-Eriksson, Ann-Marie Alborn, Claes Nordburg, Daniel Peterson, and Fred Gage, "Neurogenesis in the Adult Human Hippocampus," *Nature Medicine* 4, (1998): 1313–1317; Stephan Harzsch, Julie Miller, Jeanie Benton, and Barbara Belz, "From Embryo to Adult: Persistent Neurogenesis and Apoptotic Death Shape the Lobster Deutocerebrum," *Journal of Neuroscience* 19, no. 9 (1999): 3472–3485; Daniel Goleman, Richard Boyatzis, and Annie McKee, *Primal Leadership: Realizing the Power of Emotional Intelligence* (Boston: Harvard Business School Press, 2002).

12.   Losing neural capacity to learn: The inhibition of neurogenesis and destruction of existing neural tissue decreases the capability of the brain to absorb new material or learn. See the references in endnote 11 (above); Arturo Alvarez-Buylla and Sally Temple, "Stem Cells in the Developing and Adult Nervous System," *Journal of Neurobiology* 36, (1998): 105–110; and Elizabeth Gould, Anna Beylin, Patima Tanapat, Alison Reeves, and Tracey J. Shors, "Learning Enhances Adult Neurogenesis in the Hippocampal Formation," *Nature and Neuroscience* 2, (1999): 260–265.

13.   Uncertainty, uncontrollable situations, and social evaluation arousing stress: Dickerson and Kemeny, "Acute Stressors."

14.   The link between thoughts, feelings, and action: Psychologists Aaron Beck and Martin Seligman have explained the interaction of cognition, affect, and behavior and their relation to our effectiveness—and happiness—in life. In the now landmark work *Depression: Clinical, Experimental, and Theoretical Aspects* (New York: Harper and Row, 1967), Aaron Beck outlined for the first time what came to be called cognitive behavioral therapies—processes for enabling people to change through revising their thoughts and thought patterns while focusing on breaking the chain of thoughts and dysfunctional behaviors. His work was a foundation of Martin Seligman's early research and writing on the impact of negative and positive cognition on one's effectiveness in life (see Martin E. P. Seligman, *Learned Optimism: How to Change Your Mind and Your Life*, (New York: A.A. Knopf, 1991). In the past several years, Seligman and his colleagues have moved dramatically away from a focus on dysfunction toward a focus on positive experience, prevention, and mental health as opposed to sickness. This movement,

called "positive psychology," has at its core the belief that building on our strengths is as, if not more, important to our mental, emotional, and spiritual health than is compensating for our weaknesses and overcoming psychological dysfunction. For more on this, see Jane E. Gillham and Martin E. P. Seligman, "Footsteps on the Road to Positive Psychology," *Behavior Research and Therapy* 37 (1999): 163–173, Martin E. P. Seligman and Mihaly Csikszentmihalyi, "Positive Psychology: An Introduction," *American Psychologist* 55, (2000): 5–14; and Martin E. P. Seligman, *Authentic Happiness: Using the New Positive Psychology to Realize Your Potential for Lasting Fulfillment* (New York: Free Press, 2002).

15. Self-efficacy: Albert Bandura, in his many works on the impact of self-efficacy on human behavior and effectiveness, has been a driving force in enabling us to see how our beliefs about our ability to impact events affect what we do and the outcomes (see Albert Bandura, *Social Learning Theory* (Englewood Cliffs, NJ: Prentice Hall, 1977)); "Self-evaluative and Self-efficacy Mechanisms Governing the Motivational Effects of Goal Systems," *Journal of Personality and Social Psychology* 45, no. 5 (1977): 1017–1028; "Human Agency in Social Cognitive Theory," *American Psychologist* 44, (1989): 1175–1184; *Self-efficacy: The Exercise of Self-control* (New York: W.H. Freeman, 1997).

16. Mark R. Leary on maintaining positive self image: See "The Self and Emotion: The Role of Self-Regulation in the Generation and Regulation of Affective Experience," in Davidson, Scherer, and Goldsmith, *Handbook of Affective Sciences*, 773–786.

17. The fundamental attribution error: This was first articulated as a result of a classic study conducted by Jones and Harris in 1967. The study looked at the attributions people made about speech-givers speaking on a controversial topic. Even when the listeners knew that speakers took a position based merely on a flip of a coin, they attributed the expressed opinion to what "kind" of person the speech-giver was, rather than the fact of how positions were assigned; see Edward E. Jones and Victor Harris, "The Attribution of Attitudes," *Journal of Experimental Social Psychology* 3, (1967): 1–24. Subsequent studies have supported the initial findings, and in fact the "fundamental attribution error" is one of the bedrock concepts in the field of social psychology; see David Trafinow, Monica Armendariz, and Laura Madson, "A Test of Whether Attributions Provide for Self Enhancement or Self-defense," *Journal of Social Psychology* 144, (2004): 453–463; and John A. Wagner and Richard Z. Gooding, "Equivocal Information and Attribution: An Investigation of Managerial Sensemaking," *Strategic Management Journal* 18, (1997): 275–286.

18. CEO disease: First described by John Byrne in "CEO Disease," *Business Week*, April 1, 1991, 52–59; see also Michelle Conlin and Kathleen Kerwin, "CEO Coaches," *Business Week*, November, 11, 2002: 98–104.

19. Leadership behavior and the impact on individuals and group climate: A database on leadership behavior, style, and climate has been compiled by McBer & Company (now The Hay Group). This database was originally analyzed by Stephen Kelner Jr. See Stephen Kelner Jr., Christine Rivers, and Kathleen O'Connell, *Managerial Style as a Behavioral Predictor of Organizational Climate* (Boston: McBer & Company, 1996). The sample included leaders from Europe, Africa, North America, Australia, and the Pacific Rim; half were American.

20. Diseases from chronic stress: See appendix A for a detailed discussion and references to professional literature documenting these relationships.

21. Ineffective leaders: John Kotter showed that 53 percent of *Fortune* 500 CEOs did not have the skills to do their jobs adequately (John Kotter, *The Leadership Factor* (New York: Free Press, 1988)); analysis of the data reported in Richard Boyatzis, *The Competent Manager: A Model for Effective Performance* (New York: John Wiley & Sons, 1982), suggests that over half of the people in management jobs are not adding value to their organizations.

Chapter Four

1. "Ought self": In *The Hungry Spirit: Beyond Capitalism: A Quest for Purpose in the Modern World* (London: Hutchinson, 1997), Charles Handy described the traps we fall into when we live our lives based on the "shoulds" we have internalized. See also Richard Boyatzis, R. E. Murphy, and Jane Wheeler, "Philosophy as a Missing Link between Values and Behavior," *Psychological Reports* 86 (2000): 47–64.

2. For a review on the effects of negative emotions on physical and psychological functioning, see Daniel Goleman, *Destructive Emotions: How Can We Overcome Them? A Scientific Dialogue with the Dalai Lama*, (New York: Bantam Books, 2003).

3. Renewal: See appendix A for a detailed description of the internal processes and references.

4. Power, stress, and the power of positive emotions: See the references on power, stress, and power stress in notes 1, 3, 4, and 5 in chapter 3; note 15 in chapter 3 on the power of positive emotion; and appendix A. See also Goleman, *Destructive Emotions*.

5. Subjective well-being: Subjective well-being is a measure of one's own (subjective) evaluation of one's overall life. It is marked by the frequent presence of positive emotions, and the ratio of positive to negative emotions.

Subjective well-being research focuses on understanding what can help people live happier and more rewarding lives, rather than focusing on pathology or illness. For more on subjective well-being see: Ed Diener, Eunkook Suh, Richard Lucas, and H. Smith, "Subjective Well-being: Three Decades of Progress," *Psychological Bulletin* 125 (1999): 276–302; Ed Diener and Richard Lucas, "Subjective Emotional Well-being," in *Handbook of Emotion*, 2nd edition, ed. Michael Lewis and Jeannette Haviland-Jones (New York: Guilford, 2000), 325–337; Daniel Kahneman, "Objective Happiness," in *Well-Being: The Foundations of Hedonic Psychology*, ed. Daniel Kahneman, Ed Diener, and Norbert Schwarz (New York: Russell Sage Foundation), 3–25; Ed Diener and Martin E. P. Seligman, "Beyond Money: Toward an Economy of Well-being," *Psychological Science in the Public Interest 5*, (2004), 1–31.

6. Positive emotions and effectiveness: See Goleman, *Destructive Emotions*. See also Brian Knutson, Grace Fong, S. Bennett, Charles Adams, and Daniel Homer, "A Region of Mesialprefrontal Cortex Tracks Monetarily Rewarding Outcomes: Characteristics with Rapid Event-related fMRI," *Neuroimage* 18, (2003): 263–272.

7. Positive emotions and effectiveness: See Goleman, *Destructive Emotions*; Barbara Fredrickson and Christine Branigan, "Positive Emotions Broaden the Scope of Attention and Thought-action Repertoires," *Cognition and Emotion* (in press); Michele Tugade and Barbara Fredrickson, "Resilient Individuals Use Positive Emotions to Bounce Back from Negative Emotional Experiences," *Journal of Personality and Social Psychology* (in press); Barbara Fredrickson, "Gratitude, Like Other Positive Emotions, Broadens and Builds," in *The Psychology of Gratitude*, ed. Robert Emmons and Michael McCullough (New York: Oxford University Press, forthcoming); Barbara Fredrickson, Michele Tugade, Christian Waugh, and Gregory Larkin, "What Good Are Positive Emotions in Crises?: A Prospective Study of Resilience and Emotions Following the Terrorist Attacks on the United States on September 11th, 2001," *Journal of Personality and Social Psychology* 84 (2003): 365–376; Barbara Fredrickson, "Positive Emotions and Upward Spirals in Organizational Settings," in *Positive Organizational Scholarship*, ed. Kim Cameron, Jane Dutton, and Robert Quinn (San Francisco: Berrett-Koehler, 2003); B. L. Fredrickson, "The Role of Positive Emotions in Positive Psychology: The Broaden-and-build Theory of Positive Emotions," *American Psychologist* 56 (2001): 218–226.

8. Seven-year cycle: Erik Erikson, *The Life Cycle Completed: A Review* (New York: W.W. Norton & Co, 1985); Daniel Levinson with Charlotte Darrow, Edward B. Klein, Maria H. Levinson., and Braxton McKee,

The Seasons of a Man's Life (New York: Knopf, 1978); Daniel Levinson, in collaboration with Judy Levinson, *The Seasons of a Woman's Life* (New York: Knopf, 1996); Edgar Schein, *Career Dynamics: Matching Individual and Organization Needs* (Reading, MA: Addison-Wesley, 1978); Gail Sheehy, *New Passages: Mapping Your Life Across Time* (New York: Random House, 1995).

9. Cycle of excitement and boredom: Richard Boyatzis and David A. Kolb, "Performance, Learning, and Development as Modes of Growth and Adaptation Throughout Our Lives and Careers," in *Career Frontiers: New Conceptions of Working Lives*, ed. Maury Peiperl, Michael Arthur, Rob Goffee, and Tim Morris (London: Oxford University Press, 1999): 76–78. See also Levinson et al., *The Seasons of a Man's Life*; Levinson and Levinson, *The Seasons of a Woman's Life*; and Erickson, *The Life Cycle Completed*.

10. Burnout: Richard Boyatzis, Melvin Smith, and Nancy Blaize, "Developing Sustainable Leaders through Coaching and Compassion," *Academy of Management Learning and Education* (in press); Steven Berglas, *Reclaiming the Fire: How Successful People Can Overcome Burnout* (New York: Random House, 2001).

11. Wake-up calls: Richard Boyatzis, Annie McKee, and Daniel Goleman: "Reawakening Your Passion for Work," *Harvard Business Review* (April 2002): 87–94. Here we make the point that most people, especially leaders or others who have significant responsibility, periodically go through periods of discontent, restlessness, and possibly rejuvenation. Our research and experience showed us that there are clues that indicate when personal and or professional change is really necessary for us to continue to be effective or happy in life and work. These tend to be a rumbling sense of unease or a sudden enlightenment when we experience a traumatic event such as a death, divorce or major failure, or even a positive event such as the birth of a child. Once awakened, there are several strategies for managing the process of reflection and change, including: calling a time-out; enrolling in a new and challenging educational program; creating what we call reflective structures; working with a coach; or reframing how we are engaging in the various roles in our lives, rethinking how best to enact those roles, and consciously begin to practice new ways of being.

12. See "Stocking a Global Pantry: An Interview with Unilever's Niall FitzGerald," *Wall Street Journal*, May 24, 2004, B-1.

13. CEO disease: First described by John Byrne in "CEO Disease," *Business Week*, April 1, 1991, 52–59; see also Michelle Conlin and Kathleen Kerwin, "CEO Coaches," *Business Week*, November 11, 2002, 98–104.

14. Destructive emotions: See Goleman, *Destructive Emotions*.

15. Positive emotions and effectiveness: Ibid.; also see notes 5 and 7 for this chapter.

16. The power of positive emotions and power stress: Ibid.

17. Resilience and hardiness: Karen Reivich and Andrew Shatte, *The Resilience Factor: How Changing the Way You Think Will Change Your Life for Good* (New York: Broadway Books, 2002).

18. The "self": Philosophers, priests, and psychologists have been preoccupied with the nature of the self for thousands of years. See Aristotle, *De Anima*, in *The Works of Aristotle*, vol. 3, ed. W. D. Ross, (Oxford: Clarendon Press, 1931); Dalai Lama, *The Art of Happiness* (New York: Riverhead Books, 1998); Charles Darwin, *The Expression of Emotion in Man and Animals*, 2nd edition, (Chicago: Chicago University Press, 1965); Margaret Mead, *Coming of Age in Samoa: A Psychological Study of Primitive Youth for Western Civilization* (New York: Morrow, 1928/1988); Carl Jung, *The Integration of Personality* (New York: Farrar & Rhinehart, 1939); Thomas Merton, *New Seeds of Contemplation* (New York: Plough Publishing, 1974). See Mark R. Leary, "The Self and Emotion: The Role of Self-Regulation in the Generation and Regulation of Affective Experience" in *Handbook of Affective Sciences*, ed. Richard J. Davidson, Klaus R. Scherer, and H. Hill Goldsmith (New York: Oxford University Press, 2003).

19. Positive affect and adaptability: See Gregory F. Ashby, Alice M. Isen, and U. Turken, "A Neuropsychological Theory of Positive Affect and Its Influence on Cognition," *Psychological Review* 106, no. 3 (July 1999): 529–550. Excellent summaries of the research are to be found in Davidson, Scherer, and Goldsmith, *Handbook of Affective Sciences*.

20. Imagining the future: Early research in the field of management focused heavily on goal-setting theory. Results of many studies indicate that people who can envision a goal and then articulate it in a way that is realistic, challenging, and specific are likely to achieve that goal. But recent studies have suggested a "learning goal" orientation is more effective in uncertain situations than specific targets. For the classic work in this area, see Edwin Locke, "Toward a Theory of Task Motivation and Incentives," *Organizational Behavior and Human Performance* 3 (1968): 157–189; John Hollenbeck and Howard J. Klein, "Goal Commitment and the Goal Setting Process: Problems, Prospects, and Proposals for Future Research," *Journal of Applied Psychology* 40 (1987): 213–220; Gerald H. Seits, Gary P. Latham, Kevin Tasa, and Brandon W. Latham, "Goal-setting and Goal Orientation: An Integration of Two Different Yet Related Literatures," *Academy of Management Journal* 47, no. 2, (2004): 227–239. Annie McKee's research ("Individual Differences in Planning for the Future" (PhD diss.,

Case Western Reserve University, 1991) indicated that beyond setting specific measurable goals, some people can find a powerful vision of the future through holding certain values and beliefs as "guiding lights" to their planning. These people demonstrate a sense of self-efficacy and feelings that they can, indeed, impact their destiny. Richard Boyatzis has been studying the impact of envisioning an ideal state for many years, beginning as early as 1970 in early work on goal setting (see David A. Kolb and Richard E. Boyatzis, "Goal Setting and Self Directed Change," *Human Relations* 23, no. 5 (1970): 439–457). His more recent work includes several articles in press; "Intentional change theory from a complexity perspective," (forthcoming) and "The Ideal Self as a Driver of Change," with Kleio Akrivou-Naperksy, *Journal of Management Development* (forthcoming).

21. Reflecting on values exercises: This exercise was adapted and further developed from numerous exercises and instruments used to assess one's values based on the ideas of Milton Rokeach, described in *The Nature of Human Values* (New York: Free Press, 1973).

Chapter Five

1. Intentional Change Theory: Richard Boyatzis, "Intentional Change Theory from a Complexity Perspective," *Journal of Management Development* (forthcoming); Daniel Goleman, Richard Boyatzis, and Annie McKee *Primal Leadership: Realizing the Power of Emotional Intelligence* (Boston: Harvard Business School Press, 2002); Richard Boyatzis and Kleio Akrivou-Naperksy, "The Ideal Self as a Driver of Change" *Journal of Management Development* (forthcoming); Richard Boyatzis, Cindy Frick, and Ellen Van Oosten, "Developing Leaders Throughout an Entire Organization by Developing Emotional Intelligence Competencies, " in *The Talent Management Handbook: Creating Organizational Excellence by Identifying, Developing, and Positioning High-Potential Talent*, ed. Lance Berger and Dorothy Berger (New York: McGraw-Hill, 2003); Richard Boyatzis "Developing Emotional Intelligence," in *The Emotionally Intelligent Workplace*, ed. Cary Cherniss and Daniel Goleman (San Francisco: Jossey-Bass, 2001); Richard Boyatzis, "Stimulating Self-directed Learning through the Managerial Assessment and Development Course," *Journal of Management Education*, 18, no. 3 (1994), 304–323; David A. Kolb, and Richard E. Boyatzis, "Goal setting and Self-directed Behavior Change," *Human Relations* 23, no. 5 (1970): 439–457.

2. Longitudinal studies of learning and developing management and leadership competencies: These were reviewed in chapter 6 of Goleman, Boyatzis, and McKee, *Primal Leadership*. The key references include: Richard

Boyatzis, Elizabeth C. Stubbs, and Scott N. Taylor, "Learning Cognitive and Emotional Intelligence Competencies through Graduate Management Education," *Academy of Management Learning and Education* 1, no. 2 (2002): 150–162; Richard E. Boyatzis, Scott S. Cowen, and David A. Kolb, *Innovations in Professional Education: Steps on a Journey from Teaching to Learning* (San Francisco: Jossey-Bass, 1995); Ronald Ballou, David Bowers, Richard E. Boyatzis, and David A. Kolb, "Fellowship in Lifelong Learning: An Executive Development Program for Advanced Professionals," *Journal of Management Education* 23, no. 4 (1999): 338–354; Henry Cutter, Richard Boyatzis, and David D. Clancy, "The Effectiveness of Power Motivation Training for Rehabilitating Alcoholics," *Journal of Studies on Alcohol* 38, no. 1, (1977): 131–141; Richard Boyatzis, "Power Motivation Training: A New Treatment Modality," *Work in Progress on Alcoholism: Annals of the New York Academy of Sciences* 273, ed. Frank A. Seixas and Suzie Eggleston (New York: New York Academy of Sciences, 1976), 525–532; Cary Cherniss and Mitchell Adler, *Promoting Emotional Intelligence in Organizations: Make Training in Emotional Intelligence Effective* (Washington, DC: American Society for Training and Development, 2000); *Learning That Lasts: Integrating Learning, Development, and Performance in College and Beyond*, ed. Marcia Mentkowski and Associates, (San Francisco: Jossey-Bass, 2000); Richard E. Boyatzis., David Leonard, Kenneth Rhee, and Jane V. Wheeler, "Competencies Can Be Developed, but Not the Way We Thought," *Capability*, no. 2 (1996): 25–41; David C. McClelland and David G. Winter, *Motivating Economic Achievement* (New York: Free Press, 1969); David Miron and David C. McClelland, "The Impact of Achievement Motivation Training on Small Business," *California Management Review* 21, no. 4 (1979): 13–28; Jane V. Wheeler, "The Impact of Social Environment on Self-directed Change and Learning," (PhD diss., Case Western Reserve University, 1999); David Leonard, "The Impact of Learning Goals on Self-directed Change in Education and Management Development," (PhD diss., Case Western Reserve University, 1996); and Kenneth Rhee, "Journey of Discovery: A Longitudinal Study of Learning During a Graduate Professional Program," (PhD diss., Case Western Reserve University, 1997).

3. Maslow's hierarchy of needs: One of the better known, if not thoroughly validated, theories of human motivation was put forth in 1954 by Abraham Maslow in *Motivation and Personality*, 2nd edition (New York: Harper & Row, 1970). Maslow postulated that people first need to meet basic physiological needs—food, water, etc. Then they are free to consider safety needs, then belongingness, followed by esteem, and finally self-actualization.

4. Positive emotional attractor: See the discussion of positive versus negative attractors in chapter 7.

5. The power of vision: See chapter 7 in Goleman, Boyatzis, and McKee, *Primal Leadership*.

6. Emotion and vision: It is believed that the potency of focusing one's thoughts on the desired end state is driven by the emotional components of the brain. See Daniel Goleman, *Emotional Intelligence: Why It Can Matter More Than IQ for Character, Health and Lifelong Achievement* (New York: Bantam Books, 1995).

7. Self-protection and delusion: See Daniel Goleman, *Vital Lies, Simple Truths: The Psychology of Self-deception* (New York: Simon & Schuster, 1985); Delroy L. Paulhus and Karen Levitt, "Desirable Responding Triggered by Affect: Automatic Egotism," *Journal of Personality and Social Psychology* 52, no. 2 (1987): 245–259; Phebe Cramer, "Defense Mechanisms in Psychology Today: Further Processes for Adaptation," *American Psychologist* 55, no. 6 (2000): 637–646; George E. Vaillant, *The Wisdom of the Ego* (Cambridge, MA: Harvard University Press, 1993); Goleman, *Emotional Intelligence*.

8. Leadership style: For a review of leadership styles and their link to emotional intelligence and resonance, see Daniel Goleman, "What Makes a Leader?" *Harvard Business Review* (November–December, 1998): 93–102; and Goleman, Boyatzis, and McKee, *Primal Leadership*.

9. The book on emotional intelligence: The book Ellen's boss handed her was Daniel Goleman's *Working with Emotional Intelligence* (New York: Bantam Books, 1998).

10. 360-degree feedback on emotional intelligence: Self-assessment of emotional intelligence may be useful as a tool for reflection, but it is not likely to be an accurate measure of the associated behaviors. The reason is simple. Self-awareness is a cornerstone of emotional intelligence. It will be unlikely, if not impossible, that a person deficient in this area will accurately assess his or her own emotional intelligence. According to research on the Emotional Competence Inventory, average internal consistency of self-ratings is .75, and the average internal consistency of total others' rating is .85. Therefore, we recommend 360-degree feedback as a way to get a comparative perspective on a person's emotional intelligence. This instrument, designed by Richard Boyatzis and Daniel Goleman and distributed by the Hay Group, has been thoroughly researched for construct validation, reliability, and performance validity; see Fabio Sala, "Emotional Competence Inventory (ECI) Technical Manual" (HayGroup, McClelland Center for Research and Innovation, June 2000). Also see Richard Boyatzis and

Fabio Sala, "Assessing Emotional Intelligence Competencies" in *The Measurement of Emotional Intelligence*, ed. Glenn Geher (Hauppauge, NY: Novas Science Publishers, 2004).

11.   The power of a learning plan: Creating a learning plan results in people setting personal standards of performance, rather than "normative" standards that merely mimic what others have done; see J. Matthew Beaubien and Stephanie Payne, "Individual Goal Orientation as a Predictor of Job and Academic Performance: A Metanalytic Review and Integration," paper presented at the meeting of the Society for Industrial and Organizational Psychology, Atlanta, April 1999. Meanwhile, a performance orientation evokes anxiety and doubts about whether or not we can change; see Gilad Chen, Stanley Gully, Jon-Andrew Whiteman, and Robert N. Kilcullen, "Examination of Relationships among Trait-like, Individual Differences, and Learning Performance," *Journal of Applied Psychology* 85, no. 6 (2000): 835–847. As one of the longitudinal studies at the Weatherhead School of Management showed, MBAs who set goals to change on certain competencies changed significantly on those competencies, compared with other MBAs (David Leonard, "The Impact of Learning Goals on Self-directed Change in Education and Management Development," (PhD diss., Case Western Reserve University, 1996)). See also Edwin Locke and Gary P. Latham, *A Theory of Goal Setting and Task Performance* (Upper Saddle River, NJ: Prentice Hall, 1990).

12.   Learning activities that work and those that do not: See David A. Kolb, *Experiential Learning: Experience as the Source of Learning and Development* (Englewood Cliffs, NJ: Prentice Hall, 1984); Richard Boyatzis, "Stimulating Self-directed Change."

13.   Where to practice new behaviors: Christine Dreyfus studied managers of scientists and engineers who were considered superior performers. Once she documented that they used considerably more of certain abilities than their less effective counterparts, she then pursued how they developed some of those abilities. One of the distinguishing abilities was *team building*. She found that many of these middle-aged managers had first experimented with team-building skills in high school and college, in sports, clubs, and living groups. Later, when they became "bench scientists and engineers" working on problems in relative isolation, they still practiced this ability in activities outside of work, in social and community organizations such as 4-H Clubs, as well as in professional associations, planning conferences, and similar activities; see Christine Dreyfus, "The Characteristics of High Performing Managers of Scientists and Engineers" (PhD diss., Case Western Reserve University, 1990).

14. Learning in "safe space": See Kolb and Boyatzis, "Goal Setting and Self-directed Behavior Change"; Wheeler, "The Impact of Social Environments on Self-directed Change and Learning"; Jeffrey LePine, Marice LePine, and Christine Jackson, "Challenge and Hindrance Stress: Relationships with Exhaustion, Motivation to Learn, and Learning Performance," *Journal of Applied Psychology* 89, no. 5 (2004): 883–891; Rex Wright, Jody Dill, Russell Geen, and Craig Anderson, "Social Evaluation Influence on Cardiovascular Response to a Fixed Behavioral Challenge: Effects across a Range of Difficulty Levels," *Annals of Behavioral Medicine* 20, no. 4 (1998): 277–285; David E. Conroy, "The Unique Psychological Meanings of Multidimensional Fears of Failing," *Journal of Sport and Exercise Psychology* 26, no. 3 (2004): 484–491. For an excellent review of the role of care and support and their impact on learning, see Melissa Herb, "A Study of Care and Support Among Teachers and Students in a Small Suburban Middle-Senior High School" (PhD diss., University of Pennsylvania Graduate School of Education, 2005).

15. Social awareness: The ability to read and understand individuals, groups, and organizational cultures. See Goleman, Boyatzis, and McKee, *Primal Leadership*; Perrine Ruby and Jean Decety, "How Would You Feel Versus How Do You Think She Would Feel? A Neuroimaging Study of Perspective Taking with Social Emotions," *Journal of Cognitive Neuroscience* 16, no. 6 (2004): 988–999.

16. Reference groups: In sociology, groups that we rely on to help define ourselves are called reference groups. These relationships create a context within which we interpret our progress on desired changes, the utility of new learning, and even contribute significant input to formulation of the ideal (see Kathy E. Kram, "A Relational Approach to Careers," in *The Career is Dead: Long Live the Career*, ed. Douglas T. Hall (San Francisco: Jossey-Bass, 1996),132–157).

17. The power of relationships in the change process: Jane Wheeler analyzed the extent to which the MBA graduates worked on their goals in multiple "life spheres" (i.e., work, family, recreational groups, etc.). In a two-year follow-up study of two of the graduating classes of part-time MBA students, she found those who worked on their goals and plans in multiple sets of relationships improved the most and more than those working on goals in only one setting, such as work or within one relationship (see Wheeler, "The Impact of Social Environment on Self-directed Change and Learning"). In their study of the impact of the year-long executive-development program for doctors, lawyers, professors, engineers, and other professionals (referenced in

note 2 for this chapter), Ballou et. al. found that participants gained self-confidence during the program. Even at the beginning of the program, others would say these participants were very high in self-confidence. The explanation came from follow-up questions in which they explained the evident increase in self-confidence as an increase in the confidence to change. Their existing reference groups (i.e., family, groups at work, professional groups, community groups) all had an investment in them staying the same, meanwhile the person wanted to change. The executive development program allowed them to develop a new reference group that encouraged change.

Chapter Six

1. Much of the information about John Studzinski comes from author interviews, personal conversations, and correspondence with him during 2004–2005.

2. John Studzinski was made a knight of the order of St. Gregory by Pope John Paul II in 2001 for his humanitarian work with the homeless. More recently, he was made Commander of Saint Sylvester by the Vatican for his work in promoting ecumenism in Kosovo. In 2000, he received the Prince of Wales Ambassador Award in recognition of his work with the homeless.

3. Mindfulness and cognitive psychology: See Ellen J. Langer, *The Power of Mindful Learning* (Reading, MA: Perseus Books, 1997); Ellen J. Langer, *Mindfulness* (Cambridge, MA: Perseus Publishing, 1989).

4. Mindfulness, Buddhist philosophy, and health: Jon Kabat-Zinn, *Full Catastrophe Living: Using the Wisdom of Your Body and Mind to Face Stress, Pain, and Illness* (New York: Dell Publishing, 1990). Kabat-Zinn and his colleagues have combined Buddhist traditions, modern psychology, and medicine in creating methodologies for people to deal with stress, illness, and the trials of everyday life. At the Stress Reduction Program at the Center for Mindfulness in Medicine, Healthcare and Society at the University of Massachusetts, people are trained to use mindful practices such as meditation, breathing techniques, and yoga to discover inner strengths and coping mechanisms in order to deal more effectively with their particular situations. Also see Jon Kabat-Zinn, *Wherever You Go There You Are: Mindfulness Meditation in Everyday Life* (New York: Hyperion, 1994); and Saki Santorelli, *Heal Thy Self* (New York: Random House, 1999); Richard Davidson, Jon Kabat-Zinn, Jessica Schumacher, Melissa Rosenkranz, Daniel Muller, Saki F. Santorelli, Ferris Urbanowski, Anne Harrington, Katherine Bonus, and John F. Sheridan, "Alterations in brain and immune

function produced by mindfulness meditation," *Psychosomatic Medicine* 65 (2003): 564–570.

5. The medicine wheel: Using the medicine wheel as an organizing framework for leadership development is discussed in Clint Sidle, *Five Archetypes of Leadership* (New York: Palgrave Macmillan, in press). For more on this, see Angeles Arrien, *The Fourfold Way: Walking the Paths of the Warrior, Teacher, Healer and Visionary* (San Francisco: Harper, 1993). Arrien's work bridges anthropology, psychology, religion, and organizational dynamics to provide us with unique insights about human development and relationships.

6. Mindful living: See Tara Bennett-Goleman, *Emotional Alchemy: How the Mind Can Heal the Heart* (New York: Harmony Books, 2001); and Kabat-Zinn, *Full Catastrophe Living*.

7. Self-awareness: The ability to monitor one's thoughts, feelings, and responses enables us to engage more effectively with others. See Daniel Goleman, Richard Boyatzis, and Annie McKee, *Primal Leadership: Realizing the Power of Emotional Intelligence* (Boston: Harvard Business School Press, 2002).

8. Much of the information about Judi Johansen in this chapter is taken from author interviews and correspondence, 2004.

9. Recognizing emotional clues and cues: See Paul Ekman, *Emotions Revealed: Recognizing Faces and Feelings to Improve Communication and Emotional Life* (New York: Times Books, 2003).

10. Emotional reality: We first used this term in *Primal Leadership*. The term refers to the subtle emotional undercurrent that is present in any human group. The emotional reality informs a group's culture and climate, and individuals' behavior. For more on this see Annie McKee and Fran Johnston, "The Impact and Opportunity of Emotion in Organizational Development" in *The NTL Handbook of Organizational Development and Change* (San Francisco: John Wiley & Sons/Pfeiffer, 2005).

11. Langer, *The Power of Mindful Learning*.

12. Thoughts, feelings, and cognitive categories: Our mental categories are actually a very complex system of emotional reactions, memories, and thought patterns. They are extremely useful to us as we take in information. As we take it in, we filter it through our existing cognitive categories. We either assimilate the information, (e.g., fit it into our existing categories) or we accommodate to it (e.g., change our cognitive categories to fit the new information). This is an elegant system and yet sometimes, there can be problems: our system of categorization is not always accurate and assimilation is often

easier than accommodation. For more information on this see Langer, *The Power of Mindful Learning*; Langer, *Mindfulness*.

13. Mindfulness and cognitive psychology: Ellen Langer's work has been instrumental in helping us understand how we human beings make sense of our world and our place in it. See Langer, *The Power of Mindful Learning*; Langer, *Mindfulness*; and Ellen J. Langer and Lois Imber, "When Practice Makes Imperfect: The Debilitating Effects of Overlearning," *Journal of Personality and Social Psychology* 37 (1979): 2014–2025.

14. Brain functioning and emotions: Emotions, as well as thoughts, guide how we categorize information and make sense of what is happening to us and in our environment. In addition to the Langer reference in note 12, see Daniel Goleman, *Emotional Intelligence* (New York: Bantam, 1995); Daniel Goleman, *Working with Emotional Intelligence* (New York: Bantam, 1998); and Goleman, Boyatzis, and McKee, *Primal Leadership*.

15. Much of the information about Patrick Cescau is from author interviews, conversations, and correspondence during 2004–2005.

16. Shoulds and oughts: See Charles Handy, *The Hungry Spirit: Beyond Capitalism: A Quest for Purpose in the Modern World* (London: Hutchinson, 1997).

17. Noble purpose, noble goals: We have been inspired by our colleagues at SixSeconds, a not-for-profit organization that brings researchers and practitioners together to put the science of emotional intelligence into practice. Josh Freedman and Anabel Jensen use the term "noble goal" to describe that underlying, most important purpose in our lives. See also Clair Nuer, "Shifting to the Ecosystem," *EQ Today*, 2000, http://www.eqtoday.com/archive/ecosystem.html.

18. Optimal self-esteem: Michael H. Kernis, in his article "Toward a Conceptualization of Optimal Self Esteem" (*Psychological Inquiry* 14, no. 1 (2003): 1–26), reviews the literature on self-esteem and makes the argument that the construct is more complex than originally thought. He states that until recently, low self-esteem has been linked with negative feelings of self-worth, high self-esteem with positive ones. Recent research indicates that people with low self-esteem may in fact have some positive self-regard, and less negative perceptions about themselves than previously believed. Such people are, however, characterized by inconsistency in their views of themselves and a lack of stability in their self-concepts. More pertinent to our work with leaders, who generally seem to have a good deal of positive self-regard, Kernis and colleagues (1993) argue that there are at least two "types" of high self-esteem that until recently have often been considered to be the

same. People with "fragile" high self-esteem often operate from a sense of vulnerability and act to protect their self-image; they defend their self-image, often through a process of constantly comparing themselves with others to be sure they are still "better." These individuals may be very proud of their achievements, while attributing their failures to the environment. They often expend much time and energy (psychological and otherwise) to maintain and even enhance their positive perceptions of themselves and overall self-concept. Individuals with "secure" high self-esteem, on the other hand, are characterized by a positive, but balanced and realistic, set of perceptions about themselves. They accept themselves—both strengths and weaknesses—and do not need to feel superior to others in order to maintain their sense of positive self-regard. In our work with leaders, we notice that those individuals who, over a period of many years, do not get accurate feedback on themselves—and in fact are only given information that bolsters their self-esteem—often end up with fairly "fragile" self esteem. At some level, they may know that they are not being given the full picture, and yet it is the only one they have. This self-image can become increasingly important over the years, leading to unrealistically positive feelings of self-worth and defensive postures to protect the image; see Michael H. Kernis, David P. Cornell, Chien-ru Sun, Andrea Berry, and Thomas Harlow, "There's More to Self-esteem than Whether It's High or Low: The Importance of Stability of Self-esteem," *Journal of Personality and Social Psychology* 65 (1993): 1190–1204.

19. Imposter syndrome: See Steven Berglas, *The Success Syndrome: Hitting Bottom When You Reach the Top* (New York: Plenum, 1986); Pauline Clance, *The Imposter Phenomenon: Overcoming the Fear That Haunts Your Success* (New York: Peachtree Publishing, 1985); Kathy Oriel, Mary Beth Plane, and Marlon Mundt, "Family Medicine Residents and the Imposter Phenomenon," *Family Medicine* 36, no. 4 (2004); Peggy McIntosh, *Feeling Like a Fraud* (Wellesley, MA: Stone Center, 1985).

20. Old Arabic sayings: See *Sahara, Land Beyond Imagination*, photography by Frans Lemmens, text by Martijn de Rooi (Dutch Publishers, 2004), 29.

21. Mental imagery and physiology: Liz Roffe, Katja Schmidt, and Edzard Ernst, "A Systematic Review of Guided Imagery as an Adjuvant Cancer Therapy," *Psycho-oncology* (January 2005) DOI: 10.1002/pon.889; Lisa Manniz, Rohit Chadukar, Lisa Rybicki, Diane Tusek, and Olen Solomon, "The Effect of Guided Imagery on Quality of Life for Patients with Chronic Tension-type Headaches," *Headache: Journal of Head and Face Pain* 39 (1999): 326–324.

22. Josie Harper: Much of the information about Josie Harper was gathered through author interviews, personal converstions, and correspondence during 2004–2005.

23. Much of the information about Paul McDermott was gathered through author interviews, personal conversations, and correspondence during 2004–2005.

24. Mindfulness, emotional intelligence, and results: While Paul McDermott did not engage in a formal research study, it is worth noting that during the period that he and his team dedicated themselves to enhancing their leadership capabilities—specifically emotional intelligence—and while they focused on developing healthy, mindful relationships, common and well-known measures of customer and employee satisfaction, as well as measures of EI and revenue, rose considerably: The J.D. Power customer satisfaction rating rose to 8.6 on a 10-point scale, the Gallup Q12 employee engagement score ranked in the top 1 percent of government and industry, their EQ assessment score improved by 51 percent while revenue rose 53 percent.

Chapter Seven

1. Mrs. Zikhali: Much of the information about Mrs. Zikhali and the Nkomo Primary School was gathered through conversations and correspondences with the authors during 2004–2005.

2. Positive affect and behavior: See Alice M. Isen, "A Role for Neuropsychology in Understanding the Facilitating Influence of Positive Affect on Social Behavior and Cognitive Processes," in *Handbook of Positive Psychology*, ed. C. R. Snyder and Shane J. Lopez (New York: Oxford University Press, 2002).

3. Healing power of hope: Jerome Groopman, *The Anatomy of Hope: How People Prevail in the Face of Illness* (New York: Random House, 2004).

4. Ibid.

5. Contagious emotions: Thomas Lewis, Fari Amini, and Richard Lannon, *A General Theory of Love* (New York: Random House, 2000); Janice Kelly and Sigal Barsade, "Mood and Emotions in Small Groups and Work Teams," *Organizational Behavior and Human Decision Processes* 86 (2001): 99–130; Brooks B. Gump and James A. Kulik, "Stress Affiliation and Emotional Contagion," *Journal of Personality and Social Psychology* 72, (1997): 305–319.

6. Hope and resiliency, coping, health, and healing: Bill Moyers, *Healing and the Mind* (New York: Doubleday, 1993); Karen A. Matthews, Katri Raikkonen, Kim Sulton-Tyrell, and Lewis H. Kuller, "Optimistic Attitudes

Protect Against Progression of Carotid Atherosclerosis in Healthy Middle-aged Women," *Psychosomatic Medicine* 66, (2004): 640–644.

7. Hope and college and athletic performance: C. R. Snyder, Kevin L. Rand, and David R. Sigmon, "Hope Theory: A Member of the Positive Psychology Family," in Snyder and Lopez, *Handbook of Positive Psychology*, 257–276; see also Lewis Curry, C. R. Snyder, David Cook, Brent Ruby, and Michael Rehm, "The Role of Hope in Academic and Sport Achievement," *Journal of Personality and Social Psychology* 73, (1997): 1257–1267.

8. Positive affect and behavior, social interaction, and cognitive functioning: See Isen, "A Role for Neuropsychology"; also see Daniel Goleman, *Destructive Emotions: How Can We Overcome Them? A Scientific Dialogue with the Dalai Lama* (New York: Bantam Books, 2003); Victor S. Johnston, *Why We Feel: The Science of Human Emotions* (Cambridge, MA: Perseus Books, 1999); Jim Loehr and Tony Schwartz, *The Power of Full Engagement: Managing Energy, Not Time, Is the Key to High Performance and Personal Renewal* (New York, Free Press, 2003); Snyder and Lopez, *Handbook of Positive Psychology*; and Richard J. Davidson, Klaus R. Sherer, and H. Hill Goldsmith, eds., *Handbook of Affective Sciences* (New York: Oxford University Press, 2003).

9. See Isen, "A Role for Neuropsychology"; and Snyder and Lopez, *Handbook of Positive Psychology*.

10. Historical definitions of hope: James Ludema, "Narrative Inquiry: Collective Storytelling as a Source of Hope, Knowledge, and Action in Organizational Life (PhD diss., Case Western Reserve University, 1996).

11. Hope theory: Snyder, Rand, and Sigmon have written a comprehensive review of the development of "hope theory" and put forth their own inclusive theory in "Hope Theory: A Member of the Positive Psychology Family"; see also C. R. Snyder, "Hope Theory: Rainbows in the Mind," *Psychological Inquiry* 13, no. 4 (2000): 149–275.

12. Definitions of hope: Some psychologists believe that hope is composed of a cognitive element and an affective one. C. R. Snyder studies hope and believes that it includes a goal, a perceived path to the goal and agency (the ability to put things into action) and measures it as both a trait and state, C.R. Snyder, "The Past and Possible Futures of Hope" *Journal of Social and Clinical Psychology* 19, no. 1 (2000): 11–28; Groopman says it is "the elevating feeling we experience when we see—in the mind's eye—a path to a better future" (*The Anatomy of Hope*, xiv); Richard Davidson says, "hope involves what I would call affective forecasting—that is, the comforting, energizing, elevating feeling that you experience when you project in your mind a positive future" (Groopman, *The Anatomy of Hope*, 193).

13. Hope theory: See Snyder, Rand, and Sigmon, "Hope Theory: A Member of the Positive Psychology Family"; Snyder, "Hope Theory: Rainbows in the Mind."

14. Bjoerndalen is a winning biathlete: Charles Le Duff, "A pile of medals for a positive thinker," *New York Times*, February 21, 2002, C-17.

15. Mental rehearsal: As we mentioned in *Primal Leadership*, Laura Wilkinson had a taped foot when she won the 10-meter platform diving gold medal in Sydney. She had broken it just months before the Olympics, and she attributed her win to the visualization that her coach made her do. As her ankle healed, she sat by the pool for up to six hours a day, mentally watching herself walk to the ladder, climb it, get set for the dive, dive, enter the water, swim to the edge of the pool, get out and do it again, and again and again (Goleman, Boyatzis, and McKee, *Primal Leadership*). See also Jim Loehr and Tony Schwartz, "The Making of the Corporate Athlete," *Harvard Business Review* (January/February, 2001): 120–128; and Ingo Meister, Timo Krings, Henrik Foltys, B. Boroojerdi, M. Muller, R. Topper, and Armin Thron "Playing the Piano in the Mind—An fMRI Study on Music Imagery and Performance in Pianists," *Cognitive Brain Research* 19, no. 3 (2004): 219–228.

16. Visual imaging prepares the brain for action: Gabriel Kreiman, Christof Koch, and Itshak Fried, "Imagery Neurons in the Human Brain," *Nature* 408, (2000): 357–361. Using neural connections over and over strengthens them: Gerald M. Edelman, *Neural Darwinism: The Theory of Neuronal Group Selection* (New York: Basic Books, 1987), 58; Cameron Carter, Angus Macdonald, Stefan Ursu, Andy Stenger, Myeong Ho Sohn, and John Anderson, "How the Brain Gets Ready to Perform," presentation at the thirtieth annual meeting of the Society of Neuroscience (New Orleans, November, 2000); Tara Bennett-Goleman, *Emotional Alchemy: How the Mind Can Heal the Heart* (New York: Harmony Books, 2001).

17. Mind and Life Institute: This organization has sponsored meetings to explore Buddhist and western thought on a variety of topics since 1987. They are based in Louisville, Colorado; R. Adam Engle is the chairman.

18. The science, philosophy, and spirituality of emotions: Daniel Goleman, *Destructive Emotions: How Can We Overcome Them? A Scientific Dialogue with the Dalai Lama* (New York: Bantam Books, 2003).

19. Emotion and the brain; Sharon Begley, "This Year, Try Getting Your Brain in Shape," *Wall Street Journal*, January 10, 2003, B1.

20. Boyatzis's Theory of Intentional Change: Richard Boyatzis, "Intentional change theory from a complexity perspective" *Journal of Management Development* (forthcoming); Goleman, Boyatzis, and McKee, *Primal*

Leadership; Richard Boyatzis and Kleio Akrivou-Naperksy "The Ideal Self as a Driver of Change" *Journal of Management Development* (forthcoming); and note numbers 1 and 2 for chapter 5.

21. Complexity theory: Complexity theory is the current name for a type of analysis of natural systems. First called "catastrophe" theory, then "chaos" theory, it began as a study of the abrupt changes observed in weather, crystals, metal fatigue and failure, and investment behavior. Complexity theory is now applied to human and organizational dynamics as well. See Margaret J. Wheatley, *Leadership and the New Science: Discovering Order in a Chaotic World* (San Francisco: Berrett-Koehler, 1999); and Margaret J. Wheatley, *Finding our Way: Leadership for an Uncertain Time* (San Francisco: Berrett-Koehler, 2005). The theory has been popularized by books such as James Gleick's *Chaos: Making a New Science* (New York: Viking, 1987) and in some of the fiction of Michael Crichton.

22. Set-up-to-fail syndrome: Jean François Manzoni, *The Set Up to Fail Syndrome* (Boston: Harvard Business School Press, 2002).

23. Positive psychology: Martin E. P. Seligman and Mihaly Csikszentmihalyi, "Positive Psychology: An Introduction," *American Psychologist 55*, (2000): 5–14.

24. Optimism and positive psychology: Martin E. P. Seligman, *Authentic Happiness: Using the New Positive Psychology to Realize Your Potential for Lasting Fulfillment* (New York, Free Press, 2002).

25. Learned helplessness: Martin E. P. Seligman, Steven F. Maier, and James H. Geer, "The Alleviation of Helplessness in Dogs," *Journal of Abnormal Psychology* 73 (1968): 256–262; Steven F. Maier and Martin E. P. Seligman, "Learned Helplessness: Theory and Evidence," *Journal of Experimental Psychology: General* 105 (1976): 3–46; and Martin E. P. Seligman, *Helplessness: On Depression, Development and Death*, 2nd edition (New York: W. H. Freeman, 1991).

26. Optimism: For thorough review of the concepts, see Seligman, *Authentic Happiness*; and Martin E. P. Seligman, *Learned Optimism: How to Change Your Mind and Your Life* (New York: Pocket Books, 1998). See also Charles S. Carver and Michael F. Scheier, "Optimism," in Snyder and Lopez, *Handbook of Positive Psychology*. 231–243.

27. Optimism as a leadership competency: See Goleman, Boyatzis, and McKee, *Primal Leadership*.

28. Optimism, resilience, and effectiveness: See Goleman, Boyatzis, and McKee, *Primal Leadership*; and Karen Reivich and Andrew Shatte, *The Resilience Factor: How Changing the Way You Think Will Change Your Life for Good* (New York: Broadway Books, 2000).

29. The Pygmalion effect and self-fulfilling prophecy: See Robert Rosenthal and Lenore Jacobson, *Pygmalion in the Classroom: Teacher Expectation and Pupils' Intellectual Development* (New York: Rhinehart and Winston, 1968; New York: Irvington Publishers, 1992). See also Dov Eden, *Pygmalion in Management: Productivity as a Self-fulfilling Prophecy* (Lexington MA: Lexington Books, 1990).

30. CNN Special: "CNN Presents the Gap: Fifty Years after Brown vs. The Board of Education," aired May 16, 2004. For more on expectations and black students' performance and experience of school, see Luis Ottley, "Outsiders Within: The Lived Experience of African American Children at the Shipley School" (PhD diss., University of Pennsylvania, Graduate School of Education, 2005).

31. Ibid.

32. Self-fulfilling prophecy: Robert Merton, "The Self-fulfilling Prophecy," *Anitoch Review* 8 (1948): 193–210.

33. The will and human volition: William James, *The Principles of Psychology* (New York, Henry Holt, 1890); William James, *The Will to Believe* (Cambridge, MA: Harvard University Press, 1979; original work published in 1897); Hsun Tzu, in *Hsun Tsu: Basic Writings*, translated by Burton Watson (New York: Columbia University Press, 1996); Avicenna, in Sayyed Hossein Nasr, *Three Muslim Sages: Avicenna-Suhrawardi-Ibn 'Arabi* (Cambridge, MA: Harvard University Press, 1964); René Descartes, "Treatise on Man," in *The Philosophical Writings of Descartes*, vol. 1, translated by John Cottingham, Robert Stoothoff, and Dugald Murdoch (Cambridge: Cambridge University Press, 1985; original work published 1664).

34. Self-efficacy: Albert Bandura has coined the term self-efficacy and defined the research agenda for many years. Bandura noted that self-efficacy is the belief that one can produce certain actions—and that personal efficacy is a critical element of human agency. See Albert Bandura, *Self-Efficacy: The Exercise of Control*, (New York: Freeman, 1997); "Self-efficacy: Toward a unifying theory of behavioral change," *Psychological Review* 84 (1977): 191–215; *Social Foundations of Thought and Action* (New York: Prentice Hall, 1986). See also J. E. Maddux, "Self-Efficacy Theory: An Introduction," in *Self-Efficacy, Adaptation, and Adjustment: Theory, Research, and Application*, ed. J. E. Maddux (New York: Plenum, 1995), 3–33; and Stephen J. Zaccaro, Virginia Blair, Christopher Peterson, and Michelle Zazanis, "Collective Efficacy," in Maddux, *Self-Efficacy, Adaptation, and Adjustment*, 305–330.

35. Self-efficacy, optimism, and pessimism: See Maddux, *Self-Efficacy, Adaptation, and Adjustment*; and Seligman, *Learned Optimism*.

36. Enhancing self-efficacy: Martin Seligman and colleagues at the University of Pennsylvania have developed clear processes for developing cognitive skills to enhance, among other things, self efficacy. See Seligman, *Learned Optimism*; and Reivich and Shatte, *The Resilience Factor*. Jon Kabat-Zinn also presents ways for people to enhance their sense of control over specific events and situations in their lives in *Full Catastrophe Living: Using the Wisdom of Your Body and Mind to Face Stress, Pain, and Illness* (New York: Delta Books, 1990); see also Stress Reduction Program at the Center for Mindfulness in Medicine, Healthcare, and Society at the University of Massachusetts.

37. Collective efficacy: See J. E. Maddux, "Self-Efficacy Theory: An Introduction" in Maddux, *Self-Efficacy, Adaptation, and Adjustment*, 3–33; Stephen J. Zaccaro, Virginia Blair, Christopher Peterson, and Michelle Zazanis, "Collective Efficacy" in Maddux, *Self-Efficacy, Adaptation, and Adjustment*, 305–328.

38. Hope and spirituality: Po Bronson's *What Should I Do with My Life?* (New York: Random House, 2002) reveals an alternative to self- or even collective efficacy—one's efficacy through God. The increase in spiritual practices, both formal religious services and less formal personal prayer, meditation, and similar activities has been dramatic in recent years. Rick Warren's *The Purpose-Driven Life* (Grand Rapids, MI: Zondervan, 2002), a book based in Christian religious values, set new records in publishing, selling over 20 million copies by 2005, and was a major best seller in the *New York Times* self-help category (while Po Bronson's book was on the nonfiction best seller list, as noted by Karen Sandstrom, "Growing with God," *The Plain Dealer* (Cleveland, OH), April 10, 2004, E1); see also Lynda H. Powell, Leila Shahabi, and Carl E. Thoresen, "Religion and Spirituality: Linkages to Physical Health," *American Psychologist* 58, (2003): 36–52.

39. Spirituality versus religiosity: Psychologists William Miller of the University of New Mexico and Carl Thoresen of Stanford University make the distinction between "religiosity" and "spirituality." People high in religiosity are proponents of the practices and values of a specific religion. Those who are spiritual focus on more ephemeral aspects of their beliefs not expressed through socially prescribed practices (e.g., going to church, temple, or mosque services regularly). Miller and Thoresen cited other studies showing how seeing yourself as more religious than spiritual was associated with a view of God as a "judging creator." Those who saw themselves as more spiritual than religious tended to see their God as "loving, forgiving, and nonjudgmental." See William R. Miller and Carl E. Thoresen, "Spirituality,

Religion and Health: An Emerging Research Feld," *American Psychologist* 58, (2003): 28.

40.   Effect of prayer: See Claudia Kalb, "Faith and Health," *Newsweek*, November 10, 2003, 44–56.

41.   Spirituality and religious practice effects on health: Miller and Thoresen, "Spirituality, Religion and Health"; Powell, Shahabi, and Thoresen, "Religion and spirituality"; Teresa E. Seeman, Linda Fagan Dubin, and Melvin Seeman, "Religiosity/Spirituality and Health: A Critical Review of the Evidence for Biological Pathways," *American Psychologist* 58, (2003): 53–74.

42.   Typical arguments against optimism in organizations: David L. Cooperrider and Diana Whitney, *Collaborating for Change: Appreciative Inquiry* (San Francisco: Berrett-Koehler, 2000).

43.   Mental brakes on thought: William B. Swann and Brett W. Pelham, "The Truth about Illusions: Authenticity and Positivity in Social Relationships," in Snyder and Lopez, *Handbook of Positive Psychology* 366–381.

44.   My hope not being your nightmare: Elie Wiesel, commencement address at Case Western Reserve University, May 16, 2004.

45.   Demagogues versus resonant leaders: Goleman, Boyatzis, and McKee, *Primal Leadership*.

46.   Turning to others in trying times: See Elaine Hatfield, John Cacioppo, and Richard Rapson, *Emotional Contagion* (New York: Cambridge University Press, 1994); also see Paul Ekman, Joseph J. Campos, Richard J. Davidson, and Frans DeWaals, *Emotions Inside Out*, Annals of the New York Academy of Sciences, vol. 1000 (New York: New York Academy of Sciences, 2003); and Lyndall Strazdins, "Emotional work and emotional contagion," in *Emotions in the Workplace: Research, Theory and Practice*, ed. Neal Ashkanasy, Wilfred Zerbe, and Charmine Hartel (Westport, CT: Quorum Books, 2000), 232–250.

47.   Leadership and a major crisis: The examples in this section are adapted from Richard E. Boyatzis, Diana Bilimoria, Lindsey Godwin, Margaret Hopkins, and Tony Lingham, "Effective Leadership in Extreme Crisis," in *9/11: Public Health in the Wake of Terrorist Attacks*, ed. Raz Gross, Yuval Neria, Randall Marshall, and Ezra Susser, (New York: Cambridge University Press, 2004). We are grateful to our colleagues for the research we used to develop these examples and the permission to use them here.

48.   Evacuating American Express during September 11, 2001: Patrick McGeehan, "Sailing into a Sea of Troubles: No Grace Period for New Chief of American Express," *New York Times*, October 5, 2001, C1; John Byrne and Heather Timmons, "Tough Times for a New CEO" *Business Week*, October 29, 2001, 64.

49. Chenault's attributes as a leader: "Tough Times for a New CEO: How Ken Chenault of AmEx Is Being Tested in Ways Few Could Have Imagined," *BusinessWeek*, October 29, 2001, 64; and "Twenty-Five Most Influential Personalities in Financial Services," *BusinessWeek*, May 2001, 20; also see Patrick McGeehan, "Sailing into a Sea of Troubles—No Grace Period for New Chief of American Express," October 5, 2001, *New York Times*, C-1.

50. American Express town hall meeting: Byrne and Timmons, "Tough Times for a New CEO."

51. We introduced several of these exercises in abbreviated forms in Goleman, Boyatzis, and McKee, *Primal Leadership*. They are sufficiently powerful in invoking or evoking one's dreams that we wanted to repeat and expand them here.

Chapter Eight

1. Much of the information about Lechesa Tsenoli is taken from author interviews, conversations, and correspondence, 2003–2005.

2. Definition of compassion: *Webster's New Collegiate Dictionary* (1963) defines compassion as, "Sympathetic consciousness of others' distress together with a desire to alleviate it." The *American Heritage Dictionary* (1969) defines it as, "The deep feeling of sharing the suffering of another in the inclination to give and or support, or show mercy." The Buddhist definition, quoted by Matthieu Ricard, contrasts it with love, "The wish that others may be free from suffering and the causes of suffering, while love is defined as the wish that others be happy and find the causes for happiness" (in Daniel Goleman, *Destructive Emotions: How Can We Overcome Them? A Scientific Dialogue with the Dalai Lama* (New York: Bantam Books, 2003), 143). See also Peter Frost, *Toxic Emotions at Work: How Compassionate Managers Handle Pain and Conflict* (Boston: Harvard Business School Press, 2003); Peter Frost, Jane Dutton, Monica Worline, and Annette Wilson, "Narratives of Compassion in Organizations," in *Emotions in Organizations*, ed. Stephen Fineman (Beverly Hills, CA: Sage Publications, 2000), 25–45; Thomas Bateman and Chris Porath, "Transcendent Behavior," in *Positive Organizational Scholarship: Foundations of a New Discipline*, ed. Kim Cameron, Jane E. Dutton, and Robert E. Quinn (San Francisco: Berrett-Koehler, 2003), 122–137; Jason Kanov, Sally Maitlis, Monica Worline, Jane E. Dutton, Peter Frost, and Jacoba Lilius, "Compassion in Organizational Life," *American Behavioral Scientist* 47, no. 6 (2004): 808–827.

3. Confucian definition of compassion, specifically the concept of "ren": Antonio S. Cua, "Chinese Confucian philosophy," in *Routledge*

Encyclopedia of Philosophy, vol. 2, ed. Edward Craig (London: Routledge, 1998), 536–549; and Bryan W. Van Norden, Mencius, in *Routledge Encyclopedia of Philosophy*, vol. 6, ed. Edward Craig (London: Routledge, 1998), 302–304. Alternate reasons to help others may include wanting to alleviate others' relative distress from not moving toward desired goals or wanting to help them extend and reach for their dreams or new aspirations. Therefore, the experience of pain or suffering on the part of others is not a necessary condition for the demonstration of compassion as we are defining it here.

4. Need for affiliation: The early and most widely used measures still base their codes and studies on deficiency-based definitions of drives. But researchers in the early seventies started conceptualizing a positive, non-anxious basis for a different type of intimacy or affiliation drive. Research also began to consider the need for close relationships to support a manager's job. See Richard Boyatzis in *Organizational Psychology: A Book of Readings*, 2nd, 3rd, 4th, 5th, and 6th editions, ed. David A. Kolb, Irwin Rubin, and James McIntyre (Englewood Cliffs, NJ: Prentice Hall, 1974, 1979, 1982, 1990, 1995); see also Richard Boyatzis, "Affiliation Motivation: A Review and a New Perspective," in *Human Motivation: A Book of Readings*, ed. David McClelland and Robert S. Steele (Morristown, NJ: General Learning Press, 1973); Richard Boyatzis, "A Two-factor Theory of Affiliation Motivation," (PhD diss., Harvard University,); Dan McAdams, "A Thematic Coding System for the Intimacy Motive," *Journal of Research in Personality* 14 (1980): 413–432; Carol Constantian, "Attitudes, Beliefs, and Behavior in Regard to Spending Time" (PhD diss., Harvard University, 1981); Stephen Kelner, "Interpersonal Motivation: Positive, Negative, and Anxious" (PhD diss., Harvard University, 1990); David McClelland, *Human Motivation* (New York: Cambridge University Press, 1985); Roy Baumeister and Mark Leary, "The Need to Belong: Desire for Interpersonal Attachments as a Fundamental Human Motivation," *Psychological Bulletin* 117, no. 3 (1995): 497–529.

5. Morgan Lewis Bockius: Morgan Lewis Bockius employs over 1,200 attorneys in 14 U.S. offices and 5 international offices with expertise in 22 practice areas.

6. Ambiguous authority: This is a term we have become quite fond of over the years, as it captures the difficulties of managing in today's complex organizations. The phrase was born of a series of conversations during the late 1990s between Michael Seitchik, Greg Shea, and Kenwyn Smith, as they designed a course on leadership for the Wharton School's Aresty Insititute of Education.

7. Positive and negative emotions and their effects on performance: Thomas A. Wright and Russell Cropanzano, "The Role of Psychological Well-Being in Job Performance: A Fresh Look at an Age-Old Quest," *Organizational Dynamics* 33, no. 4 (2004): 338–351; Richard Lazarus, "How Emotions Influence Performance in Competitive Sports," *Sport Psychologist* 14 (2000): 229–252.

8. Georgia Bulldogs media stories: Personal communication, Mark Scott, December, 2003.

9. Georgia Tech builds Habitat home: "Football Teams Up with Habitat for Humanity," Georgia Institute of Technology Web site (www.gatech.edu), July, 2, 2004.

10. Team results: Team results listed in 2004 Outlook, "Since Richt came to Georgia, the Bulldogs are 32-8 (including 24-4 the past two seasons)." See: http://georgiadogs.collegesports.com/sports/m-footbl/spec-rel/070204aab.html

11. Mark Scott in *PRWeek*: "The In-house A-list," *PRWeek*, October 20, 2003, 18-19.

12. Spreading emotional contagion: Elaine Hatfield, John T. Cacioppo, and Richard Rapson, *Emotional Contagion* (New York: Cambridge University Press, 1994).

13. Culture of support for developing careers: Douglas T. Hall, ed. *The Career Is Dead—Long Live the Career: A Relational Approach to Careers* (San Francisco: Jossey-Bass, 1996).

14. Summa's vision: Comments by Thomas Strauss, President and CEO, Summa Health Systems of Akron, Ohio, at the Heart to Heart tenth anniversary conference in Akron, Ohio, April 28, 2003. Statement was adapted from one copyrighted by Albert Einstein Healthcare Foundation, Service Excellence Program, 1988.

15. Beneficial changes in Summa Health Systems: Information gleaned from personal interviews conducted by the authors with a number of physicians and nurses who currently work for Summa, as well as several former staff.

16. Importance of compassion in times of crisis: Jane Dutton, Peter Frost, Monica Worline, Jacoba Lilius, and Jason Kanov, "Leading in Times of Trauma," *Harvard Business Review* (January 2002): 54–61; Jane Dutton and Emily D. Heaphy, "The Power of High-Quality Connections," in *Positive Organizational Scholarship*, ed. Kim Cameron, Jane E. Dutton, and Robert Quinn (San Francisco: Berrett-Koehler, 2003): 264–278.

17. Mayor Giuliani on September 11, 2001: E. Pooley, "Mayor of the World," *Time*, December 31, 2001, 1.

18. Mayor Giuliani's message: A. Ripley, "We're Under Attack," *Time*, December 31, 2001, 5; Pooley, "Mayor of the World," 2.

19. Mayor Giuliani's call for compassion: Remarks by Rudolph Giuliani following the attack at the World Trade Center, September 12, 2001. www.nyc.gov.

20. New York City is different now: Personal communication from Mary Ann Batos, a long-time resident who works in midtown Manhattan.

21. Survey of coaching: Manuel London, *Leadership Development: Paths to Self-Insight and Professional Growth* (Mahwah, NJ: Lawrence Erlbaum Associates, 2002).

22. High cost of bad hires: HayGroup, "Increasing the odds of success with outside experienced hires: A case study of competency-based assessment and selection," Hay Viewpoint working paper (Boston: The McClelland Center, 2003).

23. Role of mentors and coaches in developing leaders: Morgan W. McCall Jr., Michael M. Lombardo, and Ann M. Morrison, *The Lessons of Experience: How Successful Executives Develop on the Job* (Lexington, MA: Lexington Books, 1988); Kathy Kram, *Mentoring at Work* (Glenview, IL: Scott, Foresman, 1985); Kathy Kram and Cary Cherniss, "Developing Emotional Competence through Relationships," in *The Emotionally Intelligent Workplace: How to Select for, Measure, and Improve Emotional Intelligence in Individuals, Groups, and Organizations*, ed. Cary Cherniss and Daniel Goleman (San Francisco: Jossey-Bass, 2001), 254–285; Daniel Goleman, Richard Boyatzis, and Annie McKee, *Primal Leadership* (Boston: Harvard Business School Press, 2002); Richard Boyatzis, Melvin Smith, and Nancy Tresser, "Sustaining Leadership Effectiveness Through Coaching and Compassion: It's Not what You Think," *Academy of Management Learning and Education* (forthcoming); Richard E. Boyatzis, Anita Howard, Brigette Rapisarda, and Scott Taylor, "Coaching Can Work, but Doesn't Always," *People Management* (March 11, 2004) 26-32.

24. Benefits of social functions rather than instrumental of relationships: Herminia Ibarra, *Working Identity: Unconventional Strategies for Reinventing Your Career* (Boston: Harvard Business School Press, 2003).

25. Instrumental relationship between the leader and others: A great deal of research has described this pattern and its negative effects in what has been called *leader-member exchange theory*; See Fred Dansereau, James Cashman, and George Graen, "Instrumentality Theory and Equity Theory as Complimentary Approaches in Predicting the Relationship of Leadership and Turnover among Managers," *Organizational Behavior and Human Performance* 10, no. 2 (1973): 184–200; Fred Dansereau, George Graen,

and William Haga, "A Vertical Dyad Linkage Approach to Leadership within Formal Organizations: A Longitudinal Investigation of the Role Making Process," *Organizational Behavior and Human Performance* 13, (1975): 46–78; George Graen and Terri Scandura, "Toward a Psychology of Dyadic Organizing," *Research in Organizational Behavior* 9, (1987): 175–208; George Graen, Michael Novak, and Patricia Sommerkamp, "The Effects of Leader-Member Exchange and Job Design on Productivity and Satisfaction: Testing a Dual Attachment Model," *Organizational Behavior and Human Performance* 30, no. 1 (1982): 109–131; George Graen and Mary Uhl-Bien, "Relationship-Based Approach to Leadership: Development of Leader-Member Exchange (LMX) Theory of Leadership over 25 Years: Applying a Multi-Level Multi-Domain Perspective," *Leadership Quarterly* 6, no. 2 (1995): 219–247; George Graen and J. Cashman, "A Role-Making Model of Leadership in Formal Organizations: A Developmental Approach," *Leadership Frontiers*, ed. James G. Hunt and Lars L. Larson (Kent, OH: Kent State University Press, 1975): 143–165.

26. Weak ties from instrumental coaching: Kathy Kram, *Mentoring at Work* (Glenview, IL: Scott, Foresman, 1985): 143–165; Monica Higgins and Kathy Kram, "Reconceptualizing Mentoring at Work: A Developmental Network Perspective," *Academy of Management Review* 26, (2001): 264–288.

27. Definition of coaching: Richard Boyatzis, "Notes from a Coaching Workshop," (unpublished paper, Weatherhead School of Management, Case Western Reserve University, 2003).

28. Effects of social isolation: Boyatzis, Smith, and Tresser, "Sustaining Leadership Effectiveness Through Coaching and Compassion," *Academy of Management Learning and Education* (forthcoming).

29. Competencies of effective coaches: Richard Boyatzis, "Core Competencies in Coaching Others to Overcome Dysfunctional Behavior," in *Linking Emotional Intelligence and Performance at Work: Current Research Evidence*, ed. Vanessa Druskat, Fabio Sala, and Gerald Mount (New York: Lawrence Erlbaum Associates, in press).

Chapter Nine

1. Johann Wolfgang von Goethe, *Faustus; The Bride of Corinth; The First Walpurgis Night*, 2 vols., translated by John Anster (London: Longman, Rees, Orme, Brown, Green, and Longman, 1835), 303.

Appendix A

1. The sacrifice syndrome and renewal cycle in detail: This section is taken substantially from Richard Boyatzis, Melvin Smith, and Nancy Blaize,

"Developing Sustainable Leaders Through Coaching and Compassion" *Academy of Management Learning and Education* (forthcoming).

2. Leadership and power: John P. Kotter, *The General Managers* (New York: Free Press, 1982); David C. McClelland, *Human Motivation* (Glenview, IL: Scott, Foresman & Co., 1985); Gary A. Yukl and David Van Fleet, "Theory and Research on Leadership in Organizations," in *Handbook of Industrial and Organizational Psychology*, 2nd edition, vol. 3, ed. Marvin D. Dunnette and Leaetta M. Hough (Palo Alto, CA: Consulting Psychologists Press, 1990): 147–197.

3. Leadership and dependence: John P. Kotter, *Power in Management: How to Understand, Acquire, and Use It* (New York: AMACOM, 1979).

4. Leadership effectiveness and power: David McClelland and Richard Boyatzis, "The Leadership Motive Pattern and Long Term Success in Management," *Journal of Applied Psychology* 67 (1982): 737–743; Alan F. Fontana, Roberta L. Rosenberg, Jonathan L. Marcus, and Robert D. Kerns, "Type A Behavior Pattern, Inhibited Power Motivation, and Activity Inhibition," *Journal of Personality and Social Psychology* 52 (1987): 177–183; McClelland, *Human Motivation*; Ruth L. Jacobs and David McClelland, "Moving Up the Corporate Ladder: A Longitudinal Study of the Leadership Motive Pattern and Managerial Success in Women and Men," *Consulting Psychology Journal: Practice and Research* 46 (1994): 32–41; Sharon R. Jenkins, "Need for Power and Women's Careers Over 14 Years: Structural Power, Job Satisfaction, and Motive Change," *Journal of Personality and Social Psychology*, 66 (1994): 155–165.

5. Power stress: McClelland, *Human Motivation*.

6. Factors leading to stress arousal: Sally S. Dickerson and Margaret E. Kemeny, "Acute Stressors and Cortisol Responses: A Theoretical Integration and Synthesis of Laboratory Research," *Psychological Bulletin* 130, no. 3 (2004): 355–391.

7. Anticipation of stressful events leads to stress: Paul Martin, *The Healing Mind: The Vital Links Between Brain and Behavior, Immunity and Disease* (New York: Thomas Dunne Books, St. Martin's Griffin, 1997).

8. Effective leaders use self-control: McClelland and Boyatzis, "The Leadership Motive Pattern and Long Term Success in Management"; David McClelland, *Power: The Inner Experience* (New York: Irvington Press, 1975).

9. Self-control is stressful: Roy Baumeister, Todd Heatherton, and Diane Tice, *Losing Control: How and Why People Fail at Self-Regulation* (New York: Academic Press, 1994); Robert Sapolsky, "The Physiology and

Pathophysiology of Unhappiness" in *Well-Being: The Foundation of Hedonic Psychology*, ed. Daniel Kahnemann, Edward Diener, and Norbert Schwarz (New York: Russell Sage Foundation, 1999), 453–469.

10. Aspects of power stress: Robert S. Steele, "The Physiological Concomitants of Psychogenic Motive Arousal in College Males" (PhD diss., Harvard University, 1973); Robert S. Steele, "Power Motivation, Activation, and Inspirational Speeches," *Journal of Personality* 45 (1977): 53–64; McClelland, *Human Motivation*; David McClelland and John B. Jemmott III, "Power Motivation, Stress, and Physical Illness," *Journal of Human Stress* 6, no. 4 (1980): 6–15; David C. McClelland, Grace Ross, and Vandana Patel, "The Effect of an Academic Examination on Salivary Norepinephrine and Immunoglobulin levels," *Journal of Human Stress* 11 (1985): 52–59; David C. McClelland, Erik Floor, Richard J. Davidson, and Clifford Saron, "Stressed Power Motivation, Sympathetic Activation, Immune Function, and Illness," *Journal of Human Stress* 67 (1980): 737–743; Oliver C. Schultheiss, "Psychophysiological and Health Correlates of Implicit Motives," paper presented at the 107th Annual Convention of the American Psychological Association, Boston, Massachusetts, August 1999; Oliver C. Schultheiss and Joachim C. Brunstein, "Inhibited Power Motivation and Persuasive Communication: A Lens Model Analysis," *Journal of Personality* 70 (2002): 553–582; Oliver C. Schultheiss and Wolfgang Rohde, "Implicit Power Motivation Predicts Men's Testosterone Changes and Implicit Learning in a Context Situation," *Hormones and Behavior* 41 (2002): 195–202; Joseph LeDoux, *Synaptic Self: How Our Brains Become Who We Are* (New York: Viking, 2002); Robert M. Sapolsky, "Why Stress Is Bad for Your Brain," *Science*, August 9, 1996, 749–750; Bruce S. McEwen, "Protective and Damaging Effects of Stress Mediators," *New England Journal of Medicine* 338 (1998): 171–179.

11. Stress and SNS arousal: W. Cannon, "Stresses and Strains in Homeostasis," *American Journal of Medical Science* 189 (1935): 1–14.

12. Allostatic load and strain: Sally Dickerson and Margaret Kemeny, "Acute Stressors and Cortisol Responses"; Oakly Ray, "How the Mind Hurts and Heals the Body," *American Psychologist* 59, no. 1 (2004): 29–40; Suzanne C. Segerstom and Gregory E. Miller, "Psychological Stress and the Human Immune System: A Meta-analytic Study of 30 Years of Inquiry," *Psychological Bulletin* 130, no. 4 (2004): 601–630.

13. SNS and HPA Axis: Robert M. Sapolsky, *Why Zebras Don't Get Ulcers*, 3rd edition (New York: Harper Collins, 2004); LeDoux, *Synaptic Self*.

14. SNS arousal and blood pressure: Sapolsky, *Why Zebras Don't Get Ulcers*; LeDoux, *Synaptic Self*; V. DeQuattro and M. Feng, "The Sympathetic Nervous System: The Muse of Primary Hypertension," *Journal of Human Hypertension* 16 (2002): S64–S69.

15. SNS arousal and blood flow: Sapolsky, *Why Zebras Don't Get Ulcers*.

16. SNS arousal and left prefrontal cortex activation: LeDoux, *Synaptic Self*; Richard J. Davidson, Daren C. Jackson, and Ned H. Kalin, "Emotion, Plasticity, Context and Regulation: Perspectives from Affective Neuroscience," *Psychological Bulletin* 126 (2000): 890–909; Richard J. Davidson, personal communication, 2003.

17. Cortisol and the immune system: McEwen, "Protective and Damaging Effects of Stress Mediators"; Clifford Saper, "The Central Autonomic Nervous System: Conscious Visceral Perception and Autonomic Pattern Generation," *Annual Review of Neuroscience* 25 (2002): 433–469; Melissa A. Rosenkranz, Daren C. Jackson, Kim M. Dalton, Isa Dolski, Carol D. Ryff, Burt H. Singer, Daniel Muller, Ned H. Kalin, and Richard J. Davidson, "Affective Style And In Vivo Immune Response: Neurobehavioral Mechanisms," *Proceedings of the National Academy of Sciences*, 100 (2003): 11148–11152.

18. Cortisol effect on neurogenesis and neural narcosis: Bruce McEwen, "Protective and Damaging Effects of Stress Mediators"; Sapolsky, *Why Zebras Don't Get Ulcers*; LeDoux, *Synaptic Self*; Sapolsky, "Why Stress Is Bad for Your Brain"; James E. Zull, *The Art of Changing the Brain: Enriching Teaching by Exploring the Biology of Learning* (Sterling, VA: Stylus, 2002); Peter S. Erikson, Ekaterina Perfilieva, Thomas Bjork-Eriksson, Ann-Marie Alborn, Claes Nordburg, Daniel A. Peterson, and Fred H. Gage, "Neurogenesis in the Adult Human Hippocampus," *Nature Medicine* 4 (1998): 1313–1317; Richard Davidson, personal communication, 2003.

19. Arousal of SNS and right prefrontal cortex activation: Richard J. Davidson, Paul Ekman, Clifford D. Saron, Joseph A. Senulis, and Wallace V. Friesen, "Approach-Withdrawal and Cerebral Asymmetry: Emotional Expression and Brain Physiology I," *Journal of Personality and Social Psychology* 58, no. 2 (1990): 330–341.

20. Feeling stressed and neural activation: Andrew J. Tomarken, Richard J. Davidson, Robert E. Wheeler, and Robert C. Doss, "Individual Differences in Anterior Brain Asymmetry and Fundamental Dimensions of Emotion," *Journal of Personality and Social Psychology*, 62, no. 4 (1992): 676–687.

21. Immunosuppressive effects of cortisol: Sally Dickerson and Margaret Kemeny, "Acute Stressors and Cortisol Responses"; Segerstom and Miller, "Psychological Stress and the Human Immune System"; Nikolai Petrovsky, "Towards a Unified Model of Neuroendocrine-Immune Interaction," *Immunology and Cell Biology* 79 (2001): 350–357; Gregory E. Miller, Sheldon Cohen, Sarah Pressman, Anita Barkin, Bruce S. Rabin, and John J. Treanor, "Psychological Stress and Antibody Response to Influenza Vaccination: When Is the Critical Period for Stress, and How Does It Get Inside the Body?" *Psychosomatic Medicine* 66, no. 2 (2004): 215–223.

22. Power, self-control and immunoglobulin: See David McClelland and Richard Boyatzis, "Leadership Motive Pattern and Long Term Success in Management, *Journal of Applied Psychology* 67, no. 9 (1982): 737-743; David C. McClelland, S. E. Locke, R. M. Williams, and M. W. Hurst, "Power Motivation, Distress and Immune Function" (unpublished manuscript, Harvard University, 1982).

23. Chronic stress and immune disorders: Ibid.

24. SNS arousal and disease: Richard Davidson, personal communication, 2003; Sapolsky, *Why Zebras Don't Get Ulcers*; McEwen, "Protective and Damaging Effects of Stress Mediators."

25. SNS arousal and heart disease: DeQuattro and Feng "The Sympathetic Nervous System."

26. Effect of PSNS: Sapolsky, *Why Zebras Don't Get Ulcers*; McEwen, "Protective and Damaging Effects of Stress Mediators."

27. Recovery and renewal due to PSNS activation: Ibid.

28. Chronic stress and sleep and other disorders: Sapolsky, *Why Zebras Don't Get Ulcers.*

29. Chronic stress and decrease in innovation ability: McEwen, "Protective and Damaging Effects of Stress Mediators."

30. Female differences in response to stress: Shelly E. Taylor, Laura C. Klein, Brian P. Lewis, Tara L. Gruenewald, Regan A.R. Gurung, and John A. Updegraff, "Biobehavioral Responses to Stress in Females: Tend or Befriend, Not Fight or Flight," *Psychological Review* 107 (2002): 411–429.

31. Need for power: David C. McClelland, *Human Motivation* (Glenview, IL: Scott, Foresman & Co., 1985).

32. Genetic differences in stress susceptibility: Nigel Nicholson, *Executive Instinct: Managing the Human Animal in the Information Age* (New York: Crown Business, 2000).

33. Genetic expression versus genetic determination: Robert Lickliter and Hunter Honeycutt, "Development Dynamics: Toward a Biological Plausible

Evolutionary Psychology," *Psychological Bulletin* 129, no. 6 (2003): 819–835; Eric H. Davidson, *Genomic Regulatory Systems: Development and Evolution* (New York: Academic Press, 2001); Redford B. Williams, John C. Barefoot, James A. Blumenthal, Michael J. Helms, Linda Luecken, Carl F. Pieper, Ilene C. Siegler, and Edward C. Suarez, "Psychosocial Correlates of Job Strain in a Sample of Working Women," *Archives of General Psychiatry* 54 (1997): 543–548.

34. Genetic expression: Williams et al., "Psychosocial Correlates of Job Strain in a Sample of Working Women."

35. Training for genetic expression: Ibid., 621. See also Cary Cooper, Philip Dewe, and Michael O'Driscoll, *Organizational Stress: A Review and Critique of Theory, Research, and Applications* (Thousand Oaks, CA: Sage Publications, 2001).

36. Activation of the PSNS suppresses the SNS: Sapolsky, *Why Zebras Don't Get Ulcers*; LeDoux, *Synaptic Self*; Davidson et al., "Emotion, Plasticity, Context, and Regulation."

37. Caring relationships: Robert Sapolsky, *Why Zebras Don't Get Ulcers*; Andreas Bartels and Semir Zeki, "The Neural Basis of Romantic Love," *NeuroReport* 11, no. 17 (2000): 3829–3834; Thomas R. Insel, "A Neurobiological Basis of Social Attachment," *American Journal of Psychiatry* 154 (1997): 726–735.

38. Social networks reduce mortality: Ichiro Kawachi, B. Kennedy, and R. Glass, "Social Capital and Self-Rated Health: A Contextual Analysis," *American Journal of Public Health* 89 (1999): 1187.

39. Owl monkeys: John Allman, Aaron Rosin, Roshan Kumar, and Andrea Hasenstaub, "Parenting and Survival in Anthropoid Primates: Caretakers Live Longer," *Proceedings of the National Academy of Science* 95 (1998): 6866–6869.

40. Effect of pets on cardiac recovery: E. Friedmann, A. Katcher, J. Lynch, and S. Thomas, "Animal Companions and One-Year Survival of Patients Discharged from a Coronary Care Unit," *Public Health Reports* 95 (1980): 307–312.

41. Response of PSNS: Jay Schulkin, *Neuroendocrine Regulation of Behavior* (New York: Cambridge University Press, 1999); Sapolsky, *Why Zebras Don't Get Ulcers*; McEwen, "Protective and Damaging Effects of Stress Mediators."

42. Oxytocin and vasopressin: Insel, "A Neurobiological Basis of Social Attachment"; Schulkin, *Neuroendocrine Regulation of Behavior*; C. Sue Carter and Margaret Altemus, "Integrative Functions of Lactational Hormones in

Social Behavior and Stress Management," *Annals of the Academy of Science* 807 (1997): 164–174.

43. Positive effects of oxytocin: Insel, "A Neurobiological Basis of Social Attachment"; LeDoux, *Synaptic Self.*

44. Social interactions help the PSNS: Lisa Diamond, "Contributions of Psychophysiology to Research on Adult Attachment: Review and Recommendations," *Personality and Social Psychology Review* 5 (2001): 276–295.

45. Left versus right prefrontal cortex activation through mindfulness and compassion: Daniel Goleman, *Destructive Emotions: How Can We Overcome Them? A Scientific Dialogue with the Dalai Lama* (New York: Bantam Books, 2003); Richard J. Davidson, "Toward a Biology of Positive Affect and Compassion," in *Visions of Compassion: Western Scientists and Tibetan Buddhists Examine Human Nature*, ed. Richard J. Davidson and Anne Harrington (New York: Oxford University Press, 2002), 107–130; Rosenkranz et al., "Affective Style and In Vivo Immune Response."

46. Sense of elation: Paul Ekman, Richard J. Davidson, and Wallace V. Friesen, "The Duchenne Smile: Emotional Expression and Brain Physiology II," *Journal of Personality and Social Psychology* 58, no. 2 (1990): 342–353; F. Gregory Asby, Alice M. Isen, and U. Turken, "A Neuropsychological Theory of Positive Affect and Its Influence on Cognition," *Psychological Review* 106, no. 3 (1999): 529–550; Jerome Groopman, *The Anatomy of Hope: How People Prevail in the Face of Illness* (New York: Random House, 2004); Tomarken et al., "Individual Differences in Anterior Brain Asymmetry . . ."; Davidson et al., "Approach-Withdrawal and Cerebral Asymmetry"; Richard Davidson, Jon Kabat-Zinn, Jessica Schumacher, Melissa Rosenkranz, Daniel Muller, Saki F. Santorelli, Ferris Urbanowski, Anne Harrington, Katherine Bonus, and John F. Sheridan, "Alterations in Brain and Immune Function Produced by Mindfulness Meditation," *Psychosomatic Medicine* 65 (2003): 564–570.

47. Nucleus accumbens: Esther M. Sternberg, *The Balance Within: The Science of Connecting Health and Emotions* (New York: W.H. Freeman and Company, 2001).

48. Hope and LPFC: Insel, "A Neurobiological Basis of Social Attachment."

49. Loved ones versus friends: Bartels and Zeki, "The Neural Basis of Romantic Love."

50. Arousal of PSNS: David C. McClelland and C. Kirshnit, *Effects of Motivational Arousal on Immunofunction* (unpublished manuscript,

Harvard University, 1982); Jemmott, "Psychosocial Stress, Social Motives and Disease Susceptibility."

51. Positive emotions on attentiveness and openness: Barbara L. Fredrickson and Christine Branigan, "Positive emotions broaden the scope of attention and thought-action repertoires," *Cognition and Emotion* (in press); Michelle M. Tugade and Barbara L. Fredrickson, "Resilient individuals use positive emotions to bounce back from negative emotional experiences," *Journal of Personality and Social Psychology* (in press); Barbara L. Fredrickson, "Gratitude, like other positive emotions, broadens and builds," in *The Psychology of Gratitude*, ed. Robert A. Emmons and Michael E . Mc-Cullough (New York: Oxford University Press, forthcoming); Barbara L. Fredrickson, Michelle M. Tugade, Christian E. Waugh, and Gregory Larkin, "What good are positive emotions in crises?: A prospective study of resilience and emotions following the terrorist attacks on the United States on September 11th, 2001," *Journal of Personality and Social Psychology* 84 (2003): 365–376; Barbara L. Fredrickson, "Positive Emotions and Upward Spirals in Organizational Settings," in *Positive Organizational Scholarship*, ed. Kim Cameron, Jane Dutton, and Robert Quinn (San Francisco: Berrett-Koehler, 2003).

Appendix B

1. Copyright © Richard E. Boyatzis, 1992. For in-depth reading about the test and its theoretical base as well as statistical reliability and validity, see Richard E. Boyatzis, Angela Murphy, and Jane Wheeler, "Philosophy as the missing link between values and behavior," *Psychological Reports* 86 (2000) 47–64.

achievement
  motivation, 48–50, 182
  orientation, 181
acute stress, 41
affiliation need, 179
allostatic load, 207
ambiguous authority, 182
amygdala, 128, 129, 213
Anatomy of Hope, The, 150
attractors in complexity theory,
  154–157
attunement to others, 120–121.
  See also empathy
Azevedo, Belmiro, 161

Barrett, Colleen
  conscious process of renewal,
    32–33
  contagious resonant leadership,
    25–26
  impact of her mood on workers,
    24–25
  resonance creation, 19–22, 27–28

use of EI to sustain resonance,
  30–32
Bjoerndalen, Ole Einar, 152–153
boiling frog syndrome, 94
Boyatzis, Richard, 71, 87
burnout, 32, 43–44. *See also*
  power stress

career rhythms, finding, 84–85
cases
  becoming mindful of others,
    96–100
  compassion in action, 181–184
  compassion linked to hope,
    175–178
  cultivating compassion, 187–192
  dissonance followed by renewal
    (*see* Fitzgerald, Niall)
  hopefulness, 157–160
  indications of renewal need,
    65–70
  intentional change (*see* Nicastro,
    Roberto)

cases (*continued*)
  mindless executive, 125–126
  NGO executive's fall to disso-
    nance, 13–17, 26–28
  positive role of compassion,
    184–187
  professional services executive's
    fall to dissonance, 35–40,
    48–50
  resonant leadership (*see* Barrett,
    Colleen)
  slipping into mindlessness,
    132–134
CEO Disease, 50–51, 66
Cescau, Patrick, 131, 138–141
Chenault, Kenneth, 170–172
chronic stress. *See also* power stress
  easing through renewal, 61–63
  inherent nature of leadership
    and, 41–42
  lack of self-awareness and,
    47–48
  physical effects, 52, 93
  physiological response to,
    207–209
coach, personal, 98, 100, 102, 153
coaching
  benefits to leaders, 193–195
  mentoring and teaching versus,
    192–193
  skills for becoming a great coach,
    195–198
collective hope, 166–167
compassion
  in action example, 181–184
  coaching and, 193–195
  cultivating by listening, 187–189
  culture and, 189–192
  described, 9, 178–181

exercises for practice, 198–200
  linking to hope example,
    175–178
  positive role in business,
    184–187
  psychological effects of, 213
  as a source of renewal, 77–78
competencies in emotional intelli-
    gence, 4, 28, 29, 30
complexity theory, 154–157
contagious emotions, 24–26
corticosteroids, 43
cortisol, 207
crisis
  compassion and, 190–192
  feasible hope and, 170–172
  inspiring hope and, 172
culture
  compassion and, 189–192
  creating and preserving reso-
    nance, 20–22
  emotional interactions within,
    124–125
  impact of leader's mood on
    workers, 24–25
  organizational creation of disso-
    nance, 48–51
  at Southwest Airlines, 20–22,
    30–32
Cycle of Sacrifice and Renewal.
    See also renewal; Sacrifice
    Syndrome
  described, 7–8, 18
  sources of renewal, 211–213
cynicism, 155

defensive routines
  coping attempts, 46

destructiveness of, 44–45

fundamental attribution error
and, 46–47

identification exercise, 230–232

negative self-talk, use of, 45

Destructive Emotions, 154

dissonance

case studies, 13–17, 35–40,
57–61

contagious nature of, 26

defensive routines and, 44–48

elements contributing to, 18–19

factors leading to, 7–8

failure to see relationships and,
16

lack of EI in, 30, 32

lack of self-awareness and,
47–48

organizational creation of, 48–51

power stress as a cause, 40–44

response to leader's moods,
26–28

Sacrifice Syndrome and, 6, 41,
51–52, 54–55

self-awareness shortfall, 18–19

dreams

feasible hope and, 169–171

finding your own, 91

honesty and, 75

leadership and, 152

optimism and efficacy, 164–166

sustaining nature of, 158, 162

vision and, 162–164

Eduardo (NGO executive), 13–19,
26, 27–28, 32

EI. *See* emotional intelligence

Ekman, Paul, 123

emotional contagion, 24–26

emotional intelligence (EI)

coaching and, 195–196

cognitive competencies and, 28,
30

domains and competencies, 4,
28, 29

resonance and, 2–3

sustaining resonance with,
30–32

emotions

attractors, negative and positive,
154–157

contagious nature of resonance,
25–26

emotional reality of a situation,
16

impact of a leader's mood on
workers, 24–25

impact on behavior, 151

impact on well-being, 154

nature of, 23

empathy

compassion and, 77, 179–181

learning, 98, 99

epinephrine, 42

Erikson, Eric, 64

exercises for practice

compassion, 198–200

defensive routines identification,
230–232

holistic balance, 228–229

hope, 173–174

intentional change, 106–109

mindfulness, 144–146,
227

observing relationships, 236

operating philosophy, 215–224

renewal need recognition, 80–86

exercises for practice (*continued*)
  Sacrifice Syndrome self-assessment,
    54–55
  vulnerabilities and, 226

faith, religious or spiritual,
    167–168
fantasy job exercise, 106–108
feedback
  coaching with compassion and,
    195
  to gain self-awareness, 96, 97, 99
Fitzgerald, Niall
  early career success, 57–58
  family relationships, 68–69
  final wake-up call, 69–70
  friendship losses, 67–68
  new sustaining of resonance,
    78–80
  re-engagement of mindfulness,
    74
  return to hope, 75–76
  showing of compassion, 77–78
  slip into dissonance, 59–61
  work wake-up call, 65–66
Fredrickson, Barbara, 213
fundamental attribution error,
    46–47

gaps
  determination of, 95–96
  learning agenda and, 88, 89,
    104
Ghannoum, Mahmoud, 157–160
Giuliani, Rudolph W., 190–192
glucocorticoids, 209
Goleman, Daniel, 2, 153
Groopman, Jerome, 150

Harper, Josie, 141–142
The Hay Group, 243, 249
Higgins, Monica, 194
holistic balance exercise, 228–229
hope
  collective and self-efficacy,
    166–167
  definition of, 151–152
  described, 9
  example in action, 147–150
  exercises for practice, 173–174
  expectations and, 165–166
  feasible, 169–171
  impact of positive emotions on
    our behavior, 151
  impact on well-being, 154
  inspiring when performance is
    poor, 160–162
  inspiring without a crisis, 172
  leadership example, 170–172
  need for a meaningful vision,
    162–164
  optimism and, 164–165
  positive effect example,
    157–160
  positive emotional attractors use,
    156–157
  renewal through, 74–76,
    151–152, 203–204
  using positively, 168–169
  visualization and, 152–153
humanistic philosophy, 223
hypothalamic-pituitary-adrenal
    (H-P-A) axis, 207

Ibarra, Herminia, 194
ideal self discovery, 90–91,
    95–96
imposter syndrome, 134–136

ineffective leadership, 52–53
inspiration
    being inspirational, 105–106
    imparting a shared vision,
        162–164
    personal transformation and,
        204
intellectual philosophy, 222–223
intentional change
    coaching and, 194
    discovery cycle model, 88, 89
    enlisting help, 103–104
    exercises for practice, 106–109
    experimentation and practice
        use, 101–103
    finding your ideal self, 90–91,
        95–96
    finding your strengths and weak-
        nesses (see real self discovery)
    impact on resonance, 104–106
    understanding your personal
        challenges, 96–101

Johansen, Judi, 121–123

Kabat-Zinn, Jon, 113
Kernis, Michael, 135
Kram, Kathy, 194

Langer, Ellen, 112–113
leaders
    actions associated with optimism,
        165
    coaching with compassion,
        193–195
    dissonance due to ineffective
        leaders, 52–53

example of bringing hope,
    170–172
impact of mood on workers,
    24–25, 26–28
leadership defined, 6
motivating use of hope, 155
personal transformation use,
    201–202, 204
power stress and, 41, 205–207
renewal and (see renewal)
resonance and (see resonance)
Sacrifice Syndrome (see Sacrifice
    Syndrome)
susceptibility to CEO Disease,
    50–51
leadership
    dissonant (see dissonance)
    effective, 63
    ineffective, 52–53
    resonant (see resonance)
    sustainable, 114–115
    toxic (see dissonance)
learning agenda
    creating, 98–101
    described, 88, 89, 101
learning and mindfulness, 131,
    133
learning style, 101
left prefrontal cortex (LPFC), 207
legacy exercise, 108
Lennick, Doug, 170
Levinson, Dan, 64
life cycle, 88, 89. See also Cycle of
    Sacrifice and Renewal
life rhythms discovery, 85–86
limbic brain, 41–42

Manzoni, Jean François, 155
McClelland, David, 210

McDermott, Paul, 142–143
mindfulness
    attending to one's self holistically,
        115
    basis in self-awareness, 120
    cultivating the capacity for,
        114–115
    cultivating through reflection,
        138–141
    cultivating through supportive
        relationships, 141–144
    cultivating with self-awareness,
        137
    described, 8–9, 112–113
    example, 111–112, 116–118
    exercises for practice, 144–146
    observing emotional realities,
        123–125
    slipping into mindlessness (see
        mindlessness)
    as a source of renewal, 73–74
    using to understand people and
        environments, 120–123
    using when navigating the un-
        known, 118–120
mindlessness
    being unaware of using stereo-
        types, 130
    constant multitasking and, 131
    doing what you think you
        should, 132–134
    executive example, 125–126
    imposter syndrome, 134–136
    over-intense focusing, 127–130
moral core, 82–84
Motivation, 210

negative emotional attractor,
    154–157

negative self-talk, 45
neurogenesis, 43, 63, 211–213
neurology and stress
    basis of power stress, 41–42
    choices based on experience,
        128–129
    emotional attractors and,
        154–156
    physical and psychological effects
        of stress, 42–43, 205–207
    response to renewal, 62–63
    Sacrifice Syndrome impact,
        207–210
Newton, Schalon, 163–164
Nicastro, Roberto
    background, 89–90
    learning agenda development,
        101
    personal transformation use,
        100–101
    recognition that past strengths
        have become liabilities, 92–94
Nkomo Primary School, 147–150

operating philosophy, 215–224
optimism and hope, 164–165
oxytocin, 211

parasympathetic nervous system
    (PSNS), 62, 155, 209, 211
pattern recognition, 28, 30, 196
personal vision exercise, 108
Philosophical Orientation Ques-
    tionnaire, 216–224
planning, 101
Polet, Robert, 123–124
positive emotional attractor,
    154–157

power stress, 7
   as a cause of dissonance, 40–44
   chronic nature of, 41–42, 47–48,
      52, 61
   nature of leadership and, 41
   neurological basis of, 41–42
   physical and psychological effects
      of, 42–43, 205–207
   risk of creating dissonance,
      43–44
pragmatic philosophy, 222
Primal Leadership, 2, 169, 196
PSNS (parasympathetic nervous
      system), 62

real self discovery
   engaging in mindfulness and, 92
   human tendency to not see our-
      selves clearly, 94–95
   learning agenda development,
      101
   recognition that past strengths
      have become liabilities, 92–94
   strengths and gaps determina-
      tion, 95–96
reflection and mindfulness,
      138–141
relationships and mindfulness,
      138–141
renewal
   cycle of, 61, 62–63
   elements of, 8–9
   finding rhythms in your career,
      84–85
   finding rhythms in your life,
      85–86
   need for self-awareness, 63–65
   neurological response to, 62–63
   recognition of renewal need

example, 65–70
   recognizing a wake-up call,
      80–82
   sources of, 211
   sustaining resonance example,
      78–80
   through compassion, 77–78
   through hope, 74–76, 151–152,
      203–204
   through mindfulness, 73–74
   understanding your moral core,
      82–84
   using mindfulness, hope, and
      compassion, 71–72
resonance
   characteristics of a resonant
      leader, 2–3, 22
   company culture and, 20–22
   contagious nature of, 25–26
   described, 4–5
   difficulty in sustaining, 3–4, 5–6
   EI used to sustain, 2–3, 30–32
   elements of renewal, 8–9
   factors leading to dissonance,
      7–8
   intentional change and, 104–106
   qualities essential for leaders,
      203
   sparking in concurrence with
      problems, 161
rhythms in life and career, 84–86
Richt, Mark, 185, 186
right prefrontal cortex (RPFC), 207
Riveros, Pedro, 187–189

Sacrifice Syndrome
   as a cause of dissonance, 41
   defensiveness and (*see* defensive
      routines)

Sacrifice Syndrome (*continued*)
  described, 6
  due to ineffective leaders, 52–53
  illustrated by NGO executive,
    17, 26
  impact on physical health, 52
  impact on well-being, 207–210
  results of, 51–52
  self-assessment, 54–55
Scott, Mark, 185–186
self-awareness
  coaching with compassion and,
    196
  dissonance and lack of, 18–19,
    47–48
  mindfulness and, 120, 137
  need for in renewal, 63–65
  personal transformation and,
    100–101, 113
self-efficacy and hope, 166–167
self-esteem and imposter syndrome,
  135
self-talk, 45
Seligman, Martin, 164
sense of well-being, 62
Sharbough, Tom, 181–183
Sheehy, Gail, 64
SNS. *See* sympathetic nervous
  system
Snyder, C. R., 151–152
Sonae, 161
Sontag, Dan, 119
Southwest Airlines
  culture instilled by leader's reso-
    nance, 20–22, 30–32
  impact of leader's mood on
    workers, 24–25
  resonance from leader, 20
Strauss, Thomas, 189–190

strengths
  determination of, 95–96
  in real self discovery, 92–94
stress. *See* chronic stress; power
  stress
Studzinski, John, 111–112, 114,
  115, 116–118
Summa Health Systems, 189–190
sustainability
  difficulty in sustaining resonance,
    3–4, 5–6
  emotional intelligence and,
    30–32
  of leadership through mindful-
    ness, 114–115
  renewal and resonance and,
    78–80
  resonance case study, 78–80
  sustaining nature of dreams, 158,
    162
sympathetic-adrenal medullary
  axis, 207
sympathetic nervous system (SNS),
  42–43, 62, 155, 207, 210, 211
systems thinking, 28

Tembe, Isaac, 149
traits, personality, 164–165
Trebino, Juan, 196–198
Tsenoli, Lechesa, 175–178, 187

ulcers, peptic, 209

values
  ignoring due to mindlessness,
    47–48

moral core exercises, 82–84
relying on core beliefs, 119–120
vision
    finding for yourself, 91, 100
    ideal self and, 88
    inspiration of a shared vision,
      162–164

Wager, Nadia, 24
wake-up call
    becoming aware of not being
      aware, 63–65, 125

case study, 65–70
creating new habits, 79
exercises for practice, 80–82
weaknesses
    finding yours (see real self
      discovery)
    ideal versus real self, 88, 89
well-being and hope, 154
Wiesel, Elie, 168–169
Williams, Redford, 210

Zikhali, Mrs., 147–150, 151, 163

Richard E. Boyatzis is Professor in the Departments of Organizational Behavior and Psychology at Case Western Reserve University and a Visiting Professor in Human Resources at ESADE in Barcelona. For 2005 and 2006, he is also Visiting Professor of Organizational Behavior at the London Business School. While at Case Western, he has served as Associate Dean of Executive Education and Chair of the Department of Organizational Behavior. Before becoming a professor, he was CEO of McBer and Company (an HR research consulting company) for eleven years and COO of Yankelovich, Skelly & White (a market research company) for two years. He is the author of more than 125 articles on behavior change, leadership, competencies, and emotional intelligence. His books include: *The Competent Manager; Transforming Qualitative Information;* and *Innovations in Professional Education: Steps on a Journey from Teaching to Learning* (with Scott Cowen and David Kolb). He is coauthor of the international best-seller, *Primal Leadership: Realizing the Power of Emotional Intelligence* with Daniel Goleman and Annie McKee, published in twenty-seven languages. Boyatzis has a BS in Aeronautics and Astronautics from MIT and a MS and PhD in Social Psychology from Harvard University.

Annie McKee is Co-Chair of the Teleos Leadership Institute, an international consulting firm serving leaders of *Fortune* 100 businesses and major not-for-profit organizations such as the United Nations. She also teaches in the Graduate School of Education at the University of Pennsylvania and at the Wharton School's Aresty Institute of Executive Education.

McKee's work focuses on leadership, culture, and strategy. She designs innovative approaches to leadership development and works internationally with senior executives as a personal adviser, focusing on the intersection of leadership and strategy as well as organizational transformation.

McKee is an active public speaker and writer, and makes presentations to executives around the world. Before *Resonant Leadership,* she coauthored the international bestseller, *Primal Leadership,* with Daniel Goleman and Richard Boyatzis. She has written numerous articles on management and leadership including articles for the *Harvard Business Review.* All these works address the development of emotional intelligence in leaders and the creation of vibrant, focused, resonant organizations.

Before cofounding the Teleos Leadership Institute, McKee was director of management development services for The Hay Group. She also served for several years as the managing director of the Center for Professional Development at the University of Pennsylvania and taught in the Wharton School MBA Program. Her research interests focus on leadership, executive development, and organizational change. She contributes to her field through continued writing, research, reviewing, and editing professional journals, and by providing pro bono services for international nongovernmental agencies and in the Philadelphia community.

McKee received her baccalaureate degree *summa cum laude* from Chaminade University of Honolulu and her doctorate in Organizational Behavior from Case Western Reserve University. She has continued the study of her discipline with the Gestalt Institute of Cleveland and the Institut für Gestaltorientierte Organisationsberatung of Frankfurt, Germany.

McKee lives in Elkins Park, Pennsylvania, with her husband and three children.